SWEDEN AND THE EUROPEAN UNION EVALUATED

Sweden and the European Union Evaluated

Edited by Lee Miles

CONTINUUM

London and New York

Dedicated to John and in memory of Samuel Bernard Smith

D
1065
.S34
S94
2000

Continuum
The Tower Building, 11 York Road, London SE1 7NX
370 Lexington Avenue, New York, NY 10017–6503

First published 2000

British Library Cataloguing-in-Publication Data
A catalogue record for this book is available from the British Library.

ISBN 0-8264-4868-2 (hardback)
    0-8264 4869-0 (paperback)

Library of Congress Cataloguing-in-Publication Data
Sweden and the European Union evaluated / edited by Lee Miles
    p. cm.
  Includes bibliographical references and index.
  ISBN 0-8264-4868-2 – ISBN 0-8264-4869-0 (pbk.)
    1. European Union countries–Foreign relations–Scandinavia.   2. Scandinavia–Foreign
relations–European Union countries.   I. Miles, Lee, 1969–

D1065.S34 S94 2000
327.48504–dc21

                                                                        00-031400

Typeset by YHT Ltd, London

Printed and bound in Great Britain by TJ International, Padstow, Cornwall

Contents

Figures

Tables

Contributors

Hans E. Andersson is a PhD student at the Department of Political Science, Göteborg University, Sweden. He is completing his PhD thesis on Nordic cooperation since Sweden and Finland joined the EU.

Dr Arthur Gould is Reader in Swedish Social Policy in the Department of Social Sciences, Loughborough University, UK.

Dr Jan Hallenberg is Associate Professor of Politics in the Department of Strategic Studies, National Defence College, Stockholm. He is also a member of the Graduate Faculty at the Department of Political Science, Stockholm University.

Dr Michael Karlsson is Assistant Professor of Political Science at the Södertörn University College, Stockholm. He received his PhD in Political Science from Stockholm University in 1995.

Dr Mats Kinnwall is Chief International Economist at *Svenska Handelsbanken*, Stockholm.

Professor Rutger Lindahl is Jean Monnet Chair in European Political Science and Director of the Centre for European Research, Göteborg University, Sweden.

Dr Lee Miles is a Senior Lecturer in Politics and Deputy Director of the Centre for European Union Studies (CEUS) in the Department of Politics at the University of Hull, UK. He is also Director of the Svenska Institutet Programme in Politics at the University of Hull.

Katarina Molin is a Research Associate of the Centre for European Union Studies (CEUS) at the University of Hull, UK.

Dr Ulrika Mörth is a Researcher at the Stockholm Centre for Organizational Research (SCORE), Sweden. She also heads the Master's Programme in European Politics at the Department of Political Science, Stockholm University.

Dr Ewa Rabinowicz is Research Director of the Swedish Institute for Food and Agricultural Economics, Lund, Sweden.

Professor Olof Ruin is Lars Hierta Emeritus Professor of Government, Stockholm University.

Professor Bengt Sundelius is affiliated with the Department of Government, Uppsala University, and with the Swedish National Defence College in Stockholm. In addition, he is a member of the board of governors of the Swedish Institute of International Affairs.

Dr Anders Widfeldt is a Lecturer in Nordic Politics at the University of Aberdeen, UK.

Dr Rüdiger K. W. Wurzel is a Lecturer in Politics in the Department of Politics, University of Hull, UK.

Foreword

Sweden is one of the oldest nation-states in Europe. Its geographical composition has varied over the centuries from being a relatively small state during the medieval era centred round central and southern Sweden, to the 1600s when it was probably, apart from Russia, Europe's largest nation, in terms of area.

While Sweden, of course, has always maintained some form of relationship with continental Europe, a more active involvement in European politics began only in 1630 when King Gustav Adolphus decided to intervene in the Thirty Years War to defend Protestantism against the Counter-Reformation, and to extend Stockholm's influence well beyond its borders. The decision to intervene, the reasons for which have been extensively debated, entailed a 200-year long involvement in European politics and participation in many wars. It ended with the loss of a third of Sweden's territory in 1809 to Russia, of what now is Finland, and the new union with Norway in 1814.

That period was followed by an almost as long political withdrawal from continental European high politics that ended when Prime Minister Ingvar Carlsson announced in 1990 that Sweden intended to apply for membership of the European Community. Swedish cooperation with Europe was evidently not totally ruptured. Our country did participate in such projects that were functional, such as the OEEC, Council of Europe and EFTA, but not in military or political alliances or such organizations that could be seen as supranational.

This very compressed overview of Swedish relations with the continent is a necessary background to this new volume on Swedish European Union policy. The pervading theme in this book is the reluctance of Swedish public opinion even after five years of membership to engage fully in EU affairs. When confronted with questions about the reservations of my fellow citizens when it comes to the EU, I reply that it is not possible to change the direction of a ship of state very quickly. It is, no doubt, true that since Sweden's accession in 1995, public opinion has, as is shown in Rutger Lindahl's contribution to this volume, been more reserved than when the application was filed in Brussels. To some extent this is clearly due to the very difficult economic situation in the country in the early to mid-1990s when the country experienced very large budgetary deficits and high unemployment. There was in the eyes of many Swedes a connection made between accession to the EU and the stringent policies that had to be applied to get public finances in order, whether Sweden joined the EU or not.

But I believe that a negative reaction would have followed, even if the times had not been that bad. If you have followed and actively tried to pursue a doctrine of neutrality since the Napoleonic wars it is not all that easy to adapt immediately to an active participation in a political alliance such as the EU.

If there is thus a visible degree of scepticism among many Swedes in relation to the EU, or as Lee Miles describes the whole thing in the introductory chapter of the book, the Swedish state might be ready for the EU, but Swedish society is not, there are reasons for that. It might not be a coincidence that the United Kingdom and Sweden (and Denmark) are among the older nation-states and monarchies in Europe, situated on the periphery of the continent.

As Sweden has now been a member for five years, it is very timely that Lee Miles and his co-authors have decided to follow up his earlier book *Sweden and European Integration* (1997a) with a new volume where various experts analyse relevant aspects of Swedish policy and performance, to gauge how fast, if at all, Swedish politics are being 'Europeanized'. As Lee Miles himself underlines in his concluding chapter, Sweden's agenda has been very much conditioned by its priorities in the accession negotiations. In fact, given the historical background that I have sketched above, it could hardly be otherwise. The European experience of frequent wars and occupation by other states of their respective territories is not the Swedish one. Our country has by design and/or good luck avoided the pitfalls of war and occupation for almost 200 years. While Swedish support for the current European efforts to create a crisis management capability within the EU shows a growing involvement in and warming to the idea of common preoccupations in this field, it is no wonder that the debates about accession to the Union as well as the current development of Swedish priorities have been focusing on the direct economic consequences of accession (or non-accession), with the sovereignty and identity issues looming in the background.

Interesting questions are raised in the contributions by Olof Ruin and Anders Widfeldt as to the adaptation of the domestic political system. The EU debate has very much come to dominate the political discourse both as a matter that tends to separate the 'Left' and the 'Right' of the political spectrum and, at the same time, to split some parties down the middle. As most of the Left, broadly conceived, sees EU membership as a threat to cherished values of the welfare state, they oppose further integration and at least in theory advocate 'exit' rather than 'voice', to use Albert Hirschman's classic phrases, basically because they see values pertaining in the Union as incompatible with those of the Swedish social model that have, at least since the 1930s, been guiding Swedish society.

A decisive change that has taken place since 1961 when the issues were first discussed (cf. Bergquist 1970) is that the Social Democratic Party, although still divided, is now more positively inclined towards the EU. No victory in the 1994 accession referendum could have been achieved without SAP support. Similarly, their position on the European Monetary Union (EMU) will tip the scale.

Lee Miles and Bengt Sundelius are touching upon an important Swedish priority when they discuss the enlargement process, especially in relation to our three Baltic neighbours. It is very much in our interest, also in terms of national security, that these countries are firmly anchored in the Union to ascertain their reacquired independence and democracy. That is a goal shared by the whole political spectrum in Sweden and thus probably the least controversial aspect of the EU issue.

The most controversial is the EMU, where developments in the UK and Denmark are most important for our position (Greece's accession is, in as far as it is discussed, taken for granted as soon as that country meets the Maastricht criteria). This will, in all probability, remain the most debated issue in Swedish politics for some years to come. It is ultimately a very political question of how one wants to see the Union develop, in a more 'federalist' direction or not.

Lee Miles's new book is, in my view, a timely contribution towards the explaining of the current Swedish position on EU issues. It is, therefore, my hope that it will be widely read and thus dispel some of the misperceptions of Swedish EU policy.

Mats Bergquist,
Ambassador of Sweden in the UK,
London,
January 2000

Preface

The year 1999 is, in many ways, an appropriate time for the completion of a new book on Sweden and its relationship with the European Union (EU). First, the country has been a full member of the Union for almost five years, and thus 1999 represents a useful juncture for a closer examination of Sweden's initial experiences of full membership. Second, Sweden joined the Union as part of the 1995 enlargement 'convoy'. The country acceded to a Union that is probably more dynamic and certainly more ambitious than the comparable situation of the European Community (EC) in 1973, 1981 and 1986, when previous 'rafts' of new members swelled the ranks. In short, the Union's 'acquis communautaire' and 'finalité politique' are more substantial and wide-ranging than ever before. It imposes ever greater demands on countries to ensure a smooth transition on the parts of new member states.

In addition, what will hopefully set this book apart from other studies on Sweden is that it employs a common conceptual framework – the 'Membership Diamond' – and four research questions as means of uniting the book's constituent chapters. This should, hopefully, reduce the chances of the usual criticisms of edited books – that they tend to be rather disjointed in places and chapters vary in relevance and in quality – from being attributed to this one. Moreover, the 'Membership Diamond' concept – first introduced by myself in 1997 and refined in various other publications ever since – should be put to the test. Surely the 'big test' for any framework developed by a 'non-Swede' to explain the influences on Swedish policy-makers and their attitudes is for that framework to be examined against a comprehensive cross-section of Swedish political issues and policy sectors and for those evaluations to be conducted by prominent Swedes. This approach is exactly what this book seeks to use.

However, I would also like to thank a number of people for, as always, the end result is never the product of one person. In the first place, I would like to thank the contributors to this volume, not only for the excellent quality of their individual contributions, but also for their inputs into the design of the project. In particular, I would like to thank those contributors present at the editorial meeting held at the Swedish Institute of International Affairs in Stockholm in December 1998 for their help with the framing of the four research questions. In addition, thanks should be given to Karl-Magnus

Johansson of the Swedish Institute of International Affairs and Lund University for his critique of the 'Membership Diamond' in *Cooperation and Conflict* (Johansson 1998) and the encouragement he indirectly gave to what was, by that time, an ongoing project. Particular thanks are extended to Ambassador Mats Bergquist for finding the time to write the Foreword for the book. His comments are most welcome. My gratitude should also be expressed to Holly Atkinson for her technical expertise and contribution to the editing in this book.

Finally, and as always, I would like to thank my long-suffering wife, Lesa, and our two children, Anna and John, for, once again, putting up with the usual anxieties, frustrations and inhospitable work schedule that I, like most academics, draw up when completing this kind of project.

Lee Miles

CHAPTER I

Introduction

Lee Miles

When the Swedish population tentatively approved their country's accession to the European Union narrowly by 52.2 per cent on 13 November 1994, the first chapter in Sweden's new relationship with the EU was finally closed (Gustavsson 1998; Ingebritsen 1998; Miles 1997a). The last major obstacle to Sweden joining the Union as a full member on 1 January 1995 was effectively removed. However, this did not mean that Sweden's participation in European integration was going to be plain sailing during the years after 1995. Ever since, Sweden has maintained a reputation of having one of the most sceptical domestic populations (as regards their country's EU involvement) of the existing member states. Successive Swedish governments have been shackled by divisions back home principally between and within the political parties and key interest groups and, most importantly, by opposition to the EU from the majority of the mass population.

At the same time, Sweden's status as a new member ensures that the country's political institutions and economic structures need to (and continue to) adapt to the pressures emanating from the obligations of full EU membership. Moreover, this process has been shaped by, and accelerated by, the fact that the EU has been once again reconsidering its future direction beyond the 1990s over the last few years. Certainly, most of the EU's future direction was outlined in the 1992 Treaty on European Union (TEU) – otherwise known as the Maastricht Treaty – and accepted by the Swedish governing elite before the country joined the Union on a full-time basis. However, the process of defining the EU's future policy avenues remains incomplete, and within two years of Sweden joining, the country participated in the next round of 'deepening' EU integration, culminating in the June 1997 Amsterdam Treaty (see Miles 1997a, 1998a, 1998b).

On top of this, Swedish EU policy has been drawn quickly into an examination of – what will surely amount to being the largest step forward in the process of European integration – the EU's single currency programme and more specifically whether the country should participate fully in the third stage of Economic and Monetary Union (EMU). In addition, the Union has been setting out the frameworks in which future European security cooperation, collaboration in police and criminal matters and the eventual expansion of the EU can take place – all of which require Swedish responses. If the debates on EU membership before 1995 were fraught with controversy, then it seems equally likely that the discussions on Sweden's future role in the Union will be as exciting and heated, especially since that agenda has been largely 'inherited' by Sweden as one of the EU's newest members. The country – both at the state and societal levels – has many unanswered questions relating to its evolving relationship with an expanding European Union. As Ekengren and Sundelius have argued recently, the 'Swedish state' may have joined the Union, but it is far less certain whether 'Swedish society' has come to terms with the country's participation in the EU (Ekengren and Sundelius 1998).

To some extent, the objective of this book is to begin to examine some of these unanswered questions. In particular, the book assesses Swedish experiences of full membership in the first five years of the 'post accession' period (1995–99). Not only does this represent an exciting period from the Swedish and EU perspectives, but it is also a reasonable time period in which to analyse the nature of Swedish experiences, the country's EU policy formulation, the institutional changes arising from membership and the Swedish impact on the European Union. The editor has invited a number of prominent (and mostly Swedish) academics to consider various aspects of the Swedish–EU relationship and the book attempts to structure their various analyses on Swedish perspectives on the European Union using several approaches.

If this book is to examine many of the concrete achievements and uncertainties surrounding Sweden's early experiences of full membership, it is worthwhile trying to elucidate on the nature of these key questions relating to Sweden and European integration. Given the large number of sub-fields covered by this book – which are essential in order to enable it to be a relatively comprehensive analysis of Swedish full membership of the EU – each contributor was asked to consider four research questions or 'themes' when examining their respective areas of the Swedish–EU relationship.[1] The defining of these research questions provides a common basis on which to consider the Swedish–EU relationship, whilst at the same time, allowing the contributors sufficient discretion to draw individual conclusions from their respective case study analyses. These four broad research questions or 'themes' are:

1. *What are the main Swedish priorities regarding European integration and to what extent do existing Swedish institutions and policies 'fit' into the general process of European integration?* The focus of this research theme is to ascertain what are the main Swedish governmental priorities towards the development of the European Union and in what ways the country has influenced the evolution of the EU at the supranational level. After all, it is commonly acknowledged that Swedish policy and motives towards the European Union have tended to be essentially pragmatic and cautious. The country's policy-makers have refrained from developing or adopting a specific or unique Swedish 'view' or 'vision' on the future of the European Union. Nonetheless, it has been

equally evident that successive Swedish governments have targeted a number of key issues and championed a number of major areas for future EU development. Contributors were therefore asked to consider how these priorities (such as transparency and openness, employment, environmental protection) are reflected within their respective subject areas.

2. *To what degree has Sweden been 'Europeanized'?* The primary focus of this research theme was for contributors to consider how and in what form pressures emanating from the European Union have impacted upon Swedish political actors and the country's institutional and economic structures. This includes the effectiveness of institutional changes to the Swedish political system designed to cope with external pressures, such as to the executive's organization and/or parliamentary procedures, alterations to the ethos behind policy formulation and implementation and alterations to the perspectives of influential political actors.

3. *Has Sweden adjusted fully to being an EU member state and can Sweden still be regarded as a 'new' member of the European Union?* This research theme seeks to consider whether Swedish experiences of membership (and any domestic adjustments arising from EU obligations) operate on a 'time' dimension. In effect, whether the EU has short-term, medium-term and long-term impacts on Swedish institutional procedures and governmental policy. This incorporates notions of whether EU membership itself is still controversial, or whether it is the case that domestic debates and actors are now largely concerned with how the country participates in further EU integration.

4. *What are the potential scenarios for future Swedish institutional and policy change in relation to the European Union and are any alterations in Swedish EU policy and priorities 'elite-led' or merely 'societal-influenced' (in which they reflect the constraints imposed by, and subsequent changes in, Swedish society)?* The main attention of this research theme is to evaluate the interaction between state and societal actors in Sweden, especially since there has been clear evidence of sizeable differences of perspective and opinion towards the EU between the Swedish governmental and party elite and between these elite groups and the general public.

It should, however, be noted that the relevance of the individual questions/ themes and the significance attached to them by the respective authors varies, not surprisingly, according to the nature of their subject areas. After all, given the variety of subject areas and that each author is considering differing aspects of the Swedish–EU relationship, some will be more relevant to some areas than to others.

Moreover, for the sake of intellectual coherence, each contributor has been asked to use the same conceptual framework as a starting point for their individual discussions – namely the 'Membership Diamond'. The 'Diamond' was first introduced in *Sweden and European Integration* (Miles 1997a), but has been further modified in later published works – the most recent of which appearing in *Cooperation and Conflict* (Miles 1998b).

A common conceptual framework: considering the 'Membership Diamond'

Although focused entirely on Sweden and making no claims for wider application in other member states, the 'Membership Diamond' outlines four points which are instrumental in determining Swedish perspectives as the country grapples with the twin tasks of full membership and developing policies on the Union's future evolution (Miles 1997a). These are: (1) Sweden's fragmenting, 'Europeanized' democracy; (2) the country's declining traditions of corporatism; (3) the new challenges of economic interdependence; and (4) a security policy with a 'European identity' (see Figure 1.1). According to this, it is the dynamics operating within, and the relationship between, these four points that determine Swedish governmental perspectives towards the Union and dictate the government's effectiveness in pushing forward Swedish policies at the EU level.

It should be made very clear right from the start that the Diamond aims to explain *the influences upon* Swedish EU policy-making and decision-takers. It does not seek to explain *how* Swedish EU policy and decision-making is made. The Diamond therefore offers a framework for outlining the general parameters of Swedish EU policy, and offers the contributors in the book (dealing with aspects of foreign relations (Part I), the country's political system (Part II), policy areas (Part III) and social issues (Part IV)) a useful backdrop against which to place their more detailed and specific chapter evaluations. It is worthwhile outlining briefly the four 'points' of the 'Membership Diamond' for the reader.

Point 1: a fragmenting, 'Europeanized' democracy

The Diamond's first 'point' is concerned with the relationship between Swedish perceptions of democracy (see Childs 1980; Elder *et al.* 1988; Larsson 1995; Tilton 1991) and the influence of European integration on domestic decision-making processes. It has long been acknowledged that the Swedish political system is built on the principle of consensual policy-making and that policies were the outcome of lengthy and open deliberations. Moreover, Swedish governments were, for the most part, notable for their comparative stability (in spite of their often being minority administrations), the durability of the Social Democratic Party (SAP) as the main actor in governmental formation and the continuity arising from key figures holding the position of Prime Minister for long periods. All of these

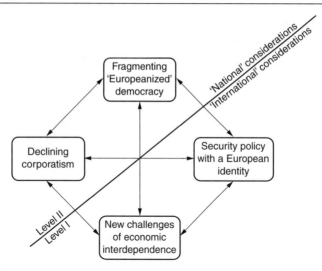

Figure 1.1 The 'Membership Diamond'

elements are incorporated into the assumptions underpinning the first 'point' of the 'Membership Diamond' (see Miles 1997a). The intention of this discussion is not, however, to deliberate upon the merits of Swedish decision-making, but rather to indicate in what ways European integration has affected it in the 1990s. Concerns, for example, over the impact of EU membership on the country's open system of 'consensual' government have been central features of the Swedish political debate.

The first 'point' contains twin dynamics – that are simultaneous sources of tension. In the first place, consensus-seeking is more difficult owing to the partial fragmentation of domestic political norms – a process complicated for government by the lack of party coherence on, and public support for, European integration in general. Although the growing volatility within Swedish politics is neither unique in Western Europe, nor particularly extreme (Katz and Mair 1994), EU-related questions as issues of 'new politics' (Jahn 1993) have complicated an already fluid domestic political scene (Svåsand and Lindström 1996; Widfeldt 1996a). As Hinnfors (1997: 159) comments, 'recent research holds that consensus has yielded to a more conflict-ridden climate'.

This is reflected in the comparatively recent changes to the country's party system, which underpins and influences the effectiveness of Sweden's 'consensual democracy'. The long-standing five-party system for instance – already transformed into a seven-party variant (excluding New Democracy; Widfeldt 1997) – has experienced greater difficulties partly because of inter- and intra-party divisions on EU issues. There are stark differences between mainstream pro-EU and peripheral anti-EU political parties on important issues relating to European integration. The Left Party and Greens, for instance, have kept the 'anti-EU voice' alive – a profitable tactic given the Union's unpopularity amongst a fair proportion of Swedish voters. Indeed, since the September 1998 general election, the Left and the Greens are now in the position to limit the government's ambitions in the EU area as they are supporting Persson's Social Democratic administration in the parliament.[2]

The impact of European integration can be seen at the intra-party level as well. The resilience of the Social Democratic Party (SAP) for example – traditionally the country's largest and most influential political party – has been especially tested by EU-related questions (Aylott 1997; Miles 2000).[3] Ironically, the main losers (in terms of party unity) from 'EU cleavages' have been the parties of the political centre, such as the Social Democrats and the Centre Party, which in spite of being essential components of any EU policy-making consensus have been vulnerable to internal disunity. As in other member states, EU questions are now constant (and rather divisive) features of domestic politics and have no doubt contributed to the more conflict-ridden climate of Swedish politics that Hinnfors suggests.

Nevertheless, EU membership makes the search for (at least elite) consensus (as the very minimum) in support of governmental policy towards the Union very important for it is certainly true that governments, of whatever political creed or colour, operate more effectively in the Union if there is domestic support for their policies at home. Political fragmentation has not prevented, and may have even spurred on, governmental, administrative and parliamentary attempts at adapting to EU membership. Structural changes in Swedish–EU relations have not only offered the state a new role as 'an outward-looking centralized European negotiator' (Ekengren 1996: 393), but further 'Europeanization' of decision-making is essential if the government is to formulate effective and popular policies on EU-related questions. The executive and parliament have engineered reforms facilitating consensual policy-making on EU matters in order to channel governmental input into the EU's evolving system and accommodate the growing number of political actors involved in Swedish EU policy since accession – in part reflecting the continuing 'domestication' of Swedish foreign policy (Karvonen and Sundelius 1987; 1990).

At the executive level at least, the 'Europeanization' is relatively well-advanced, dating back to before participation in the European Economic Area (EEA). The net effect has been 'a certain bureaucratic centralisation' and the consolidation of the Foreign Ministry's responsibilities in directing EU policy (Mouritzen 1997: 82). To a limited extent, this illustrates the ongoing impact of interdependence on political structures and government accountability – elements of what Stenelo and Jerneck have identified as a *bargaining democracy* (Stenelo and Jerneck 1996). Yet, as part of this process, 'Europeanization' has also introduced 'new autonomy dangers', since the necessity for speedy governmental responses may accelerate the de-parliamentarization of domestic EU-related policy-making (Mouritzen 1997). Nevertheless, this trend should not be (at least for the present) exaggerated. The Riksdag has also been an integral part of the 'Europeanization' process, with its Advisory Committee on EU Affairs enabling it to present the 'parliamentary view' on EU questions (Hegeland and Mattson 1996).

The first 'point' of the Diamond therefore incorporates elements of what Swedish governments need to harness if their EU policies are to be success-ful at the domestic and EU levels. They need to strike a delicate balance between, on the one hand, the desire for overarching elite consensus in favour of governmental EU policy (in order to strengthen Swedish influence at the EU level) and, on the other, a more fluid domestic political scene that makes its achievement far more complex and difficult.

Point 2: declining corporatism

The Diamond's second 'point' addresses the impact of the Union on industrial relations and Swedish 'exceptionalism' (see Lawler 1997) and, in particular, the role of interest groups in influencing governmental EU policy. First, EU membership has become synonymous with wider govern-ment changes in economic policy. It was continually portrayed by domestic parties, interest groups and the media as a partial antidote to severe recession in the early 1990s and as a supplement to economic restructuring (Miles 1995). Second, the role of key interest groups has altered, largely as a consequence of developments affecting Swedish industrial relations, which began in the 1980s, but accelerated in the 1990s. This decade marked the era not only of EU accession, but also the time when the last remnants of the 'Swedish model' (Lane 1993) were abandoned (Iversen 1996; Pontus-son and Swenson 1996). The influence of traditional interest groups, such as the blue-collar trade union congress (LO) and, to a lesser extent, the employers' federation (SAF), on government policy has been affected by disagreements amongst these organizations and between them and govern-ment, especially at a time when unemployment remains high (averaging 8 per cent in 1997).

As a consequence of the widening gulf between key groups' interests, there have been substantial differences between them regarding European integration issues (Gustavsson 1998; Miles 1997a) – restricting govern-mental manoeuvre and making the incorporation of their views into a 'balanced' Swedish EU policy increasingly complex. On the one hand, the employers' and farmers' associations are enthusiasts of full membership and in the case of 'big business' of Swedish participation in the single currency. In contrast, the trade union movement has been at best divided, and at worst, hostile to European integration – with some prominent union lead-ers, such as Kenth Pettersson (*Handels*), opposing even full membership. The net outcome has been that successive governments find it more difficult to develop wide-ranging interest group support for key EU policies. In particular, Social Democratic governments have been unable to count on the support of their traditional trade unionist allies to support their policies relating to European integration – something that is likely to continue given that Economic and Monetary Union (EMU) is also controversial.

Point 3: the new challenges of economic interdependence

The third 'point' deals with the influence of essentially economic-driven issues and priorities on Swedish EU policy and actors. Whilst the significance of economic interdependence arguments in shaping Swedish attitudes towards the EU is widely accepted (see Fagerberg and Lundberg 1993; Stålvant 1990), the third 'point' suggests that governmental economic objectives have altered since accession:

- With some simplification, it is no longer merely access to EU policies that is important (for this has been secured by accession), but rather securing the fullest utilization of benefits for Sweden from those policies. These new challenges of economic interdependence centred initially on the potential opportunities for attracting Foreign Direct Investment (FDI – see EU Consequences Committee 1994; Lindbeck *et al.* 1994) and later, the most controversial issue since joining, whether the country should participate in EMU (see Calmfors Commission – Calmfors *et al.* 1997).
- The second objective lies (at least for the moment) within the realms of EU external relations. It concerns Sweden's influence upon the formulation of the Union's policy regarding third states and, more specifically, on further EU enlargement. In this respect, successive Swedish governments have been keen to ensure that the three Baltic Republics (Estonia, Latvia and Lithuania) are jointly placed at the forefront of EU aid programmes to non-member states and are priority candidates for any future EU enlargement. This strategy (which includes common policies amongst the Nordic EU states) is especially significant as the Persson government has also sought a larger role in the Council of Baltic Sea States (CBSS).

In the earlier book by Miles (1997a), greater stress was placed on the first 'internal' objective – principally because his book concentrated upon the lengthy process of achieving EU membership status. With accession achieved, and despite the FDI aspect remaining important, elite and public attention turned to the prospect of Swedish participation in the Union's single currency programme, especially since the Persson governments have adopted a 'wait and see' policy and decided that the country should not be among the first wave of EMU members. However, as Miles asserts in his later works (Miles 1998a; 1998b), the second 'external objective' attained a higher profile in the IGC discussions at Amsterdam. There is now in the late 1990s a more 'balanced' distribution of influences pressing down on Swedish EU policy. The government is, for instance, responding simultaneously to the beginning of stage three of EMU in 1999 (the 'internal' objective of 'point' three) and attempts to influence the EU's 'Agenda 2000' discussions dealing with further enlargement to include the Baltic States (the 'external' objective of 'point' three). The outcome of the influence of these economic priorities has been to ensure Swedish involvement (at the elite level at least) in the European Union and, to large degree, that the arguments in favour of Swedish EU membership were and are largely portrayed in terms of benefits to the economy.

Point 4: Swedish security policy with a European identity[4]

The Diamond's fourth 'point' relates to Swedish security policy, especially since neutrality (Sundelius 1989) provided the main rationale for not joining the EC for a long time and there have been notable reforms to it in response to events affecting the continent since 1989 (Karvonen and Sundelius 1996; Miles 1997b; Sundelius 1994). The main pressure here on Sweden is how the country should react to policy initiatives set by the EU and NATO powers on future security cooperation. Given that Swedish security policy is no longer based on a strict doctrine of 'active neutrality' and has been reduced down to simply 'non-participation in military alliances', cooperation with other Western powers is both inevitable and advisable. In the post-1989 era, when governments are no longer bound by the old Cold War based language of security, the main concern of the Swedish Foreign Ministry is in what form the country will be tied to the wider security structures in Europe (Miles 1997a: 321). On the one hand, Swedish policy-makers accept (as part of their commitment to 'internationalism') that it is beneficial if the country cooperates with other powers in areas such as peacekeeping and humanitarian intervention. On the other hand, the Swedish government, largely with the support of the domestic population, still displays a commitment to non-alignment.

Hence, whilst successive governments have committed the country to being 'a full and active member of the CFSP', they remain opposed to Swedish participation in any (permanent) CFSP-related collective defence arrangement. More specifically, the Persson administration has continued with Sweden's observer status in the Western European Union (WEU) – the body designated with the task of developing the Union's future defence identity – and objected to any radical alterations of the CFSP's procedures as a means of restricting commitments to Pan-European defence. Hence, although the strict doctrine of Swedish neutrality may be long gone, it seems fair to suggest that the security parameters of the Diamond's fourth 'point' are still important in shaping Swedish EU policy and domestic perspectives towards the European Union.

Relationships between the Diamond's 'points'

The 'Membership Diamond' is a useful conceptual framework because it explains changes in emphasis placed on identifiable values by Swedish policy-makers and, to a lesser extent, the mass population. It is not, however, a static, insular framework, nor one that seeks to describe a constant, stable process. Rather, its points are of changing strength, influence Swedish policy-makers to varying degrees at differing times, and are not immune from external pressures being set by the Union as a whole.

There are, of course, direct links between each of the four 'points'. In particular, the first and second 'points' – those of a fragmenting, 'Europeanized' consensual democracy and declining levels of corporatism – are closely interrelated. The emphasis of the first 'point' on policy-making by consensus assumes a participatory role for important Swedish interest groups and, consequently, changes in the profile of these interest groups (assumed in the second 'point') has implications for the practice of consensual policy-making in the first 'point'. The Social Democratic Party has, for instance, discontinued 'collective affiliation' allowing (at least in principle) for a looser relationship between the governing Social Democrats and their colleagues in the labour movement, Second, the abolition of centralized collective bargaining of wage levels at the national level since 1990 has removed one of the key roles of the trade union congresses and employers' association(s) in contributing to the formulation of Swedish economic policy. 'De-corporatization' has changed indirectly the relationship between interest groups and the government. Hence, although Swedish interest groups still participate in the traditional consensual policy-making procedures of government, their roles have altered in a qualitative sense. Third, the Swedish industrial relations scene is more fluid than it used to be. The divisions within the trade union movement (such as between the blue-collar and white-collar trade union congresses), the growing divide between the movement as a whole and their counterparts in the Swedish business community and the increased tensions between the labour unions and the Social Democratic government on the future direction of Swedish economic and welfare policies have also reduced the impact of interest groups on government policy. It is now much harder for Swedish interest groups to speak with a unified voice underpinned by a very close relationship between them and government.

Indeed, there is also a clear relationship between 'points' one and two on the one side, and the third 'point' (new challenges of economic interdependence) on the other. First, the new economic issues (of FDI and EMU) are central elements of any discussion on the future of the Swedish welfare state and have provided additional rationales for the stringent fiscal and monetary policy stance on the part of successive Swedish governments in the 1990s. Second, these essentially 'economic-based' issues have continued to shape Swedish political debates on the country's participation in European integration and consolidated existing divisions on EU policies in the Swedish party system ('point' one). The Left Party and Greens, for example, have been able to maintain their anti-EU membership stances (which have been popular with voters) precisely because they have been able to argue that government policy and cuts in the 1990s have been (at least partially) influenced by the desire to attract foreign 'capitalist' investors, increase its popularity in EU circles and, most importantly, keep the option of EMU membership for Sweden open. Third, the new challenges of economic interdependence ('point' three) have become interwoven elements of the Swedish debate on 'de-corporatization' ('point' two). The Swedish business community, and the SAF in particular, have regularly argued that EU-related pressures, such as the need to reduce the chances of Swedish firms moving abroad due to the country's high wages and marginal status on the EU's periphery, were important reasons why the national bargaining on wages had to be abandoned and 'de-corporatization' should continue.

There is also a notable link between the fourth 'point' and the other three. In the first place, the challenges confronting Swedish security policy have dramatically altered in the 1990s and so, accordingly, has policy. The decline in consensus between the main political parties on security issues, and the fact that the more fluid international environment has allowed for limited fragmentation of the domestic consensus surrounding Swedish security policy ('points' one and four). Parties now take differing stands on the future of Swedish security policy, complicating any government attempts at striving for a new consensus on security issues ('points' one and four). Given that the Liberals and Moderates have talked openly of Swedish NATO membership, and that the Left Party, the Greens and Centre Party remain equally convinced of the merits of non-alignment, the minority Social Democratic governments of Göran Persson have charted a tentative approach on say the CFSP for domestic reasons. There is now a greater propensity for a wide-ranging debate on Swedish security policy, even if all parties recognize that security policy has been 'Europeanized' in the last decade (the second element of the Diamond's first 'point'). At least for the foreseeable future, Swedish security policy will be shored up by the EU's adoption of PfP and the 'Petersberg Tasks' as the basis for CFSP evolution (see Miles 1998a; 1998b). A more subtle and indirect process can also be seen within the Swedish interest groups (point 'two' – see Miles 1998b).

Most important is the relationship between the third and fourth 'points'. While it is true to say that the fourth 'point' is now less influential, and Swedish EU policy is driven in general by aspects relating to the third 'point', the two 'points' (in conjunction) provide the main external ratio-nales for Swedish involvement in the EU. Moreover, the tension between the two 'points' has also shaped general EU policy at the governmental level and provides the main basis for the country's selective policy on further EU integration. Even now in the 1990s, the governing Social Democrats remain cautious on the future development of the CFSP, but favour more ambitious supranational integration on selected issues such as monetary policy, the Single European Market (SEM) and environmental and employment policies.

Enhancing the 'Membership Diamond' through the application of double-edged diplomacy

The 'Membership Diamond' has also been enhanced through the provision of a more tangible connection with diplomacy theory (Miles 1998b). More specifically, the interaction between international and domestic influences in Swedish foreign policy-making is clarified through the analytical linkage of the 'Diamond' with Putnam's concepts of 'two-level games' and 'double-edged diplomacy (see Evans *et al.* 1993; Putnam 1988). Putnam and others have argued that 'double-edged diplomacy' requires national political leaders to conduct foreign policy by simultaneously managing contending political pressures and constraints in the international (Level I) and national (Level II) environments (Evans *et al.* 1993; Putnam 1988).[5]

The 'Membership Diamond' therefore provides a useful correlation to Putnam's theory by providing a clearer conceptual explanation of forces in the Swedish case. The 'Diamond' should not be perceived as a theory in its own right, but, more correctly, as a supplementary explanatory conceptual framework, reinforcing the general trends within the existing literature towards the usage of two-level games and the conclusion drawn recently by Lantis and Queen (1998) that a greater focus on the interaction between external bargaining strategies (Level I) and internal constraints (Level II) is essential. In the Swedish case, the strength of the 'Diamond' lies in its ability to elucidate the factors impinging on Putnam's Level I and Level II negotiations.

The Diamond's third and fourth 'points' are roughly salient at Putnam's Level I. Indeed, it is widely recognized that external variables and 'shocks' are often vital to the process of foreign policy change (see Gustavsson 1998; Hermann 1990; Jerneck 1993; Sundelius 1994). Furthermore, 'economic interdependence multiplies the opportunities for altering domestic coalitions (and thus policy outcomes)' – so-called *synergistic linkage* (Putnam 1988: 447). According to Putnam, political leaders must manage the pressures of the Level I international environment – the greatest of which (according to the Diamond) are those of growing economic interdependence (through EU membership) and the continent's changing security architecture. Ultimately, the Diamond's third 'point' has been the central driving force as regards closer Swedish–EU relations, with full membership portrayed domestically and (rightly or wrongly) as 'complementary medicine' to cure Sweden's economic problems (Gustavsson 1998). In the years since 1995, the EU's main agenda item – the single currency – has done little to dispel these illusions.

In part, the security concerns of Swedish policy-makers have also substantially altered (Huldt 1994; Jerneck 1993; Sundelius 1994), transforming the Diamond's fourth 'point' and proving that it is not a major obstacle to participation in new EU initiatives since accession. Any friction between the Diamond's third and fourth 'points' is 'internalized' by EU membership with successive governments following a 'mixed' approach on European integration questions (Lindahl 1996a: 43). With some simplification, the third 'point' promotes Swedish involvement in supranational EU-based policies (such as on environmental matters), whilst the fourth 'point' restricts it, emphasizing intergovernmental tendencies (illustrated by Swedish attitudes towards the CFSP). In any case, the two 'points' are now complementary in defining elite perspectives on European integration, for at the elite level, and with the exception of the Left Party and Greens, the main priority is influencing EU-derived policies, rather than reconsidering full membership.

However, Putnam is also keen to highlight that 'the domestic determinants of foreign policy and international relations must stress politics: parties, social classes, interest groups (both economic and non-economic), legislators, and even public opinion and elections' (Putnam 1988: 432). Aspects of the Diamond's first and second 'points' are therefore clearly evident at Putnam's Level II. According to him, political leaders play a two-level game, whereby at the domestic level, domestic groups pursue their interest by pressuring government to adopt favourable policies and at the international level political leaders 'maximise their own ability to satisfy domestic pressures, while minimising the adverse consequences of foreign developments at the domestic level' (Putnam 1988: 434). They constantly need to build coalitions of support for foreign policy initiatives and reduce the influence of unsympathetic 'isolationist' domestic groups on their foreign/EU policies (Putnam 1988: 443). Moreover, the size of a 'win-set' is affected by levels of discipline within governing parties – if it is weak, the scope of international cooperation is also curtailed (Putnam 1988: 449). At the end of the day, the outcome of international negotiations is dependent upon the size of the Level II 'win-set', i.e. the set of all possible Level I agreements necessary to win a majority among domestic constituents when simply voting to accept or reject an international agreement (Putnam 1988: 437). Most of all, any deal cut internationally by political leaders must meet the acceptance of those that could veto its ratification back home (Knopf 1993; Lantis and Queen 1998).

The Diamond's first and second 'points' are equally useful in clarifying the nature of these domestic constituents and the problems when the respective Swedish 'win-set' accepts high degrees of domestic disagreement. The lack of party agreement on EU questions, combined with the transitional changes affecting the Diamond's first and second 'points', ensure that the Union is seen, at the public level, as an appendage to a larger debate on Swedish political and corporate traditions and levels of welfare provisions. The size of the Swedish 'win-set' remains relatively small and the Swedish elite will continue to be constrained by the domestic picture – with EU questions consciously framed within the first, second and third 'points', rather than the previously important security dimension for the foreseeable future.

As a conclusion then to this chapter, there are some general lessons that can be drawn to facilitate the application of the 'Membership Diamond' to the subsequent case studies incorporated in this book. First, that the (Level II) first and second 'points' are critical in explaining the Swedish debate on EU questions and the restrictions imposed upon policy-makers in articulating EU-related issues back home. They help explain the prioritizing by Swedish policy-makers of (what some may consider) mundane issues in other member states, and the reasons why they take on such importance in Sweden. It is most likely that it will take until well into the twenty-first century for the transitional stages affecting the first and second 'points' to be completed and, until this is done, Swedish governments will continue to find it difficult to convince public opinion of the benefits of EU participation.

Second, that the delicate balance within the (Level I) third 'point' between 'internal' EU-related aspects and the Union's external relations is important to any understanding of why Swedish policy-makers continue to pursue closer cooperation in the EU, in spite of the scepticism of fringe political parties, certain interest groups and the majority of the domestic population. The third 'point' also provides a major rationale for intra-Nordic cooperation within the Union between the existing three Nordic members (Miles 1995), especially as regards the development of EU policy towards the Baltic states.

Next, that the (essentially Level I) third and fourth 'points' are significant in explaining Swedish elite attitudes towards European integration in general. The Amsterdam IGC is a practical example of Sweden utilizing a 'mixed' approach towards EU development, with preferences for Baltic EU enlargement and incremental CFSP reform illustrating tensions between the two 'points' (see Miles 1998a; 1998b). Emphasis should be placed on this complementary, but taut, relationship between the two 'points' as they, most probably, guarantee that Swedish governments follow a 'mixed' strategy on European integration.

Overall, Sweden will define progressively its relationship with the EU well into the twenty-first century, especially since the EU's present and likely future agenda will incorporate policies that are largely deemed controversial by the country's political parties, media and public. This is unlikely to mean that the country's elite would consider withdrawing from the Union seriously, nor that Sweden will equally be at its epicentre. Rather, successive governments will continue to chart a tentative path on the rocky road of European integration. Given the present (and deep-seated) domestic constraints placed on government, the Diamond's four 'points' will remain central elements underlining Swedish perspectives towards the future evolution of the European Union.

This introduction has therefore duly set out the broad parameters and provides the context in which the respective contributors were asked to place their analysis. The text is split into four sections: an analysis of the Swedish international relations and foreign policy (Part I); an examination of the impact of European integration on the Swedish political system (Part II); a selective investigation of aspects of Swedish EU policy relating to the Union's expanding policy portfolio (Part III) and, finally, a consideration of certain significant social issues relating to Swedish EU membership (Part IV).

Notes

1. The research questions/themes were framed at a meeting of the editor and contributors held at the Swedish Institute of International Affairs in Stockholm on 1 December 1998. The editor would like to thank those contributors present for their valuable advice.
2. Cooperation between the Social Democrats on the one side and the Left Party and the Greens on the other does not include EU policy formally. Prime Minister Persson announced shortly after the election that in the areas of EU and foreign policies, the Social Democrats will seek to build consensus arrangements with the non-socialist parties in the Riksdag instead. However, they will be restricted indirectly on EU policy because they rely, for the most part, on the Left Party and the Greens to form a parliamentary majority supporting the day-to-day business of government.
3. As regards the governing Social Democrats, the division on the EU membership issue has been to a large degree resolved. At the SAP's extraordinary conference (March 1996), the pro-EU wing secured a decisive victory. However, divisions on other EU-related issues remain.
4. Although the official term 'Swedish Security Policy with a European Identity' is no longer used since 1994, it is, in the author's view, an accurate description of security policy to date.
5. Robert Putnam's concept of 'two-level games' (Putnam 1988) was further developed and given the title of 'Double-edged Diplomacy' in the edited volume by Evans, Jacobson and Putnam (see Evans *et al.* 1993).

PART I

Foreign Relations

CHAPTER 2

Swedish Foreign and Security Policy

Jan Hallenberg

Introduction

For many years after the Second World War, Swedish foreign and security policy rested on two pillars. The first was an active foreign policy strategy based upon membership of the United Nations, and activity within its framework (cf. Mörth and Sundelius 1995). The second was a security strategy that came to be expressed by the phrase – a phrase that gradually came to stand for an inflexible doctrine – 'non-alignment in peace, aiming towards neutrality in war' (see Johansson and Norman 1986: 11–43). The second strategy was nearly invariably followed by a variation on the theme that 'the policy of neutrality is supported by a strong Swedish defence'. If the first strategy implied activity and flexibility, the second implied rigidity. Swedish security policy during the Cold War was officially portrayed as a third way between the two security alliances in Europe, NATO and the Warsaw Pact. Swedish politicians tried to make sure in their speeches and in other aspects of security policy that there was absolutely no leaning either way: the country steered a course that was clear of both the Scylla of NATO and the Charybdis of the Warsaw Pact.

Research on Swedish security policy after the end of the Cold War has shown clearly that the characterizations made by Swedish politicians concerning the second strategy, at the very least, neglected to mention important aspects. The special commission given the task of analysing Swedish neutrality during the Cold War has shown that while Swedish politicians professed non-alignment, and a steadfast avoidance against leaning towards either power bloc, the highways in Sweden were built according to specifications that made it possible for NATO planes to land there. Indeed, it was a basic, if secret, tenet of Swedish policy during the years of Cold War that in the case of a Soviet attack, NATO would on short notice come to Sweden's aid (cf. SOU (1994a) – 1994: 11 *Om kriget kommit*).

Put another way, Sweden was very active before 1990 on the global, foreign policy level. Swedish Prime Minister Olof Palme supported verbally the Third World; for instance in the debates on the New International Economic Order that was carried out in the 1970s. At the same time, security policy pursued in a Nordic, and to some extent a European, context rigidly maintained the non-alignment/neutrality line. Sweden supported disarmament and nuclear-free zones in the debates on the future of European security. The Swedish historian Kent Zetterberg has aptly characterized these two strands of Swedish foreign and security policy as 'real-politik in the immediate vicinity, idealism globally' (Zetterberg 1997: 14). During the Cold War, it was difficult even for Swedish academics to question publicly whether Sweden under any conceivable circumstance really ought to pursue what came to be known as the neutrality line. Such hypothetical discussions could, according to the policy-makers, risk the credibility of this vital political strategy. Any public hints of the possibility that Sweden might, under any circumstances, apply for NATO membership was the greatest sin of all in this context.

As the Berlin Wall was torn down in 1989 and the Soviet Union collapsed in 1991 Swedish foreign and security policy had thus settled into two paths of quite different characters. The foreign policy strategy can be characterized as global, while the security strategy was self-centred, concentrating mainly upon the immediate vicinity. In this picture of Swedish foreign policy, Western Europe did not play any central role. Such was the context in which the Swedish Government decided, in the Autumn of 1990, to seek membership of the (then) European Community (cf. Sundelius 1994). This chapter evaluates what has happened to these two strategies in the period between 1995 and 1999 – that is, during the period of Swedish EU membership. It focuses on Swedish policies within the context of the EU, but other aspects of foreign and security policy, in particular that involving cooperation with NATO, is also covered. In other words, this chapter highlights explicitly what Lee Miles calls the fourth 'point' of his 'Membership Diamond' (Security Policy with a European Identity – see Chapter 1).

In addition, the chapter covers Swedish 'verbalized' policies[1] during the 1990s, to clarify to what extent the two strategies have been maintained as the pillars upon which Swedish foreign and security policy rests. Of particular interest in this context is to what degree, if any, has (what is termed in this chapter) the security strategy undergone any real changes on the 'verbal' level. The 'verbalized' policies are then contrasted to the 'non-verbalized' policies of the Swedish government during the 1990s (particularly from 1995 onwards).

One aspect that is central to this chapter is that although Sweden's foreign and security policy has, of course, been affected by EU membership, other institutional contexts have also been very important influences upon the country's foreign and security policy in the 1990s. Indeed, it is difficult to single out the role played by EU membership given the wider context of multifaceted cooperation with many 'inter-locking institutions'. The chief argument of this chapter is that the context in which Swedish foreign and security policy is made has changed profoundly since 1990. EU membership is one crucial aspect of this change, but it is, by no means, the only important alteration. The vast change in the environment in which foreign policy is conducted also means that the contents of that policy are undergoing important shifts. What here are called 'non-verbalized' policies are, at this stage, the clearest illustrations that this is the case. Swedish foreign and security policy will, however, also have to adjust gradually in other ways as well, including in terms of 'verbalized' policies.

The most lasting remnant of the old Swedish strategy in this field is the non-alignment strategy. This author argues that this strategy is already circumscribed, to a significant degree, by Sweden's external commitments during the 1990s (which are also noted in this chapter). The 'verbal' commitments to non-alignment of Swedish government(s), particularly those led by the Social Democrats, will last longer, but they are also bound to be dropped within a not too distant future.

Swedish foreign policy after 1990: an overview of verbalized policy

In October 1990 the Swedish government for the first time announced its intention to apply for membership of what was then the European Community (EC). Perhaps the first time this application was put into a broader foreign policy context was in a debate on foreign policy in the Swedish Riksdag in February 1991. The government's official position on this occasion included the following statements:

> The policy of neutrality, supported by a strong and comprehensive total defence, remains the foundation of our security policy. We decide for ourselves the actions that are compatible with neutrality policy. When our environment changes drastically, the conditions for our peacetime foreign policy also change ...
>
> The government and the parliament have during the autumn of 1990 declared that membership in the EC with preserved neutrality policy is in Sweden's national interest. (Government Declaration on Foreign Policy to Parliament, 20 February 1991, *Utrikesfrågor* 1992 (Foreign Policy Issues 1991): 14)

This very first statement dealing with the implications of Swedish EC/EU membership can be said to unite the two aspects that have characterized Swedish 'verbalized' policy on these issues ever since 1990–91. The first aspect can be implied from the above statement: namely Swedish foreign policy has to be different in a context where the country is a full EU member. The second aspect is that however important the first change may be, it does not imply that the second strategy, 'neutrality policy', has changed or that it even needs to change in the future. Statements on Swedish foreign policy in 1998 and during the first half of 1999 still maintain this dichotomy. The details describing the changes in the foreign policy strategy may be more numerous and more elaborate; however, the neutrality strategy remains largely the same. As will be further discussed, there are aspects of change surrounding even this strategy, but the ministers responsible for foreign and security policy are still emphatic when they characterize the essence of this strategy as lasting and that Sweden intends to remain non-aligned in peace in order to be able to stay neutral in case of war.

This does not mean that the security strategy, on the verbal level, has remained totally unchanged. The new fundamental formula for the non-alignment strategy is along these lines:

> The goals of Swedish security policy remain the same, but the means must be developed based on changes in the external world. Sweden's military neutrality remains unchanged, with the aim of remaining neutral in case of war in our immediate vicinity. (Government Declaration on Foreign Policy, 14 February 1996, *Utrikesfrågor* 1997 (Foreign Policy Issues 1996): 13)

As briefly described later in this chapter, the role of NATO has changed considerably during the 1990s. This has necessitated a response on the part of the Swedish government. The extent of, as well as the limits to, Swedish participation in this development is spelled out in a speech by (then) Foreign Minister Lena Hjelm-Wallén after the establishment of the Euro-Atlantic Partnership Council (EAPC) within the larger NATO framework in the Spring of 1997:

> 'The government regards the EAPC as primarily a vehicle for practical co-operation in crisis management carried out by NATO. We also value highly the possibilities offered by the Council to give us greater chances to participate in planning and decision-making regarding crisis management operations to which Sweden contributes military forces, such as in Bosnia. As before, there is a need for a mandate from the OCSE or the UN before such an operation can be undertaken.
>
> The cooperation is limited to that part of NATO cooperation that does not concern the territorial defence of the member-states or security guarantees. This is essential in deciding whether or not Sweden as a militarily non-aligned country can participate in this cooperation.' (Foreign Minister Lena Hjelm-Wallén, speech to Parliament on 3 June 1997)

This quote captures, for the most part, the degree of change evident within Swedish security policy (or at least as presented by members of government). On the one hand, Sweden has chosen to participate in most of the new structures created for cooperation in European security policy after 1990. On the other hand, it is made clear that the limits to this cooperation steer well clear of any breach of the non-alignment policy line.

One other aspect of Swedish foreign and security policy is its support for an 'all-encompassing European security order'. Foreign Minister Lena Hjelm-Wallén addressed this aspect of the Government's strategy in a response to a written question in Parliament in 1996:

> The development towards a new European security order, of which NATO is one part, is hopeful in many ways. The states of Europe already in many respects have a common agenda of security policy. It is this common agenda that forms the basis for cooperation between NATO and states outside the organization, both in the PfP and in concrete missions, such as that in Bosnia.
>
> In Bosnia, as in other contexts, Sweden has contributed to the building of a European security order. We intend to continue to do so. Military non-alignment does not mean passivity.

Against this background, the government sees no reason to abandon the military non-alignment decided upon by parliament ... It is probable that the common security agenda step by step will become more all-encompassing. At the end of that process we envisage the comprehensive European security order whose attainment the Swedish government works to accomplish. (Foreign Minister Lena Hjelm-Wallén, Response to a written question in Parliament, 7 November 1996, *Utrikesfrågor* 1997 (Foreign Policy Issues 1996): 224)

These quotes indicate one facet of current Swedish foreign and security policy. It is the sense that the whole context in which Swedish policy is being carried out is changing. The entire European security system is being transformed – while, at the same time, Stockholm remains the same as ever: peaceful, constructive, willing to cooperate, but unalterably non-aligned. It is hard not to see a tension between this external fluidity, on the one hand, and the simultaneous inflexible stability, on the other. Can Sweden remain ever steadfast in its non-alignment strategy whatever the external circumstances?

The EU context: Swedish foreign policy inside and outside the CFSP from 1995

EU membership has been highly consequential for Swedish diplomacy especially if the daily working patterns of diplomats are examined. Interviews with Swedish officials at the Foreign Ministry give the clear impression that much of the work of Swedish diplomats in the second half of the 1990s is infused by the necessity of cooperation in a European context.[2] One part of the procedural aspects of Swedish diplomacy that illustrates this general tendency is the establishment of a unit for European integration in the Ministry for Foreign Affairs in 1994–95. Another aspect of this is the close cooperation among high-ranking diplomats in the EU carried out, among other places, in the Political Committee of Political Directors (PoCo) (cf. Jørgensen 1998: 175). The Swedish diplomat active in PoCo is a very high-level official in the Ministry for Foreign Affairs (*utrikesråd* in Swedish).

It thus seems that many of the processes underpinning traditional foreign policy have changed in Sweden as a result of EU membership. 'Foreign policy' takes on a different connotation for a state that is a member of the European Union (as opposed to what the concept means for a non-member), and this is taken for granted here. Such aspects are not further analysed in this chapter.

What should be mentioned, however, is the particular role played by the Ministry for Foreign Affairs in times when foreign policy is quite different from traditional diplomacy. It is clear that EU membership has meant that most, if not all, Swedish ministries have become involved in what was formerly the preserve of the Ministry for Foreign Affairs. This creates a dilemma for a ministry that wants to keep its crucial role in all aspects of

Sweden's foreign relations. On the one hand, EU membership creates many new opportunities for Swedish diplomats to act in an international framework. On the other hand, the multifaceted nature of Sweden's new patterns of interaction in the EU ensures that it is, in practice, impossible for the Ministry for Foreign Affairs to control the definition of what is 'foreign policy' in the Europe of the 1990s. The loss of this ability means that the Ministry no longer has the same strong role in the process of foreign policy-making in Sweden as it had before 1995. Still, even in its new capacity as a coordinator of many aspects of Swedish EU policy, the Ministry for Foreign Affairs retains a central position in the foreign policy process.

Swedish policies pursued within the EU in the realms of traditional foreign policy can be characterized as focusing on four types of issues (see Regeringens skrivelse 1995/96; 1996/97; 1997/98; 1998/99). The first is strong support for further EU enlargement, in which the aspirations of the three Baltic nations are highlighted. Strongly linked to this is a second line of action, which is Swedish support for the various cooperative ventures that have started in the Baltic Sea Region (see Chapter 3). Third, the Swedish government has as an EU member sought to further a traditional area of interest – the liberalization of international trade. This is manifested in Sweden's strong support for the WTO and by its striving to liberalize the behaviour of the Union as regards global free trade. A fourth issue became more important as the negotiations for (what became) the Amsterdam Treaty got under way in 1996. This is the ability of the Union, and of individual members of the EU, to partake in operations termed 'military crisis management'.

In this context Sweden cooperated with the government of Finland in efforts to create a framework in which the two non-aligned countries could contribute to peacekeeping operations in Europe within the context of the Western European Union (WEU) or in the broader NATO context. The eventual result of the negotiations on the Amsterdam Treaty were in essence identical to the joint Swedish and Finnish position, in that the so-called 'Petersberg tasks' were incorporated into the framework of the Common Foreign and Security Policy (CFSP). These tasks were also to be discussed within the WEU, in which Sweden and Finland have observer status. (On the Amsterdam negotiations on these issues see Gourlay and Remacle 1998: 86–90; Miles 1998b.) This is another instance where the workings of the fourth 'point' of the Miles 'Membership Diamond' (Security Policy with a European Identity) manifests itself.

In short, the four priorities mentioned above constitute the answer to the first research question/theme posed in Chapter 1: namely what are the main Swedish priorities regarding European integration? In the field of foreign policy, these have to do with EU enlargement, with ties to the Baltic States, with increasing liberalization of international trade and with a greater role for the EU in flexible 'military crisis management'. The first three of these are not that controversial in the domestic political context, while the fourth issue has potentially wider ramifications, particularly if the EU's role in international security affairs becomes more wide-ranging than that allowed by the fairly narrow Swedish conception. As noted in this chapter, the representatives of the Swedish government have a clear tendency to portray the agreements within the EU on the future of the CFSP, for instance, those at the Cologne summit in June 1999, as having fewer ramifications for the future of the Swedish strategy of non-alignment than at least this writer estimates to be the case.

The results of the Amsterdam Treaty negotiations (as regards the fourth issue) must be regarded as a victory for the Swedish position. The final outcome ensures that Sweden will be able to participate in crisis management operations when it chooses to do so, and abstain from participating when it wants. In those operations where it chooses to participate, its representatives will also be able to take part in planning and other preparations for the related missions. This result is compatible with the essentials of Sweden's position on security strategy during the last few years. The country's representatives are prepared to play an active part in crisis management operations when they will, in its view, contribute favourably to European stability. However, Sweden will refrain from taking part when the government fears that positive results may derive from such operations.

This policy is also in line with another feature of Swedish foreign and security policy after the end of the Cold War: namely support for the creation of an all-encompassing European security system. The success of Sweden's position in the negotiations on the CFSP and the relationship between the EU and the WEU during the Amsterdam IGC can, at the very least, be said to have not made the achievement of this goal any more difficult.

More generally, Swedish foreign policy has, to a significant degree, been carried out in the context of EU membership. The crisis over Kosovo illustrates the changing context for Swedish foreign policy. NATO's military operations were (initially) undertaken without an explicit mandate from the Security Council of the United Nations, ostensibly in violation of central tenets of what has here been called the first strategy of Swedish foreign and security policy. This strategy envisaged the UN as central for issues regarding war and peace globally. As a member of the EU, an organization where 11 of the 15 members are simultaneously members of NATO, Sweden no longer has the luxury, however, of being able to judge the actions of NATO in the detached way as was the case before 1995. The dilemma for Sweden can be illustrated by a quote from a press statement issued by the Swedish Prime Minister, Göran Persson, on the start of NATO bombings over Yugoslavia in March 1999:

> From the perspective of international law, it is difficult to find a clear justification for the military operations now under way. I regret the fact that it has not been possible for a united world community to back these actions by a mandate from the UN Security Council ...

> NATO's decision to start the bombings were obviously taken with the intention to prevent a humanitarian disaster and to re-establish peace in the area ...
>
> But bombings in themselves cannot solve the Kosovo conflict. It must be solved politically. The foundation is the Rambouillet agreement. The Government in Belgrade must now choose peace. (Prime Minister Göran Persson, press statement, 24 March 1999)

The Swedish government has needed to balance the requirements of non-alignment with the new requirements placed on a state that belongs to the EU, an organization that has a very intimate relationship with NATO, in the Kosovo crisis. The fact that the government has elected to take the policy stance indicated in the quote above must be taken as an indication that Sweden's posture in international crises and wars in Europe is different after membership in the EU as compared to before. It is next to impossible to imagine a Swedish government, led by Social Democrats, that prior to the country's membership in the EU would even have contemplated accepting, let alone supporting, the bombing of a sovereign European state without an explicit mandate by the UN Security Council. In this way, aspects of the Swedish government's foreign policy have 'become Europeanized' (the second research question outlined in Chapter 1). As is so common in Swedish foreign and security policy, however, the government has elected not to discuss the many ramifications that this change of stance has for Sweden's international posture now and/or in the future.

A similar failure to address the consequences of changes in the circumstances in which Swedish foreign and security policy is conducted can be seen in connection to the EU summit in Cologne, Germany, in early June 1999. In the 'Declaration of the European Council on Strengthening the Common European Policy on Security and Defence' it is stated that:

> In pursuit of our Common Foreign and Security Policy objectives and the progressive framing of a common defence policy, we are convinced that the Council should have the ability to take decisions on the full range of conflict prevention and crisis management tasks defined in the Treaty on European Union, the 'Petersberg tasks'. To this end, the Union must have the capacity for autonomous action, backed up by credible military forces, the means to decide to use them, and a readiness to do so, in order to respond to crises without prejudice to actions by NATO.

When representatives of the Swedish government are asked to comment on what is implied in these commitments, their tendency is to respond by stating that the EU's future actions should consist of such things as 'mine-clearing operations'. Prime Minister Göran Persson published an article in *Svenska Dagbladet* in early June 1999, where he addressed the question what these developments mean in terms of the Swedish strategy of non-alignment. The Prime Minister's response is emphatic:

> Swedish Social Democracy will not abandon non-alignment. We will not sign any proposal that means that the EU gets a permanent common army or that we have defence obligations within the EU. (Persson 1999)

While verbal declarations with essentially this content are being issued, the Swedish government, as well as other Swedish representatives, are busily taking part in a host of cooperative ventures which makes it quite difficult to regard these professions of continued 'non-alignment' as having any real content. This is so at the very least if one regards non-alignment as a concept with any practical meaning, as opposed to a mantra that has to be uttered on every conceivable occasion, but that has no practical content.

Another attempt to clarify the limits of Swedish participation in the sphere of security policy is made in the most recent proposal to the Swedish Riksdag on defence issues:

> Sweden's security policy today consists of broad participation in international cooperation in security policy. The only exception is the security cooperation that entails mutual security guarantees. (Prop. 1998/99: 74: 76)

The assessment that the 'verbalized' aspects of Swedish policy in the EU context do not, in this writer's view, square with important 'non-verbalized' aspects of the same policy, raises the question of why this is so. Without delving too deeply into this question, my answer is that this has to do with the difficulties of Sweden's dominant party, the Social Democrats, in handling many aspects of Swedish politics that are gradually being transformed by EU membership and more generally by wider processes in European politics. Within the Social Democratic Party there are important elements who remain very critical regarding the behaviour of the first Social Democrat-led government, in 1990–91, that decided to apply for Swedish EU membership. Despite the fact that the issue of membership can be regarded as having been finally resolved in the 1994 referendum, many members of the Social Democratic Party continue to be rather negative towards Swedish EU membership. The strategy of non-alignment has, in many parts of the Swedish polity, not least within the Social Democratic Party, acquired the status of a national myth. This strategy is, according to this view, essential not only for Sweden's past and future stability and well-being, but also for maintaining the stability of, at the very least, the Baltic Sea Region (see Chapter 3). The present (1999) Social Democratic government is very aware of these sentiments which is the reason why its representatives are very careful indeed when they portray the likely future significance of the CFSP and the EU as an actor in foreign and security policy more generally.

Sweden and the military alliances: NATO and the WEU

The previous sections make it clear how difficult it is to separate between the ostensibly different tracks on which Swedish foreign and security policy operates in Europe after 1990. Still, it is necessary to examine also Sweden's behaviour in relation to the two remaining military alliances in Europe, NATO and the WEU. During the period after 1990 both these organizations have undergone important changes. This has presented the Swedish government with further dilemmas as to the possible incompatibility of cooperation with either or both of these organizations, on the one hand, and the continued pursuit of the strategy of non-alliance, albeit in somewhat different form, on the other. Overall, the various Swedish governments after 1990 have decided to become more active in relation to the two military alliances, while at the same time stating that these activities do not constitute a break with the strategy of non-alignment, or that they necessarily imply that this strategy will be abandoned anytime soon.

One aspect of the ever-closer Swedish integration into the various security institutions in Europe has been the participation of Swedish military forces during several stages in the conflict in Bosnia. The origins of the Swedish participation were in the traditional institutional context: as a participant in the UNPROFOR mission first established in 1992. As the conflict in Bosnia changed, international involvement altered as well, including the composition and institutional connection of the peacekeeping (and to some extent, peace-enforcing) forces. With the active intervention of the United States from 1995 on, UNPROFOR was succeeded by IFOR, a mission undertaken within the context of NATO. Given the circumstances, it was regarded as natural for the Swedish contingent to remain in Bosnia, but in a different institutional context. There is no doubt that this experience, a largely successful military cooperation with NATO and NATO forces on a peacekeeping mission, gave an impetus for further flexibility in Swedish foreign and security policy.

Outside Bosnia, Sweden had to make decisions on three tracks in which its relationship with NATO was involved. The first of these was the Partnership for Peace (PfP) initiative (Yost 1998: 97–100; see also Andrén 1997: 114–22). This was an initiative taken by NATO at the summit meeting in Brussels in January 1994. It was undertaken with two broad purposes in mind. The first was to assist in the democratization of the defence forces in the former Warsaw Pact states. The second intended to create better practical cooperation between members of NATO and PfP members for various military interventions in crisis areas, including peace enforcement operations.

For Sweden, participation in the PfP was not a controversial issue among the parties represented in Parliament. Sweden thus acceded to the PfP in May 1994. Due to the wide participation in PfP, with 27 countries having signed the PfP Framework Document as of March 1999, the decision to participate was not a difficult one for Stockholm. Even if it meant that ties to NATO were, for the first time, formally established, since so many other countries did the same it was not regarded as really problematic when seen in the context of the strategy of non-alignment. It could also be said that the broad participation in PfP made the project seem somehow linked to the long-term Swedish goal of an all-encompassing security framework in Europe (cf. Andrén 1997: 114–15).

A second problem posed for Swedish politicians regarding the new situation in European security was more directly tied to the country's EU membership: namely, what to do concerning the Western European Union (WEU)? In the Maastricht Treaty, which entered into force on 1 November 1993, the WEU had been linked to the foreign and security policy cooperation (CFSP) within the EU framework. The relevant clause on CFSP in the Maastricht Treaty is Article J.4.1 where it is stated that the CFSP 'shall include all questions relating to the security of the Union, including the eventual framing of a common defence policy, which might in time lead to a common defence'. Article J.4.2 of the same Treaty created a formal link between CFSP and the WEU by stating that 'The Union requests the Western European Union . . . which is an integral part of the development of the Union, to elaborate and implement actions which have defence implications'.

This situation created a predicament for a Swedish government that professed to continue with a 'policy of non-alignment' even as a full member of the EU, an organization which had fairly far-reaching plans for a common foreign and security policy. At the same time, Sweden had to make a decision about how to link itself to what was indisputably a defence alliance: the WEU. EU membership clearly entailed the necessity of participating in the CFSP. Since this cooperation was in the second pillar of the new Union, where intergovernmental decision-making prevailed, it was not regarded as impossible to live with. Another factor that was important was the distinction made in the Maastricht Treaty between security policy, to be carried out within the CFSP framework, and defence policy, which was to be undertaken in the WEU framework (Rees 1998: 50–3). The Swedish government regarded its repeated declaration that it intended to remain non-aligned as setting a clear, self-defined boundary as to how far Stockholm was prepared to go when it came to the CFSP.

Full membership of the WEU would have been another matter. This was never seriously considered by either the non-socialist government that was in power between the Autumn of 1991 and the Autumn of 1994, or by the subsequent governments led by the Social Democrats. While the negotiations were going on in the first half of the 1990s between the EC/EU and the four candidate countries, besides Sweden also Finland, Norway and Austria, the WEU was also changing its character in several respects. One aspect of this change was making the exact nature of a tie between the organization and an interested state more flexible. Thus, during the 1990s there were three new types of association created to the WEU. The first was Associate membership, where countries that were members of NATO, but not of the EU, could cooperate with the WEU. Turkey, Norway and Iceland belong to this category as does the Czech Republic, Hungary and Poland. A second category was the status of Observer, which first was the type of tie chosen by Denmark and Ireland, and subsequently by Sweden, Finland and Austria (ibid.: 98–9). The third type of association with the WEU, besides membership, is that of Associate Partner, a category that includes seven states that were either former Warsaw Pact members or Republics of the (then) Soviet Union.

This solution created a situation where Sweden could both participate in the bulk of WEU work – in the parlance of the WEU's 'decisions at 18' (sometimes 28) – while, at the same time, claiming that it was not a member, and could thus not be seen as breaking the non-alignment strategy.

Still another track on which the Swedish government, as well as Swedish companies, gradually becomes more involved was that of cooperation among the defence industries (see Chapter 8). It must be highlighted, however, that Sweden's multi-pronged participation in many ventures in armaments cooperation, both within the NATO and the WEU frameworks, make official Swedish declarations of continued adherence to a strategy of non-alignment increasingly difficult to take at face value.

Conclusion

Any evaluation of the foreign and security aspects of 'Sweden as a member of the EU' has to take Swedish participation in other institutions and contexts into consideration. It is obvious that several aspects of traditional foreign policy, as well as some new strands, are now carried out in an EU context. At the same time, cooperation in the larger NATO framework and Observer status in the WEU also play a role for Swedish foreign and security policy.

Among the old aspects of Swedish foreign policy that are now carried out within the EU, a continued adherence to a strong support for the liberalization of international trade in the GATT/WTO framework must be mentioned. As there are several aspects of EU trade policy that are regarded as 'protectionist' by the Swedish government, it also seeks to further a more open trade policy on the part of the Union.

EU membership has created opportunities to pursue two new policies, both of them linked to the Baltic Sea Region (see Chapter 3). The first is strong support for the early entrance of the three Baltic nations into the EU. The second is general support for the development of stronger cooperation between all the nations in the Baltic Sea Region. In the latter respect, Sweden shares this emphasis with Finland.

Cooperation between Stockholm and Helsinki has been perhaps even more pronounced when it comes to the development of the CFSP as a vehicle for flexible operations in crisis management in Europe, and for the selective participation by the two countries in the WEU in this context. It must be stressed that these aspects of the Amsterdam Treaty, which came into force on 1 May 1999, are justly seen by the Swedish government as an important success. This development has not only contributed to making the EU a more flexible actor in European security affairs, but has also meant that the Swedish goal of creating an all-encompassing framework for European security has, at the very least, remained alive.

At the same time, it must be said that there are several aspects of Swedish relations with the EU, and more broadly to other European cooperative ventures, that makes the professed continued strategy of 'non-alignment in peace' ring increasingly hollow. The first and most important aspect here is that it seems very difficult for a member of the EU, an organization that ties its member nations so very closely in so many different policy spheres, to profess that it intends to remain 'neutral in the case of military conflict in its immediate vicinity' and remain credible. Second, the ever-increasing Swedish participation in cooperative ventures involving defence industries (see Chapter 8) also serves to make the non-alignment strategy seem to be one that is continually adhered to in 'verbal' policy, while it is, at the same time, undermined by other actions of the Swedish government. The perennial question of whether an analyst of foreign policy can distinguish between what a government says and what it does is acute when it comes to Swedish foreign and security policy after 1995. While the political scientist is often wary of making this distinction, in the case at hand it can be concluded that there is, indeed, an important difference between what Swedish representatives say that they are doing in the context of participation in cooperative ventures in foreign and security policy, and what is happening, at least in this analyst's assessment, in the policy spheres that Swedish politicians are characterizing.

My conclusion is that Sweden's foreign and security policy is now carried out within a context where, in practice, the 'all-encompassing European security system' already exists. The organizations that are the main spiders in this web are NATO, the OCSE, the WEU and, of course, the EU. It should be added that on top of these formal organizations, there are several other ties linking the European states to each other and, sometimes, to the US and Canada, as well as to the European states outside the nucleus of European security. This chapter has shown that these circumstances changed the very perspective on which Swedish foreign and security policy is being conducted and based. In several ways, this new perspective is already reflected in Swedish foreign and security policy. In other respects, notably the strategy of non-alignment, the Swedish government argues that the essence of the strategy still remains the same.

It is the main contention in this chapter that even the strategy of non-alignment has by 1999 been overtaken by events in Europe, prominently including the commitments that the Swedish government has undertaken within the many European cooperative ventures. It should be highlighted that the cooperative system not only includes many organizations, but also many other aspects of cooperation that are outside the strict organizational frameworks.

It is not possible to assess strictly and differentiate between the role of Sweden in just the EU separate from the wider context. Nevertheless, Swedish EU membership is an essential part of the changes that have occurred in the Swedish foreign and security policy landscape. At the same time, Swedish interaction with other bodies, such as NATO and the WEU, is also very important to any explanation of the changes affecting these matters. In addition, the broader research context of this book must be kept in mind. The pressures for increasing cooperation and integration that are analysed fairly strictly in terms of foreign and security policy in this chapter become even more pronounced if the third 'point' of the Miles's 'Membership Diamond' (new challenges of economic interdependence) are taken into account (see Chapter 8). The pressure for further integration that they produce is, nonetheless, also relevant to this analysis.

Notes

1. Within the author's conception of 'policy', a distinction is made between 'verbalized' and 'non-verbalized' policies. The former represents all spoken and written messages issued by official representatives. The latter represents all other aspects of behaviour in the external realm. On this distinction see Goldmann (1988: 6–10).
2. Interviews with Karl Hartzell and Nicola Clase, former and, at the time, present member of the European Integration Department at the Ministry for Foreign Affairs, 24 November 1998.

CHAPTER 3

'EU Icing on a Baltic Cake': Swedish Policy towards the Baltic Sea and EU Northern Dimensions

Lee Miles and Bengt Sundelius

Introduction

Sweden has regarded itself as an important actor in the Nordic region. As the Nordic state with the largest population, the country has been able to exert influence on its neighbours, both economically and politically. At the same time, the country is not immune from pressures emanating from inside and outside the Nordic region. As Krister Wahlbäck argued way back in the early 1980s, Sweden has largely found itself this century 'in the eye of a cyclone' watching small countries to the east and west drawn into wars or entering into cooperation with different large powers. Her instinct was 'to try to keep out of conflicts, to sustain neutrality, and to maintain as much Nordic cooperation as possible while waiting for better times' (Wahlbäck 1982: 23). Indeed, with the strategic changes that affected Europe since 1989, it may have seemed, at least initially, as if Sweden would be engulfed in another (if slightly unpredictable) patch of European bad weather. Nevertheless, there are indications that the 'better times' that Wahlbäck mentioned may have arrived. Certainly, Sweden's role in its surrounding region has altered in a qualitative sense. Although Nordic cooperation remains an important element (and these aspects are largely dealt with in Chapter 13), Swedish policy on Nordic cooperation has been largely complemented in the last decade by broader concerns – namely Sweden's interests in the Baltic Sea region and within the context of the country's EU membership since 1995.

The intention of this chapter is to examine Sweden's role as a regional actor. Alongside Swedish 'national' security policy concerns associated with the country's 'non-alignment' and the country's 'internationalist' commitments to peace and global stability through the United Nations (Goldmann 1991), regional politics are an integral component of Swedish foreign policy. Indeed, the 'Membership Diamond' (presented in Chapter 1) draws attention to the importance of EU and Baltic dimensions as part of the external dimension segment of its third 'point'. This chapter therefore explores Swedish policy towards several complementary, and interlinking concepts – stability in the Baltic Sea Region, the evolution of the EU's 'Northern

Dimension' policy and the development of a common CFSP strategy with Russia. We examine Swedish governmental policy at the bilateral and multilateral levels.

A clarification should also be made at this juncture. Swedish policy towards regional cooperation and organizations, can, of course, be gauged at various levels and using numerous concepts (see Gidlund and Jerneck 2000). The focus of this chapter will essentially be on government policy and thus take more of a 'state-centric' perspective, incorporating the assumption that state policy operates on a 'two-level game' where policy is formulated in the light of a thick mixture of domestic and international influences and pressures. This does not mean disregarding 'multi-level game' approaches to Nordic and Baltic cooperation for subnational authorities often form the bedrock of such Nordic and Baltic deepened cooperation (see Miles 1999). For example, the Swedish municipalities are active participants in regional initiatives. The authors also recognize the importance of private ventures by business, trade associations, voluntary groups and professionals. Government initiatives often aim to stimulate such interactions, which make up the brunt of Swedish 'foreign' involvement in these regional settings. Rather, the division is one of emphasis, given that most regional initiatives have been, to a large degree, enacted under the auspices of 'interlocking' international institutions in which the Swedish government is the chief representative of the state.

Swedish Priorities

Sweden has been seen traditionally as one of the leading, if not the leading, power in the Nordic region. Partly this derives from Sweden's history and cultural heritage as a once imperial power, whose influence stretched right across the Nordic region and Baltic Sea, and the fact that there has always been a healthy competition between Denmark and Sweden for the title of 'Nordic champion'. However, it is also in direct recognition that Sweden, like all states, has a distinct interest in fostering cordial and peaceful relations with its direct neighbours for sound economic and political reasons. Historically, the majority of Sweden's trade has been with other Nordic countries and, as we shall see later, the Baltic Sea is an area of substantial market potential. From a political perspective, Sweden has an interest in portraying itself as a nation-state with substantial regional influence, committed to coordination with neighbouring states. This image strengthens indirectly the Swedish government's negotiating hand in European organizations and further projects the country's voice on the world stage.

Moreover, Sweden has a stake in ensuring that the Nordic and wider Baltic Sea regions remain ones of low tension as part of its government's continuing policy of non-alignment. There are several elements associated with this point. First, it is important to Sweden that the democratic and economic transitions of the ex-communist states on edges of the Baltic Sea take place as smoothly as possible. In particular, this includes the recognition and protection of the Baltic States' (Estonia, Latvia and Lithuania) newly acquired sovereignty and that potential flashpoints with Russia are reduced as this is the most probable cause of tension in the area. Second, Swedish policy seeks to develop closer relations with Russia (and the Ukraine) in order to encourage the domestic reform process taking place there. Like many others, Sweden is fearful of instability in any of the large powers in the region. The presidential election taking place in Russia in 2000, for instance, was observed closely by the Swedes.

To be able to achieve these numerous aims, Swedish policy has operated at many levels, including bilateral and multilateral approaches (see Værnø 1999), and using most of the institutional mechanisms presently on offer. Indeed, any analysis of Swedish policy needs to accommodate assumptions that the Baltic Sea is an increasingly diverse and crowded area, with a substantial number of interested nation states and a growing number of international institutions establishing a presence of some sort. At the bilateral level, the Swedish government seeks to improve diplomatic relations with neighbouring states and has established and/or improved bilateral cooperation programmes with most of them. Bilateral cooperation is neither small nor insubstantial.[1] At the multilateral level, the Swedes, like all of the Nordic states, have used international institutions, such as the Council of Baltic Sea States (CBSS), to manage appropriate regional initiatives and to nurture some kind of Baltic Sea 'civic security' community. In short, the Baltic Sea 'unites free countries and people through increasing trade, cultural exchange and political cooperation' (Ministry of Foreign Affairs 1999a: 2).

Given the growing complexity and numbers of international institutions, it seems reasonable to argue that Swedish policy operates largely, if not exclusively, through several frameworks in this particular regional setting, which help to support existing bilateral contacts. Close to home, the Swedish government has continued with formal and informal cooperation with its traditional Nordic partners, for this, as always, remains the bedrock on which regional cooperation is built (see Ministry of Foreign Affairs 1998a). However, concepts of the 'Baltic Sea' may have, albeit to a limited extent, blurred the distinctiveness of purely Nordic cooperation schemes in the 1990s. Certainly, Sweden has encouraged the inclusion of Estonia, Latvia and Lithuania in regional initiatives, including the expansion of once purely Nordic multilateral institutions to include regular joint sessions with representatives from the three Baltic States. The Swedish government has also sponsored their applications to join the EU. Moreover, Swedish notions of 'enlarged Nordic', or, more accurately, Northern cooperation is not restricted to the three Republics and incorporates the wider dimension of the 'Baltic Sea'. In particular, Poland, Russia and even the Ukraine have been identified by the Persson government as key partners. The CBSS has been regarded by the Swedes as 'an increasingly important forum for cooperation' (Ministry of Foreign Affairs 1999a: 3) as Russia, Germany, Poland and the European Commission are members.

Furthermore, since accession in 1995, cooperation with continental European partners has become a centrepiece of Swedish policy. As the third 'point' of the 'Membership Diamond' suggests, Sweden's economic policies are largely reacting to an agenda set outside the Baltic Sea region. Where the Nordic and Baltic dimensions are considered, Swedish policy aims to utilize EU mechanisms to foster further Baltic Sea cooperation, such as the channelling of assistance through the EU's PHARE and TACIS programmes. From a political and rather practical viewpoint, 'Europe' has been regarded increasingly by the Swedes as being as important as purely Nordic and/or Baltic Sea solutions. The former is certainly the preferred arena for 'crisis management' roles (see Chapter 2). As Værnø (1999: 193) comments, 'the Nordic region is being absorbed in a Baltic or Northern East European Region, and seen as a sub-region in an EU or NATO/PfP context'. However, from a more general, societal perspective, the Swedes are still hesitant towards involvement in European integration (Ekengren and Sundelius 1998). Many segments of Swedish society identify more closely with their more intimate Nordic, and also increasingly with their smaller-sized Baltic, neighbours.

Sweden and the Baltic Sea

All it takes to understand (at least superficially) the importance of the Baltic Sea region for Sweden is to take a quick look at any map of the region and its demography. The Baltic Sea area has a population of about 84 million and Sweden is centred geographically in the middle of it, with the entire region accessible from Stockholm by ship or by air. Tallinn is the closest foreign capital to Stockholm, closer in fact than even Oslo and/or Helsinki. In qualitative terms, Swedish policy (operating at both the bilateral and multilateral levels) must accommodate events and changes in this vital region.

Swedish policy-makers have seen great political opportunities in participating in Baltic affairs. As the largest of the Nordic states, an ex-imperial power and member of all the major Nordic, Baltic and now EU clubs, Sweden can, quite naturally, play a leadership role, reinforcing its 'internationalist' credentials in Europe's backyard. Turning to economic considerations, the Baltic Sea has been an area of dynamic growth – and some have called it 'Europe's economic tiger' (see *Financial Times* 1999a). The region represents, as Leif Pagrotsky, Swedish Minister for Trade, comments, 'a sea of opportunities' and a tremendous economic development for Sweden (Ministry of Foreign Affairs 1999b: 1). In GDP terms, it is about the same size as the UK and represents more than 10 per cent of Europe's total GDP, and the region's growth rate (in spite of the economic crisis affecting Russia) averaged 3.2 per cent between 1997 and 1999. The new market opportunities have, for example, begun to be exploited by Swedish companies. Volvo, ABB and Ericsson are just some of the names of high profile firms establishing operations in the region. Swedish trade with Estonia, for instance, has increased by more than 300 per cent in five years.

Baltic cooperation also provides additional methods for dealing with some of the thorniest security-related problems that have accompanied the positive changes in Central and Eastern Europe. As Hubel asserts, the Baltic Sea region links together Eastern, Northern and Western Europe – three sub-regions which previously had differing political and economic and military orientations, making up his so-called 'Baltic Triangle' (Hubel 1999). From a 'soft security' perspective, it is in the Swedish government's interest, not only to reduce tensions between neighbouring states in this 'triangular' region – for instance, between Russia and certain Baltic states over the question of the treatment of Russian minorities – but also to utilize Baltic cooperation to handle (at least partly) key 'environmental' and 'societal security' questions (Buzan 1991), such as promoting greater nuclear (military and civil) safety in the region, coordination in public health questions and initiatives aimed at restricting organized crime. Moreover, as Archer and Jones argue, the Swedes, along with the rest of the Nordic countries, have been predisposed to acceptance of 'softer' definitions of security. Aspects such as 'comprehensive security' (where security is not just about military issues), 'civic security' (implying security also includes society and civic aspects) and cooperative security (assuming that security is about resisting indeterminate forces of instability through cooperation between states) are assumptions underpinning Swedish governmental statements on the Baltic Sea region (Archer and Jones 1999: 172–6). Indeed, Dahl further argues that the importance of the Baltic Sea region may act as a catalyst for substantial changes in Swedish security doctrine and a convergence of an active role in the Baltic with diminishing concerns over maintaining a policy of 'freedom from military alliances' (Dahl 1999: 154).

The foundation of Swedish policy and, indeed, of Swedish influence in the region lay, from a very early stage, in the establishment of substantial bilateral programmes, accompanied later by increasingly focused policy objectives. In the economic sphere, the Swedes were not slow in offering development assistance to the economies in transition around the Baltic Rim – principally to Estonia, Latvia, Lithuania, Poland and Russia (see Table 3.1).

Virtually right from the start, the Swedish government focused on supporting the changes in these states by offering economic aid for various projects (starting with aid to Poland in 1989), and by the 1994/95 fiscal year some SEK 3.7 billion had been assigned for this purpose. However, it was in June 1995 that the Swedish parliament approved the first comprehensive

Table 3.1   Distribution of total Swedish support to the Baltic Sea region 1989–97

Country	%
Estonia	14
Latvia	17
Lithuania	19
Poland	14
Russia	15
Ukraine	2
Others	4
Regional	15

Source: Ministry of Foreign Affairs 1998b:9

programme for this cooperation, allocating SEK 4 billion for the following three and a half years (1995–98).[2] Between 1989 and 1998, for example, Sweden allocated a total of SEK 6.5 billion to bilateral development cooperation for Central and Eastern Europe, although this development assistance was chiefly focused on supporting 'the transfer of "know-how", creating contacts and networks between countries, institutions and people' (Ministry of Foreign Affairs 1998c: 10).

Moreover, in 1996, another separate fund of SEK 1 billion – the so-called 'Baltic Billion Fund' – was created to finance cooperation in the areas of environmental protection, education, infrastructure and the food industry (Ministry of Foreign Affairs 1997a: 2–3). This Fund, which was given an especially high profile since it was administered originally by the Prime Minister's Advisory Council for Baltic Sea Cooperation, was intended to be a finite sum distributed over three years (1996–99). However, given that the Fund has been regarded as a political and economic success, confirming Swedish desires to play an active role in the Baltic sphere, the government allocated a further SEK 1 'Baltic billion' to be distributed over the succeeding five year period in its 1998 Spring Budget Bill.[3] The economic objective of this bilateral support is, in many ways, to increase Swedish, as opposed to Nordic, influence in the Baltic Sea region and, in particular, to give the country's firms a hand in securing investment opportunities in the face of competition from other Nordic and Western rivals.

Moreover, Swedish bilateral aid has been focused increasingly around a number of other (essentially political) goals. The Riksdag (in May 1995) specified four objectives as regards cooperation with Central and Eastern Europe (and the Baltic Sea region in particular) which appeared in the government's flagship 1997 bill (Government Bill 1997/98: 70)[4] and form guiding themes for Swedish policy in the Baltic Sea region:

1. *Cooperation to promote security.* This support has primarily been given to strengthen the sovereignty of the three Baltic States and includes: aspects relating to 'comprehensive security' such as the training of diplomats from the Baltic States, cooperation and training of border

control and customs guards, police, rescue services and civilian and military defence. Sweden has also supported the Baltic peacekeeping Battalion (BALTBAT) and mine clearance operations.

2. *To deepen the culture of democracy.* Swedish objectives in this area aim to strengthen aspects of 'civic security' such as the judicial systems and local democratic traditions and authorities. Swedish non-governmental organizations, political parties and interest groups are all important components. In particular, special language and integration support for the Russian-speaking minorities of Latvia and Estonia is included as a means of supporting the first objective.

3. *To support a socially sustainable economic transformation.* Swedish intentions are to promote education, information and knowledge exchange and to provide financial aid in support of economic reform processes taking place in the ex-communist countries in the Baltic.

4. *Environmental support* in order to promote the sustainable development of the region – an example of 'cooperative security'. Swedish measures have concentrated on water purification and sewage treatment in the large cities in the Baltic Sea, and enhancement of nuclear safety and radiation protection, such as improvement of security at the Ignalina power station in Lithuania.[5]

A central part of Swedish policy is concentrated on developing closer relations with the three Baltic States (Estonia, Latvia and Lithuania). After 1991 – with the collapse of the Soviet Union, the Baltic States' independence, the EC application and a change in Swedish government – the non-socialist administration of Carl Bildt followed a more open and assertive policy towards Estonia, Latvia and Lithuania (Archer 1998: 17). This policy included intense negotiation efforts to facilitate Russian troop withdrawals from the region. With the return of the Social Democrats to power in October 1994, non-alignment was once again emphasized. Over time, policy towards the three 'Balts' has been placed firmly in the context of the EU's emerging CFSP and NATO's 'Partnership for Peace initiative'. Another notable and high-profile strategy of the Göran Persson government was to engage the USA in the development of this sub-region.

After 1996, Sweden, once again, took important steps to raise its presence in the Baltic Sea on to a higher plateau, when Prime Minister Göran Persson launched 'a Baltic offensive', aimed at promoting a more discernible political and multilateral (as opposed to economic and bilateral) role in the region. Not only was this the year when a new Prime Minister came to power in Sweden, looking for an agenda on which to imprint himself in the minds of the electorate, but this was also the time when the Swedish government held the Presidency of the CBSS, which was also reviewing its programmes. Indeed, the CBSS, which has been established since March 1992, offered numerous advantages for Sweden. Designed as a forum for close cooperation between the countries around the Baltic Sea, it remains the only body in which all the Baltic Rim states are represented together, alongside Norway, Iceland and the European Commission.[6]

The CBSS extensive action programmes for the Baltic Sea region were largely the result of negotiations shaped during the Swedish Presidency (1995–96) and the Swedes were influential during the high profile summit held in Visby in May 1996 (Ministry of Foreign Affairs 1997b: 10). The Swedes used their period holding the Presidency to ensure that the agenda of the CBSS was influenced by their priorities already shaping Sweden's bilateral programmes. Indeed, it is striking that the so-called 'Visby Process' mirrored many of the priorities emphasized in Swedish domestic programmes. The 'Baltic 21' (Agenda 21 for the Baltic Sea region) programme, for instance, included many familiar themes, such as sustainable development, close to Swedish hearts. Furthermore, at Visby, the Swedish Prime Minister was instructed to ensure the coordination of Baltic cooperation through a special office – the Baltic Sea States Support Group – which was the embryo for the CBSS Secretariat established in Stockholm in 1998. In addition, a Swedish-led Task Force on Organized Crime in the Baltic Area has also been in operation since Visby. Additional initiatives were also taken at the Riga CBSS summit in January 1998, which also included a weighty Russian presence. At that time, a programme for civil security transcending the former enemies of the Cold War was launched following a Swedish initiative.

In short, the Social Democratic government, and Persson himself, invested substantial political time in developing multilateral cooperation in the Baltic area, so that since 1996, Swedish multilateral cooperation has become comparable to prior and existing levels of bilateral contact. Swedish Baltic policy is more 'balanced' since 1996, with Sweden's well-established bilateral programmes supplemented by a gradually more prominent role in key multilateral organizations associated with the Baltic Sea. The Swedes have also tried to play a role on the Barents Euro-Arctic Council (established in 1993) and, under the Swedish chairmanship (1997), helped to push forward negotiations on, amongst other things, policy towards nuclear safety, the management of nuclear waste and on the efficient use of energy. The (then) Secretary-General of NATO, Javier Solana, attended the Foreign Ministers' meeting of the Council in early 1998.

There are obvious advantages for the Swedish elite in shaping out this role. Not only does this carve out Persson's individual contribution as Swedish premier, and reaffirm Sweden's role as a leading player in the Baltic Sea, but it also shows an effective domestic strategy. An active role in the Baltic is less controversial back home with the electorate than is the country's membership of the European Union. By stressing Swedish action under Baltic auspices, it allows the governing elite to popularize regional initiatives, which are attached to, but not entirely immersed in, the unpopular vestiges of the EU – aspects of the first 'point' of the 'Membership Diamond' (Miles 1997a; 1998b). However, under the Social Democrats the country's role in the Baltic arena is selective. It is largely based on non-military assistance and regional cooperation on functional matters, and is associated with concepts of broader 'soft security' contexts which pose much less threat to Swedish ambitions of military non-alignment and/or Russian anxieties over NATO dominance (Archer 1999: 54–5). The idea that Sweden should provide 'hard security' collective defence assurances to the Baltic states is clearly not realistic. Sweden has refused to give such assurances even with regard to her close Nordic neighbours and/or to her new political partners in the EU (see Chapter 2).

This brings us to three final points as regards multilateral cooperation in the Baltic Sea. First, the Swedes perceive the CBSS and Barents forums as offering benefits precisely because they include Russia as a member. They are seen as 'Northern' rather than purely Western orientated organizations, compatible with the country's alignment-free posture, and as potential vehicles to placate Russian fears of marginalization. Second, the US has been generally in favour of the CBSS in particular and, thus, Sweden can operate with American approval and support. Persson's 'Baltic Offensive' was launched after securing American blessing and the CBSS has avoided embroilment in many of the divisions associated with NATO and Russia. Rather, a US–Nordic–Baltic axis is being nurtured through a number of annual conferences and exercises, support of the US–Baltic Charter signed in Washington in early 1998, and high-level official meetings on defence issues. Thus, the language of Baltic cooperation is largely told using positive vocabulary similar to that usually ascribed to Nordic cooperation. Nonetheless, as Anders Bjurner comments, even Baltic cooperation 'is a supplementary process greatly dependent upon the broader all-European processes' (Ministry of Foreign Affairs 1998c: 2). Consequently, Baltic Sea cooperation also needs to be seen in the light of Sweden's other European commitments and it is to these aspects that this chapter will now turn.

Sweden in the EU

Sweden's role as a full EU member is the fastest-developing of the dimensions considered here. This section is concerned primarily with the Swedish position in relation to EU policy aspects most affecting its relations with its closest neighbours. These include Swedish policy on the accessions of the Central and Eastern European Countries (CEECs) into the EU, especially since the present applicants include the three 'Balts' and Poland. Second, Swedish attitudes towards the Finnish-inspired and now Union-adopted policy on the 'Northern Dimension' – in practice, the Union's attempt to develop a comprehensive strategy towards the Baltic and Barents regions. Finally, attention is also given to Sweden's emerging role in the EU in fostering closer relations with Russia.

Suffice to say, the Swedes have been interested for a long time in utilizing, where possible, the European Union, in order to aid the democratic and economic reform processes taking place in the Baltic Rim states. On top of its growing bilateral programmes, Sweden has also contributed to EU programmes for Eastern Europe – TACIS and PHARE – amounting to SEK 1.2 billion up to and including 1998. Like Sweden's smaller bilateral programmes, these EU funds were largely focused on aiding the Baltic Republics (initially) and (later) directed at institution-building in the Baltic Rim states more generally in order to support ongoing reforms.

However, alongside Sweden's renewed interest in the Baltic, the Persson government has placed even greater emphasis on developing EU policies on Baltic issues since joining the Union in 1995. The EU has been seen increasingly by the Swedish elite as an additional source of policy coordination on Baltic questions and of financial support for the region. This reflects partly the fact that the Union itself has a growing interest in Baltic questions, especially as there are four member states (Denmark, Finland, Sweden and Germany) since 1995 with a geographical 'toe' in the Baltic Sea. Moreover, with further EU enlargement seeming inevitable, Baltic considerations have assumed greater importance for the Union given that four of the CEEC applicants also have Baltic interests (Estonia, Latvia, Lithuania and Poland) and all are presently (or soon to start) negotiating entry terms. In addition, Finland has since 1997 championed the need for an 'EU Northern Dimension' and under its 1999 Presidency pushed for further expansion of EU provisions in this area. Alongside the Northern Dimension initiative, the EU has also agreed a common strategy for dealing with Russia in 1999. Indeed, it is Sweden, rather than Finland, that has been given special responsibility for 'fleshing out' the Union's political commitments with the Russians.

Further EU enlargement

There are several broad Swedish priorities towards the EU on Baltic questions, which, when taken together, ensure the Union is regarded by the Swedish elite as an increasingly important strand of Sweden's multilateral approaches towards the Baltic Sea region. First, the Swedish government canvasses for the entry of Estonia, Latvia, Lithuania and Poland into the European Union, broadening the 'Baltic basis' of the Union and the potential for EU policies affecting the region (Ministry of Foreign Affairs 1998d). This has been a long-standing objective of the Swedes and dates back almost from the time they joined and certainly from when the three Baltic Republics lodged their respective membership application in 1995. Much of Swedish and EU assistance to these countries is now aimed at facilitating their entry into the EU. This is also one of the key priorities listed for the Swedish European Council Presidency of 2001.

Indeed, it is easy to see why the Swedish elite, already finding it hard to convince the domestic public of the relevance of the EU, would like to see the growing markets of the Baltic Sea inside the Union (Ministry of Foreign Affairs 1998c: 90). However, there have been some political difficulties. In spite of the obvious potential for Nordic unity, a common Nordic policy on CEEC accessions has been problematic at times. From an early stage, the Swedes preferred that a joint policy between the three existing Nordic EU member states be followed, based on ensuring that the EU's Agenda 2000 programme treated the three Baltic Republics similarly and as a de facto convoy of applicants. This policy came unstuck when the Finns broke ranks and championed Estonia's sole promotion into the fast-track of EU entry – to the consternation of the Swedish Foreign Ministry.[7] However, these difficulties have been overcome since the EU agreed at its Tampere summit in 1999 to speed up the opening of accession negotiations with the remaining applicants, which include Latvia and Lithuania.

The Swedish government has been a fervent supporter of speeding up the Agenda 2000 process, arguing vigorously for extensive reform inside the existing Union, such as to the CAP. Moreover, in the government's programme entitled 'Developing Cooperation between Neighbouring Countries' (Government Bill 1997/98: 70), three tasks have been given priority for the period 1999–2001 – all of which are associated with the EU's emerging role in the Baltic Sea. The first is 'to contribute towards EU membership for Estonia, Latvia, Lithuania and Poland' (in recognition of the opening of formal accession negotiations by the EU with the Estonians and the Poles). It has been estimated, for example, that 90 to 95 per cent of Swedish financial support to these four countries is designed to facilitate their preparations for EU membership (Ministry of Foreign Affairs 1999c). The second is the further integration of Russia and the Ukraine into broader European cooperation and the third is to step up efforts in the social sector, including gender equality issues, in which the Union already has a substantial presence in terms of existing EU legislation (Ministry of Foreign Affairs 1998e). It is noticeable that in this Swedish cooperation programme, the three tasks (the first directly and the last two indirectly) are associated with EU roles – suggesting a tendency for convergence between Sweden's Baltic and EU policy portfolios.

The EU's Northern Dimension

The EU's Northern Dimension (ND) is of particular interest as the concept stretches beyond the strict borders of the EU. Consequently, the Swedes were supporters of Finnish proposals to create such a policy, suggested by them at the European Council summit in Luxembourg in late 1997, given that at the heart of the initiative was the concept that the ND could 'decrease the risk of a destabilising divide forming along the border of an enlarged Union' (Stenlund 1999). Since the Commission's report on the viability of a Northern Dimension (requested at Luxembourg) was adopted by the European Council (11–12 December 1998) at Vienna, an ND policy is virtually guaranteed.[8] However, this must be transformed into a concrete package of policies and policy guidelines.

It not hard to discern why the Swedes favoured the creation of an EU Northern Dimension. First, the ND was largely perceived by the Persson government as 'a policy and area awareness exercise' for the EU and as 'a marketing tool' in which the EU has given formal recognition to what largely amounts to ongoing activities.[9] Second, the Swedish government, like its Finnish counterpart, sees that one of the main 'cooperative security' aims of any ND policy is to keep key non-EU states, such as Russia and Norway, involved in EU policy affecting the region, especially after the Commission explicitly recognized that 'The Northern Region is also the Union's only direct geographical link with the Russian Federation' (European Commission 1998: 1). On top of this, the creation of an ND policy would strengthen the EU's future 'common strategies' (a policy instrument provided for under the Amsterdam Treaty) – the first of which deals with Russia and was agreed in 1999.

Third, the ND policy coverage is broad and flexible, helping to fill in the gaps between the activities of Nordic, Baltic and Barents cooperation, which do not, for the most part, have the attention of mainstream continental (and Mediterranean-focused) Europe. Fourth, and as a caveat on previous points, the Swedes were also contented with the fact that, despite the ND's flexibility, 'hard' security issues were not to be included, ensuring that the ND should be a 'low tension' policy. Finally, the proposed ND is largely concentrated on issues such as environmental protection, nuclear safety issues, cooperation on energy and between regional and subnational authorities, trade, transport and telecommunications and health issues, which are funded out of existing EU programmes and have no implications of increased budgetary contributions. In short, the ND is a relatively 'low-tension' and 'low-cost' option, which offers advantages for Baltic Sea countries in bringing the EU more actively into the region.

Hence, Swedish policy-makers have stressed that there are now three EU policies which deal with Baltic Sea questions. For the Swedes, Agenda 2000 – the EU policy on CEEC enlargement – deals, to a large degree, with EU relations with the Baltic States and Poland. Second, the fledgling ND policy incorporates those non-EU states (who are also not EU applicants at present), such as Russia, with key Baltic interests. However, the Swedish government is keen to ensure that the ND remains low cost and is essentially about raising the profile of 'The High North' and the Baltic within the EU, and most of all as an 'umbrella concept' for Sweden's existing work in the interlocking institutions of the CBSS and BEAC. Indeed, it is striking that most of the activity areas identified by the Commission in its 1998 ND report are already covered by the work of the CBSS and its 'Baltic 21' initiative.

The ND is regarded by most Swedish policy-makers as a supplementary concept to the existing work of the various 'interlocking institutions' covering the Baltic Sea – another mechanism to manage Hubel's 'Baltic triangle'. It is not as yet regarded by the Swedish elite as an EU replacement for other organizations, especially since Sweden has marked out a leading role for itself in the latter. In Swedish eyes, the EU is incorporating the Baltic Sea, but the Baltic Sea should not be an exclusive EU domain. Other multilateral institutions, as well as other countries, such as Norway, Russia and the USA, have legitimate stakes in the area.

Furthermore, the ND is 'a good base, but not a perfect one'.[10] The Swedish Foreign Ministry has, for example, called for greater attention to be placed on education and training issues, which were largely ignored in the 1998 Commission report. This is an area, of course, where the Swedes are already active. Many Swedish educational institutions have established links with other Baltic and Russian counterpart organizations and thus, these aspects can be included with little political or financial cost to the ND project or the Swedes.

In addition, the launch of the ND initiative has not been trouble free. The first major foreign minister's meeting on the ND held on 11–12 November in Helsinki was, to some extent, overshadowed by the civil war taking place in Chechnya. This has soured relations between certain EU member states and Russia and made moving the ND forward somewhat difficult. The meeting was also poorly attended by EU foreign ministers (partly in protest at Russian actions in Chechnya), but further doubts were also expressed about the commitment of the continental European EU states to the project. As one diplomat put it, 'The Northern Dimension is not a very sexy item for ministers. There is nothing to argue about' (*Financial Times* 1999b: 6).

Nevertheless, the political base of the ND has been consolidated. The Helsinki conference was important in recognizing the progress made under the ND umbrella in, amongst others, the environmental protection and energy sectors and the EU is now establishing a 'Northern Dimension Action Plan' (Finnish Ministry of Foreign Affairs 1999). Most importantly, the creation of the EU's ND policy has introduced a stronger focus on the EU's Northern periphery and this momentum will be continued since Sweden has already committed itself to holding a 'follow-up conference' on the ND during the Swedish EU Presidency.

Closer relations with Russia

The third EU policy which indirectly affects the Baltic Sea is the EU's CFSP 'common strategy' for dealing with Russia agreed at Cologne in June 1999, which complements the more general 'Northern Dimension' initiative. This new mechanism aims to promote coordination between member states in order to maximize their efforts and influence on Russia. It is of particular interest to the Swedish government since it has built an extensive array of bilateral contact and developmental cooperation with the evolving Russian Federation dating back to 1991. This has intensified considerably in recent years, with, for example, the Persson government adopting a new country strategy for development cooperation with Russia (1999–2001) as recently as October 1999. The new country strategy focuses on 'socially sustainable economic transition', and increases Swedish assistance to Russia in democratic, environmental, social and public health areas (Ministry of Foreign Affairs 1999d: 1). Yet, the Persson government has sought to enhance its contribution to EU policy on Russia by assembling a high-ranking inter-ministerial task force within the Swedish governmental machinery to focus on these questions (Ministry of Foreign Affairs 1998f: 5).

What is of particular interest is the fact that Sweden's important relationship with Russia has been formally recognized by the Union. The Persson administration has been given the task of further cementing the new CFSP 'common strategy' through its extensively developed cooperation with the Russians. To some degree, this is in recognition of the Persson government's desire to see relations with Russia having a central place in the CFSP. For example, Sweden was successful in ensuring the EU hearing a number of proposals relating to Russia which featured in the Commission's report to the Vienna summit in December 1998 and which formed the basis for the EU's first common strategy with Russia.

This closer Swede–Russian relationship and its transmission into EU policy has shown the first signs of fruit for the Union, with, for instance, the Swedes tabling cooperation with Russia against organized crime as an important issue for discussion at the 1999 EU Tampere summit. Indeed, the Swedish government has already indicated that relations with Russia will be a priority during Sweden's term as President of the European Council in 2001 (Ministry of Foreign Affairs 1999e: 3).

Conclusion

When analysing Swedish policy towards the respective aspects covered in this chapter – the Baltic Sea and EU Northern Dimension – then a number of preliminary conclusions can be drawn. First, Swedish policy does illustrate, albeit to a limited extent, the potential for the country to fit into the general process of European integration. Indeed, it is pretty clear that a strong Nordic and Baltic dimension within the European Union (with Sweden playing a key role) is what the Swedish elite thinks that the EU-reluctant public would like to see develop. As always Nordic cooperation remains a central plank of Swedish policy, but can also be increasingly viewed as a 'subset' of European integration. Regular manifestations of Nordic unity do help Sweden to project a larger and more coherent policy image in the Baltic and EU environments. Moreover, since Sweden joined the Union, the Baltic Sea as a region has grown in importance to the Union. Swedish policy-makers have the opportunity to ensure that Sweden plays a formative role in shaping EU policy in relation to the Baltic Sea and towards Russia.

Second, even though Nordic multilateral and bilateral cooperation remains important, Swedish policy has been based largely on projecting its perspectives and leadership profile in Baltic and EU forums by cementing its role in the CBSS/BEAC, playing a supportive role as regards further EU enlargement and the formulation of an EU Northern Dimension and an enhanced role in developing the EU's common strategy towards Russia. There has been an increasing convergence of Swedish, Nordic, Baltic and even EU viewpoints on the need for coherent approaches towards the Baltic Sea. Hence, as the EU has become more 'Balticized' so have Swedish policy-makers grasped the opportunity for leadership inside the EU and directed policy efforts at ensuring that their Baltic policy is also directed at facilitating EU objectives. With some simplification, it can be argued that, conversely, Swedish policy towards the Baltic Sea has become further 'Europeanized' and Swedish bilateral and multilateral programmes do include considerations relating to the Union.

This analysis also verifies aspects of the 'Membership Diamond', in which perspectives on the Baltic formed an integral part of its third 'point', pushing forward Swedish EU socialization and the perceived benefits as an EU member (see Miles 1997a, 1998b). Certainly, the EU provides new institutional opportunities for Baltic cooperation. Also closer relations with Russia, as well as the prospect of further EU enlargement to include the Baltic Republics and Poland, are arguments in favour of Sweden staying in the Union. An EU Northern Dimension and, even more markedly, the Union's developing relationship with Russia facilitates, albeit to a limited extent, Swedish popular acceptance of greater levels of 'Europeanization' and for the country's society to be further adjusted to life as an EU member state.

Furthermore, aspects of the Diamond's first 'point' are also vindicated by this analysis since there is general accord between the governing elite, the main political parties and even the general public that Sweden should play a role in the Baltic. There is an opportunity for the Persson government to utilize Baltic Sea questions in its fight to persuade a sceptical public and unite the political parties on the benefits of the Union ('point' 1). There is clearly the potential here for vibrant interaction between Putnam's Level I (international) and Level II (national) contexts. However, a word of caution is needed. There are criticisms within Sweden that the EU's Agenda 2000 strategy is slow and cumbersome, that essential EU reform of the CAP has been uninspiring, and that the EU's Northern Dimension policy is at a fledgling stage. The short-term impact on domestic opinion will be minimal, despite the EU representing 'a better umbrella structure covering the whole of Europe'.[11] The irony is that it has been, at least initially, the Finns, rather than the Swedes, who have been better so far in projecting themselves on Baltic questions inside the Union and thus, they have (so far) benefited most from playing the EU–Baltic card.

For this reason, the Persson government will also seek to maintain its high profile in other Baltic forums, like the CBSS. Furthermore, it will also stress

Sweden's excellent bilateral relationship with Russia as being of value to the entire Union. Nonetheless, the period up to the 2001 Swedish European Council Presidency will be a critical time, in which the Persson government will seek to enhance further its Baltic credentials and bring the work of the Baltic and EU forums together for domestic (partisan) and international (strategic) reasons.

Notes

1. In this context, bilateral cooperation refers to Sweden's relations with other individual nation states. Multilateral cooperation is defined as Sweden's policy towards international organizations and groups of states working together for mutual benefit.
2. The first government bill on cooperation with Central and Eastern Europe was presented to the Riksdag in February 1995 and resulted in its unanimous adoption later in the year.
3. Management of the Fund has also been transferred from the Prime Minister's Advisory Council for Baltic Sea Cooperation to the Ministry of Industry and Trade.
4. The Bill was approved by the Riksdag in May 1998.
5. For further details see Ministry of Foreign Affairs (1998b).
6. The members of the Council of Baltic Sea States (CBSS) are Denmark, Estonia, Finland, Germany, Iceland, Latvia, Lithuania, Norway, Poland, Russia, Sweden and the European Commission.
7. Taken from an interview with Mr Gunnar Lund, then Under-Secretary of State for Foreign Affairs, Stockholm, December 1998.
8. The European Council requested the European Commission to prepare an action plan for the Northern Dimension at the Helsinki Summit in December 1999.
9. Taken from an interview with Anders Bjurner, then Assistant State Secretary for Foreign Affairs, 23 February 1999.
10. Taken from an interview with Helena Ödmark, Ministry of Foreign Affairs, 27 February 1999.
11. Taken from an interview with Anders Bjurner, then Assistant State Secretary for Foreign Affairs, 23 February 1999.

PART II

The Political System

CHAPTER 4

The Europeanization of Swedish Politics

Olof Ruin

The Europeanization of Swedish politics has affected the country's political system, including the different actors participating in ongoing decision-making processes. This means that, amongst others, the central political institutions, political parties, interest organizations and bureaucrats have adapted to the pressures emanating from the fact that Sweden has for several years been a member of the EU. Sweden has thereby experienced new situations of a kind similar to those that older members of the Union had faced earlier in their relationships with Brussels (Mény *et al.* 1996; Rometsch and Wessels 1996).

In this chapter the emphasis will be on the institutional changes that have occurred as a consequence of EU membership. In particular, the constitution of Sweden was altered as a prerequisite for entry into the Union and the national institutions – especially the Riksdag and the government – have come to operate in a slightly different way.

The constitutional framework

The fundamental law (constitution) of Sweden, The Instrument of Government of 1974, did not, as the relevant clauses were formulated, allow for a transfer of power to the EC/EU of the magnitude that full membership was interpreted to imply. Therefore, half a year after the Social Democratic government announced its readiness to consider such a membership in October 1990, a commission of inquiry was appointed with the task of proposing constitutional changes that would make EC/EU entry legally possible. The commission consisted of parliamentarians from all the political parties and was chaired by myself as a professor of political science. Early on in the work of this body it was concluded that it was neither necessary nor desirable to change many paragraphs of the existing legal text in preparation for accession; nor had any elaborate changes been made to the fundamental laws regulating the political life of other and older members of the EC/EU at the time of their entry.

This commission did propose, however, the inclusion of a totally new paragraph in Sweden's fundamental law of a general nature, which did not have any equivalence in other constitutions of older member states (SOU (1993a) – 1993: 14). It reads as follows:

> As an agreement has been reached about Sweden joining the European communities and as the Riksdag decided to transfer decision-making rights to the Communities, the obligations, following this membership, are to apply regardless of what is stated in the constitution or in other laws.

This clause was thought to be in accordance with the constitutional philosophy existing in the country: that the written constitution should reflect as much as possible existing power-relations and the distribution of decision-making competencies between different levels and authorities. Accession was interpreted to have important political and legal consequences since European Community Law, both formally and in reality, is regarded as superior to national law (in areas where a transfer of power takes place). This very fact ought also to be expressed, it was argued, in the fundamental law of the country. In addition, the inclusion of such a general clause would make other changes in the Instrument of Government unnecessary in the future, if further steps were taken later on in the process of European integration.

The presenting of this proposal provoked an intense reaction, however (Sterzel 1993). Fears were expressed that the future position of Sweden in negotiations with the Community would be weakened if it was so clearly stated, as suggested, that European Community law had priority even in relation to the fundamental law of the country itself. A clause of this kind was accused of laying the country 'flat' in relation to the Community. Indeed, the proposal even came to be called the 'flat-laying clause' in the public debate. The government quickly decided to reject this particular clause, but after some amendment did approve what the commission had suggested concerning the very forms in which the Riksdag was to transfer power to the Communities. This amended clause, as it now stands in the Instrument of Government (Chapter 10, Art. 5), read as:

> The Riksdag may entrust the right of decision-making to the European Communities so long as these provide protection for rights and freedoms corresponding to the protection provided under this Instrument of Government and the European Convention for the Protection of Human Rights and Fundamental Freedoms. The Riksdag authorizes such delegation in a decision which has the support of at least three fourths of those present and voting. The Riksdag may also take such a decision in the manner prescribed for the adoption of a fundamental law.

From a comparative perspective, this clause is interesting in many ways. An explicit reference is made in the text to 'The European Communities'; most of the other and older member states do not mention the Union in their corresponding fundamental laws at all. Furthermore, a transfer of power is dependent on the continuous protection of a series of human rights – acting as a kind of 'safety device' in the hands of national Swedish authorities in relation to Brussels (although it remains unclear how it is to be triggered). Finally, the transfer of decision-making competencies to the Union will require the approval of a very large qualified majority in the Riksdag. The alternative form of 'entrustment' mentioned – the manner in which the fundamental laws in Sweden are adopted – requires that two parliamentary decisions on motions with identical wording have to be taken and the second one has to be preceded by elections to the Riksdag (Ruin 1997a).

Interestingly enough, this new clause was not invoked when the Riksdag in the Autumn of 1994 decided that Sweden should join the EC/EU as a full member. Rather, the first use of the clause was made some years later when the decision was taken to ratify the Amsterdam Treaty. The reason for not employing it during the crucial decision taken on EC accession in the Autumn of 1994 was that the parliament's final vote had been preceded by a referendum. Since the citizens approved full membership directly, which also presupposed a transfer of power, it was perceived as being inconsistent to uphold a rule about a parliamentary decision based on a qualitative majority. According to a special law, a simple majority was considered to be sufficient in this situation (SOU (1993a) – 1993: 14; Ruin 1997b).

Constitutionally Sweden was not bound, as, for example, in the case of Denmark, to have transfers of power to an international organization approved by the citizens in the form of a referendum. Demands for holding a referendum were, nevertheless, raised immediately in Sweden after the government's pro-EC membership announcement in October 1990. The two most EC-negative parties, the Greens and the Left Party (the former communists), were the first ones to request a plebiscite, but all the bourgeois opposition parties – even though they all appeared (more or less) EC-positive at this time – quickly followed suit. The Social Democratic Party, which had been rather sceptical initially towards this form of 'direct democracy', also accepted the need for a referendum after a while. Rather ironically, the Social Democrats came to be pleased about having such a plebiscite because of the fact that the Social Democratic orientated electorate turned out to be very divided on the EC membership issue. In holding the 1994 referendum, Sweden can be said to have adjusted to a broader constitutional pattern emerging in Europe in connection with the integration process: namely that EC/EU accession should be approved directly by the citizens of the respective country, and similar referenda were also held in the other applicant states of Austria, Finland and Norway (Todal Jenssen, Pesonen and Gilljam 1998; Ruin 1997a).

The Swedish Instrument of Government provides for two different kinds of referendum: decisive and advisory. The former type can be used only in relation to revisions of the fundamental laws and has to take place on the same occasion as general elections to the Riksdag. The latter type, four of which have been held previously in Swedish parliamentary history, can encompass all kinds of issues and take place whenever the Riksdag deems it fit to hold one (SOU (1997b) – 1997: 56). It was decided that the EC/EU membership referendum was to be of an advisory character formally. The interesting thing was, however, that all the parties promised – regardless of whether they were pro, contra or divided on the issue – to treat the outcome of the referendum as binding in practice. All the members of the Riksdag were to abide by the verdict of the citizens. The majority of the 'Yes' vote in the Swedish referendum was quite narrow – only 52 per cent – but none of the MPs who were negative to Swedish EU membership voted against. In this respect the situation was different in neighbouring Finland where the referendum also had been of an advisory character. Yet, in spite of the fact that the 'Yes' majority (56 per cent) was higher than in Sweden, almost a quarter of the members of the Finnish *Eduskunta* voted against full membership in the end (Ruin 1997b).

Constitutional issues played, in a very broad sense, a rather significant role in the EC/EU debate in Sweden, culminating in the Autumn 1994 referendum campaign. If Sweden was to join the Union a decrease would inevitably occur in the formal sovereignty of the country given that some national decision-making powers would be transferred to the EU level, encompassing representatives of all the member states. One of several commissions of inquiry, appointed with the task of assessing the possible effects of membership before the referendum took place, was assigned the specific task of evaluating what would be the consequences for Swedish democracy and the political institutions of the country (SOU (1994b) – 1994: 12) accruing from full membership. Those in the foreground were, on one hand, the Riksdag, and, on the other, the cabinet with its subordinate institutions. The Riksdag was expected to see its power reduced as had happened to the parliaments of other member states. In contrast, the cabinet was predicted to gain in influence in relation to the Riksdag but would also probably encounter new 'horizontal coordination' problems. There would certainly be changes to the central administration and to the elaborate committee system that has served the Swedish government for so long. Fears were also expressed that the well known features of 'openness' prevailing in the Swedish political system might be restricted.

Probable changes in Swedish democracy, due to future accession, were looked upon with alarm by opponents of Swedish EU entry, while its proponents expected that the losses in formal sovereignty would be compensated by greater participation in EU-wide decision-making. National sovereignty would be pooled, as they often tended to say in this pre-referendum debate, on a transnational European level (Jacobsson 1997).

The central institutions

The central political institutions – the Riksdag and the government – have experienced a 'pull' in two contradictory directions during the years since Sweden became an EU member. This general 'pull' is a consequence of two different tendencies. On one hand, representatives of Sweden have been drawn into a multitude of committees and networks established on a transnational level. Negotiations are going on continually in order to find common solutions to problems, often of a concrete and limited nature, in those policy areas where final decision-making has been transferred to the EU level. On the other hand, Sweden as a member state has sought to maintain an overview of EU proceedings and be able to formulate Swedish positions that can be viably defended and argued for in the European Council (which the Prime Minister is part of), or in the weekly meetings of the European Council of Ministers (where other members of the Swedish cabinet participate). Indeed, within the idea of this conflicting 'pull' may lie, albeit to a limited extent, an explanation of how Sweden 'fits' into the process of European integration and formulates its priorities towards the EU – one of the four research questions/themes posed by Lee Miles (see Chapter 1).

In addition, this 'pull' in various directions corresponds, to some extent, to the EU's two different dimensions: as an organization with supranational traits and, at the same time, as an association based on intergovernmental cooperation. It is clear that after Sweden became an EU member, the country's central institutions have experienced, in their daily life, both centrifugal forces and, at the same time, ambitions in the opposite direction, which can, in turn, be characterized as centripetal.

The Riksdag

The Swedish Parliament (Riksdag) has been the centre of attention during the past years as regards the effects of Swedish EU entry on the workings of the central institutions, especially since the legislative branch has traditionally played an important role in the political history of Sweden. Definite changes have now occurred in the relationship between the Riksdag and the government in those policy areas where a transfer of decision-making power to Brussels has taken place.

The government is, according to an explicit clause in the Riksdag Act, obliged to keep the Riksdag informed continually of events occurring within the framework of European Union cooperation. This has meant that the parliament has been almost flooded with material emanating from the Union; more than 1000 documents dealing with EU matters were, for example, forwarded in the 1997/98 parliamentary year (Hegeland 1999). Furthermore, the government is expected to produce so-called 'memos of facts' (*faktapromemorior*), in order to facilitate the understanding of all this material and to inform the Riksdag about the preliminary positions taken by the Swedish government during negotiations in Brussels. Finally the government also has to present an annual report about the activities of the Union (*Årsboken om EU*).

The Riksdag, for its part, deals with ongoing EU activities in various forms. Plenary discussions have been organized on aspects of these activities. Individual members have introduced private bills touching upon EU-oriented problems or posed questions concerning the EU to their own ministers. In the 1997/98 parliamentary year, for instance, 20 per cent of all private bills submitted at least mentioned the EU and more than 10 per cent of questions posed to a minister had an EU connotation (Hegeland 1999).

The views of the Riksdag on EU matters are, however, primarily exposed and formulated in two different kinds of committees: the Advisory Committee on European Union Affairs and the regular standing committees that happen to have responsibility for policy areas that come under EU jurisdiction (Hegeland and Mattson 1997). To some extent, these two types of committees in their dealing with EU matters correspond to the earlier mentioned pressures (or 'pull') that Sweden as an EU member has experienced during the past years: namely to be drawn into all kinds of preliminary and detailed negotiations on a transnational level and, trying simultaneously, to obtain an overview of all the EU-oriented activities and to formulate national stands.

The Advisory Committee on European Affairs represents, as far as the Riksdag is concerned, this latter ambition. This committee was established explicitly as a consequence of Swedish EU entry; it was originally proposed by the commission that looked into the constitutional problems connected with this entry and later endorsed by the Riksdag itself. The committee is modelled after the special European committee existing in the Danish parliament (*Markedsudvalget*), although the Swedish counterpart is given less formal power than the Danish original. The Swedish committee is not, and unlike the Danish one, entitled to bind the government explicitly but its views have to be heard before decisions are taken on an EU level (Hegeland and Matsson 1995). It consists of 17 members with 25 substitutes encompassing all the parties that are represented in the Riksdag. To be part of this committee has been seen by many parliamentarians as an important assignment and many of the present members are prominent figures in their respective parties.

Fairly precise working practices have also developed in this Advisory Committee. It is due to meet every Friday morning and the meetings tend to last from one to three hours. A few days earlier the members receive information in written form about the positions that the Swedish government is planning to take in the Council of Ministers; the Prime Minister is also expected to appear before he goes to a meeting of the European Council. At the Friday meetings, the ministers in charge of issues pending in the Council will be present (together with their assistants) and they will expound on the preliminary Swedish stands and answer questions from committee members. The chairman of the committee will sum up the discussion at the end and on behalf of the committee declare either support, with perhaps varying degrees of wholeheartedness, or no-support for the governmental position. The latter situation has until now seldom occurred, partly because of the parliamentary strength of the government during Sweden's first four years of full membership. Once when the committee did air scepticism – the question concerned tourism and the EU – and the government maintained its original position in Brussels regardless, this behaviour was explicitly criticized by the Riksdag's constitutional standing committee. The interest of Sweden was said to be best served when the government's final policy positions are in accordance with the sentiments expressed by the Advisory Committee on European Affairs – unless very good reasons motivate a deviation (Hegeland 1999). The advice given is expected evidently to be binding in practice.

The regular standing committees, which cover policy areas affected by EU activities, have, by necessity, a narrower focus than the Advisory Committee on European Affairs. Their attention is directed mostly towards assessing current events in Brussels just before an issue is ready for discussion in the Council of Ministers. To begin with, many of these committees had difficulty in finding the appropriate means of involvement in these preliminary stages but lately their positions seem to have improved somewhat. They tend now to be informed both by written material supplied by the government and by occasional briefings by governmental representatives. But a discussion still continues about further improvements to this situation, particularly concerning the need for detailed information when proposals are being prepared in Brussels (Riksdagskommitten 1999).

Relations between these standing committees and the Advisory Committee on European Affairs have been very much at the forefront in discussions about how the Riksdag exerts its influence upon the ongoing decision-making processes in Brussels. The best expertise on different policy issues is to be found in the standing committees; the best overview of the development in the Union is provided by the Advisory Committee. The question has been how to combine and coordinate the work pursued by these different types of committees. There exists a valuable overlapping of the membership; many of those on the Advisory Committee have, at the same time, central positions in the standing committees. Furthermore, there is ongoing cooperation between the secretariat of the Advisory Committee and the secretariat of the standing committees. Yet, the standing committees have encountered difficulties in finding time to formulate opinions on the issues presented to the Advisory Committee by the government. All concerned are pressed for time. On this point, discussions also continue regarding further reforms. These two types of committees, with their different focus and profile, are still attempting to find the best form of cooperation in order to make it possible for the Riksdag, as the direct representative of the Swedish people, to influence Swedish activities in Brussels.

The government

The government, for its part, has also clearly experienced a 'pull' in two contradictory directions in its work preparing the positions to be presented in Brussels. On one hand, governmental representatives have been split up in a multitude of different and even disparate EU-oriented activities. On the other, there have been efforts, from the very beginning, to obtain, on the governmental level, an overview of all these EU activities and to find means of coordinating them.

This need for coordination not only has a horizontal dimension but also a vertical one. There exists in Sweden a rather unique division between fairly small ministries and a series of autonomous agencies, subordinate to these ministries (Ruin 1990). In an EU context, it is not only a question of securing coordination between ministries involved in different activities taking place in Brussels but also between ministries or group of ministries and subordinate agencies (Beckman and Johansson 1999; Statskontoret 1996: 7; Sundström 1999). The latter also have their employees involved in these activities.

Most of the ministries and their respective agencies have been affected by EU membership although some of them, due to the Union's specific traits, are particularly involved. Central among them in Sweden, as in other member states, are the Ministries of Finance and Foreign Affairs besides the Office of the Prime Minister. All the ministries affected by EU membership are responsible for following developments in Brussels in their area of jurisdiction, for preparing Swedish governmental policy positions and, finally, as mentioned previously, to keep the Riksdag informed.

To some extent, the Swedish ministries have expanded in terms of personnel because of the extra demand placed upon them as a consequence of full membership. Yet, they remain relatively small and rely not just on their own civil servants but also on those working in the subordinate agencies for the staffing of the different committees involved in preparing EU legislation. The mixture of these two different types of civil servants in the preparatory work as well as the tendency on the ministerial level to formulate often detailed directives to be followed have, to some degree, altered the traditional lines of competence and command existing between the two levels of the central administration. Put simply, the lines have become more blurred as a result of EU accession (Beckman and Johansson 1999).

Another notable characteristic of the Swedish governmental system has also been affected by the membership. Traditionally the praxis has been that the cabinet, in preparing new legislation, first appoints a special commission of inquiry (a Royal Commission) with the task of investigating related matters and working out proposals. These commissions normally consist of parliamentarians, experts of different kinds as well as representatives of special interests. Although both the quality and the importance of this elaborate system of commissions have decreased somewhat during the past two decades, the system still plays an important role in preparing legislation that is solely national in orientation. In the preparation of Swedish involvement in EU legislation the system has, however, been used hardly at all, attracting some attention and concern – and an omission in this ongoing Europeanization process. Recently the Riksdag's constitutional committee looked explicitly into this neglect and posed questions to the ministries concerned (KU 1998/99: 10). The survey confirmed that this traditional Swedish pattern of preparing new legislation hardly featured in the EU context. Appointing special commissions of inquiry is perceived as too cumbersome as regards EU-oriented decision-making mainly because of the rapid and irregular nature of EU processes.

The activity of the individual ministers varies as to their involvement in the processes preparing EU legislation, although, at the end of the day, they take responsibility for any policy conclusions reached in their particular spheres of jurisdiction. Interestingly, those who are most affected by the EU activities have not formed any kind of group at the cabinet level – as is the case in some member states – with the aim of coordinating the work of their respective ministries. On the whole, the Swedish cabinet seldom discusses current EU issues at its regular weekly meetings. Instead, essential coordination on EU activities has, in principle, taken place on the level immediately below the ministers even though the Prime Minister, as Head of Government, has ultimate responsibility for ensuring efficient coordination.

Nevertheless, the best focal point within the governmental apparatus for the overall responsibility for coordinating Swedish EU activities has been the object of dispute over past years. Different arrangements have been tested (Beckman and Johansson 1999).

Two schools of thought existed as to this 'organizational placement' before Swedish EU accession. One school of thought, supported by the Ministry of Finance, argued that overall responsibility should be assigned to the Office of the Prime Minister. Another school wanted to have the Ministry of Foreign Affairs fulfil this coordinating function. The latter school of thought won initially and responsibility for overseeing day-to-day EU matters was placed in the Ministry of Foreign Affairs, with a special EU minister, Mats Hellström, appointed and situated in this ministry in the last Carlsson administration (1994–96). However, he remained in this capacity only until March 1996. After the resignation of the Ingvar Carlsson government, and the appointment of the new premier, Göran Persson (the former Minister of Finance), a reorganization took place. The new Prime Minister stated explicitly that overall responsibility for this activity should rest with his own office in the future. It was emphasized that EU activities could no longer be treated primarily as a foreign policy matter. The traditional dividing lines between international and domestic questions have been further blurred as far as the EU is concerned.

The intentions of the new Prime Minister were not fully realized during the following years. Although a permanent secretary (*statssekreterare*) in the Office of the Prime Minister was said to have primary responsibility for coordinating EU questions, the secretariat in charge of day-to-day EU activities remained in the Ministry of Foreign Affairs under the chairmanship of another '*statssekreterare*'. (A '*statssekreterare*' in the Swedish administrative system is a political appointee to be regarded almost as a vice-minister.) The EU secretariat, according to official regulations, was to formulate guidelines for coordinating Swedish EU activity and to ensure that there were always definite governmental views on pending EU issues. As part of its work, the secretariat was in contact both with the Swedish representation in COREPER and with EU coordinators in each individual ministry.

Three forms of interdepartmental meetings – each with a differing timing and focus – were established to guarantee the necessary inter-departmental coordination (Cirkulär 1–8; KU 1998/99: 10). One was *statssekreterargruppen för EU-frågor*, which, in principle, consisted of all the *'statssekreterare'* associated with the different ministries. This group was convened usually once a month, largely for information dissemination on, and discussions about, key EU questions, but also to enable political initiatives in EU policy areas to be taken. The *'statssekreterare'* from the Office of the Prime Minister chaired the meeting with the *'statssekreterare'* on EU issues, located in the Ministry of Foreign Affairs, serving as deputy chair. This fairly large group does not, however, seem to have been particularly active. A smaller group (*Beredningsgruppen för EU-frågor*), assigned the task of handling current EU issues, met every second week. It consisted only of representatives from the Office of the Prime Minister, the Ministry of Foreign Affairs and the Ministry of Finance, a composition reflecting the importance of these three entities in the cabinet. Finally a meeting called *EU-samrådet* took place every Tuesday afternoon, chaired by a representative of the EU secretariat. The purpose of this meeting was the most narrowly focused: namely to ensure that preparations for forthcoming policy questions to be discussed in COREPER were duly made through a conference of all the EU coordinators from the different ministries and with the help of a direct link to the Swedish representation in Brussels.

This pattern of handling EU questions at governmental level lasted for almost three years. Yet, at the beginning of 1999, another reorganization took place (Promemoria 1999). The aim is, once again (although more explicit than before), to concentrate the overall coordination responsibilities within the Office of the Prime Minister and thereby overcome the earlier unclear division of competence between this office and the Ministry of Foreign Affairs. The ideas behind this latest reorganization seem to have been taken from the arrangements existing in the British cabinet system, where the Prime Minister's Office plays a central role in the EU context.

The position as *'statssekreterare'* for EU matters in the Ministry of Foreign Affairs has been abolished and the secretariat for EU matters, which he headed, was merged with another division in the Ministry, led by a civil servant of lower status. Instead a *'statssekreterare'*, with specific responsibility for EU and international questions generally, is located in the Office of the Prime Minister. He and his staff will in the future, and according to the directives sent out by the Prime Minister's Office, have responsibility for coordinating ongoing EU activities, solving conflicts occurring between ministries, paying special attention to EU issues that are politically sensitive in Sweden and/or of great importance generally, assisting the Prime Minister in preparing for European Council meetings and, finally, taking care of preparations for the Swedish Council Presidency in 2001.

The earlier pattern of meetings has also changed somewhat. Evidently two meetings, both organized by the Office of the Prime Minister, are convened regularly with the common task of coordinating Swedish EU activities. One is the *EU-beredningen* (meeting every second Wednesday) and consisting of '*statssekreterare*' from the ministries concerned. It is chaired not by the special '*statssekreterare*' for EU questions, but rather by the Prime Minister's own '*statssekreterare*'. The other meeting, (called *Fredagsgruppen*) meets every Friday and consists not only of high-level civil servants from the Office of the Prime Minister and the Ministries of Finance and Foreign Affairs but also of people from the Swedish Permanent Representation in Brussels (who fly home for the meeting).

This concentration of different EU-oriented activities in the Office of the Prime Minister does not, of course, exclude all future involvement on the part of the Ministry of Foreign Affairs. The Foreign Minister (presently Anna Lindh) will continue to play a central role in the Council of Ministers; the ministry has ongoing responsibility for central areas of EU activity and consists of far more people than the fairly small Office of the Prime Minister. Thus, it remains to be seen if this latest reorganization overcomes the administrative tensions that have appeared in the EU context between the Ministry of Foreign Affairs and the Office of the Prime Minister and, of course, between both of them and the Ministry of Finance.

Finally, as regards the key question of who has enjoyed the best overview of Swedish EU involvement over the past years, there is a paradoxical trait. Although the government is responsible for the Swedish positions presented in Brussels, in practice it has sometimes lacked such an overview due to being split into many different entities. The Riksdag, which has less influence in shaping any policy positions taken, seems instead to have enjoyed a better overview of EU activities, which is largely due to the Advisory Committee on European Affairs receiving presentations on forthcoming governmental stances regularly every Friday morning. It can, therefore, be argued that those parliamentarians who are members of this Committee often have a better general picture of Swedish activities in the EU than individual members of the cabinet.

Fears were expressed before Swedish accession that future membership would negatively affect the practical levels of 'openness' that traditionally characterized the Swedish political system. This principle of 'openness' is based primarily on the right of free access to official documents that Swedish citizens have enjoyed for more than two hundred years – although this general right is restricted in some cases. One such instance concerns governmental relations with foreign states and/or international organizations. Indeed, the Union seemed problematic initially since the EU is an international organization, whilst, at the same time, its activities of the Union form simultaneously part of the domestic politics of the member states. Nervous questions were asked during the accession debates about the extent to which EU documents arriving in Sweden should be kept secret due to the EU's status as an international organization.

During the past few years of full membership, great attention has been given to the problem surrounding the availability of EU documents. Several investigations have been made – the latest of which was undertaken by the Riksdag's Constitutional Committee in 1998 (KU 1998/99: 10). The findings were regarded as encouraging and no further measures were deemed to be required or were taken.

The number of EU documents arriving in Sweden has increased, naturally enough, since Sweden became an EU member. Most documents have been made available even if it so happens that single sentences are deleted and kept secret due to their content. Special registers for incoming EU documents have been established at most of the ministries and these registers make it, in turn, easier for those interested to find the relevant EU documents. Furthermore, those responsible for the registration of these documents do not find, as a rule, that it is more difficult to decide which documents have full open public access (and in accordance with existing legislation) in the EU context than ordinarily. Some uncertainty does seem, however, to surround documents relating to the work of the EU committees in Brussels (which include Swedish civil servants as committee members). Nevertheless, there have only been five cases so far where EU documents, asked for by private citizens, have not been made available in line with decisions taken by the government.

This principle of public access to official records, now more than two hundred years old, has also been regarded by the Swedish government as worthy of export, and the government has sought its introduction into the EU system as a whole. It is said (by the government) to promote transparency, to be valuable from a democratic point of view, to constitute a balancing factor against the tendencies toward corruption that has plagued the Union of late and also to be conducive to a more efficient EU administration. In concrete terms, members of the Swedish government have argued that different EU institutions should establish accessible registers covering all documents, including those that institutions receive from outside (with the exception of working papers) and any reasons for keeping documents secret should be clearly stated and enumerated. These proposed rules should also apply to the different EU committees existing in Brussels because of their importance to ongoing decision-making processes.

In any discussion on the effects of EU membership on traditional Swedish political institutions, the principle of public access to official records can be seen as a somewhat special case. Here it is not only a question about the possible effects of EU membership on a cherished Swedish 'institution', but it may also have a valuable contribution to make to the Union as a whole. Swedish principles of 'openness' should be seen as an appropriate item for export (Lindh and Lejon 1999) and is clearly one example where Sweden has tried to influence and shape the development of the EU in line with the first research question/theme posed by Lee Miles, in this book's introduction (see Chapter 1).

The Swedish political system in general

In the late 1990s, greater attention than usual has focused on the state of the Swedish political system generally, and, in particular, the health and vitality of Swedish democracy. A series of changes have been registered and some of them have been regarded as leading to a deterioration in the state of Swedish democracy, with, for example, lower turnouts in national elections, party membership and the electorate's party-loyalty declining, and public trust in elected representatives seeming to be less than before. These and other similar tendencies are all contrary to the high degree of citizen participation in Sweden's democratic processes that the country was earlier known for.

A public debate continues on the possible causes of these changes and elements of this debate are associated with Swedish EU membership. The adjustment to the requirements of full membership have been seen by some as an important factor behind these negative tendencies and a perspective of this kind comes, of course, easily in a country where EU-scepticism or outright opposition to membership of the Union is still widespread. Indeed, the results of, and the low turnout for, the June 1999 election to the European Parliament testify to the persistence of these feelings. The two most EU-negative parties, the Left Party and the Greens, obtained together more than 25 per cent of votes cast and many of those who did not vote – the turnout was only 38.3 per cent – seem also to have been EU-negative.

In attempting to explain the changes that have occurred in the Swedish political system at the end of twentieth century, it is difficult to distinguish between those that may have been caused by EU membership and those that are due to general tendencies in today's societies. We know that many societies – regardless of whether they happen to be EU members or not – exhibit negative tendencies similar to those in Sweden today.

One such factor is, for example, the behaviour of mass media. Their concentration on negative and dramatic political issues in their continuous search for news is said to produce feelings of estrangement as to political participation. Another often mentioned factor might be slightly more correlated to EU membership. Originally Sweden applied for accession for essentially economic reasons and to avoid feelings of isolation in an increasingly globalized economy. New types of restrictions have appeared since

Sweden became an EU member that might influence the level of the citizen's trust in the political system. It has become difficult, for instance, for a welfare state to continue to deliver elaborate social programmes, dependent on a high degree of taxation, when the state is, at the same time, seeking to provide favourable economic conditions in order to attract new business investments in competition with other EU member states.

Moreover, as Miles (1997a) points out, changes have also occurred in the interplay of the central political actors in the Swedish political system, that is, between the political parties and the different interest organizations as part of the first and second 'points' of his 'Diamond' framework.

The Swedish party structure, earlier known to be very stable, has fragmented during the past decade, with some new parties being established. Although these tendencies occurred largely before Swedish EU entry, what accession has brought about is a new dimension of 'cleavage' in some of the parties (see Chapters 1 and 5). The Conservatives and the Liberals can be characterized as a whole as pro-EU and the reverse applies to the Left Party and the Greens, whilst three parties – the Social Democrats, the Christian Democrats and the Centre Party – remain divided in their attitudes towards the EU. To some degree these different attitudes complicate today's parliamentary situation, especially since a Social Democratic minority government relies mostly on the support of the Left Party and the Environmental Party in the Riksdag.

The Swedish corporativist pattern – that is the tendency to integrate representatives of organized interests formally in the state machinery – was both strong and elaborate a few decades ago (Hermansson 1993; Ruin 1974). It has, to some extent, weakened at the end of the twentieth century. In order to make themselves heard within the political process corporate organizations have used complementary methods such as an increased emphasis on the importance of lobbying. Possibly this type of activity has been stimulated by the fact that this phenomenon has been part of the political culture in Brussels for a long time; many Swedish organizations and enterprises today employ their own lobbyists in Brussels. It is not justified, however, to say that the weakening of the corporativist pattern of Sweden is due to the EU membership generally and Miles may focus slightly too much upon these aspects as part of point 'two' of his 'Membership Diamond'. Partly this process had already started earlier, and, in addition, there still exist many examples of the continual incorporation of organized interests within formal decision-making, including the EU context. Many such groups, for example, appointed by the ministries or the central agencies with the task of preparing Swedish positions in Brussels, include representatives of organized interests as members.

Another often emphasized trait of the Swedish political system in the past was the slow, but thorough decision-making processes. Lengthy deliberations tended to take place before decisions were taken in order to obtain both political consensus and good preparation for solving future problems

(Ruin 1982). Now these processes are generally more disjointed and piece-meal. Again these kinds of changes were visible before the 1990s and Sweden's EU entry, but certainly full membership has not been conducive to the reintroduction of a calmer policy-making 'rhythm' – in fact, rather the opposite. The pressure on politicians and civil servants has further increased because of their continual commuting between Stockholm and Brussels, and because final Swedish positions on issues to be decided in the Council of Ministers are often formulated in a hurry, against the clock.

Changes have evidently occurred in the Swedish political system at the end of the twentieth century in terms of citizen participation, the interplay of central actors and the pattern of the political process. To determine the role of the EU membership in bringing about these changes is, I repeat, difficult. It is far easier, as is done in this chapter, to study the effects of this membership on the constitution as such and on the central national institutions, namely the Riksdag and the cabinet. Due to Swedish full membership, new types of decision-making patterns have been established both inside and between these institutions and affecting their relationships with other entities. Some of these aspects could be deemed as part of a Europeanization process even if not exclusively. Certainly, a blurring of traditional lines of competence and responsibility has taken place: particularly between the Riksdag and the government as well as between the cabinet and the subordinate agencies.

Finally, there is one more trait to be emphasized with reference to the institutional side of Swedish political life. The country appears after several years as a member of the EU to be the most efficient of the fifteen members in implementing directives agreed in Brussels. This dutiful behaviour can be explained by many factors: good resources and capacities on the part of central administration, a centralized system that is not constrained by regions with a high degree of autonomy and, on top of this, an old and well established public ethos stating that public decisions, taken in accordance with existing rules, should also be implemented efficiently (Tallberg 1999). At the same time as Sweden appears in this way to be the most law-abiding member of the Union the country continues to harbour greater levels of EU scepticism than in the other member states. The predisposition to follow Brussels' directives may even be one of several explanations for these negative attitudes.

CHAPTER 5

The Swedish Party System and European Integration

Anders Widfeldt

Introduction

The 1994 referendum, which secured Swedish accession to the European Union, left scars on almost every political party in Sweden. The Social Democrats, Centre Party and Christian Democrats were openly split on EU membership, while there were small but notable minorities against the party line in the EU-positive Moderate and Liberal parties, as well as in the EU-negative Left and Green parties (Miles 1997a). The referendum was decided with a fairly small majority, and the losing 'No-side' bitterly complained about discrepancies in resources and about the perceived lack of honesty in the victorious 'Yes' campaign. The resentment was most openly represented by Per Gahrton, future MEP of the Green Party, who asked Moderate leader Carl Bildt to 'Shut Up' (*'Håll truten'*) on radio the morning following the referendum.

Sweden's first two elections to the European Parliament in 1995 and 1999 further emphasize the country's uneasiness on 'the road to Europe'. The governing Social Democratic Party has fared disastrously, the openly EU-critical Green and Left parties have performed well, and the turnouts have been very low. On the whole, it seems clear that the Swedish party system is under severe stress which, at least in part, is caused by EU-related issues. The purpose of this chapter is to investigate the impact of the EU on the Swedish parties. The extent of this impact will be studied on two levels. First, on the party system level. The main question here will be whether any significant and lasting changes have taken place in the Swedish party system since the EU accession, and whether any such changes can be attributed to EU-related issues. Second, the individual parties will be studied. In an earlier study, the development of the major Swedish parties until the 1994 referendum was studied (Widfeldt 1996a). In this chapter, events until the second Swedish EU election, on 13 June 1999, will be discussed.

The Swedish party system until 1994

Before going into the most recent developments, it will be helpful to provide a brief background to the Swedish party system. For many years Sweden was considered one of the most stable party systems in the democratic world. The five-party configuration, split into two ideological blocs, and with the Social Democrats as the dominant government party, was the norm from the 1930s until the mid-1980s. It was a historic event when a government without the Social Democrats was formed in 1976, for the first time in 40 years, but this was caused by fairly marginal shifts in party strength.

Around 1990, however, there was a period of upheaval (Arter 1999a). Three new parties entered the scene, and there was also a shift in the balance of power in the party system. The Green Party gained entry to the Riksdag in 1988 (Bennulf and Holmberg 1990). Despite losing its parliamentary status in 1991, the party cleared the 4 per cent threshold in 1994 as well as in 1998, and by the end of the 1990s appears as relatively established. The Christian Democratic Party achieved its final electoral breakthrough in 1991. Formed in 1964 as essentially a confessional party, the Christian Democrats are now part of the mainstream non-socialist bloc (Arter 1999b: 111; Pierre and Widfeldt 1994: 340). The third party to enter the scene was the right-wing populist New Democracy, which entered parliament on the crest of a wave in the 1991 election (Taggart 1996). New Democracy turned out to be a temporary phenomenon. Although it still exists, the party has been of no political significance since losing its parliamentary status in 1994.

The entry of three new parties between 1988 and 1991 proved that the party system was penetrable. Before 1988, no party had on its own gained entry to the Riksdag since 1917. There were two other significant changes. First, the dominant position of the Social Democrats was eroded. In 1991, the party received 37.7 per cent of the votes, which at the time was its worst result since 1928. Although the party recovered in 1994 to 45.2 per cent, the 1991 result and a series of poll ratings showed that they could no longer rely on a solid 'worst case' support base of over 40 per cent of the votes. Second, there have been long-term changes among the non-socialist parties. Between the 1920s and 1970s, the People's Party Liberals, Moderates and the Centre Party all enjoyed periods of dominance among the non-socialist parties, but none obtained anything like a hegemonic position. After 1979, however, it could be argued that the Moderate Party has achieved such hegemony. They have been the biggest non-socialist party, second only to the Social Democrats, in every election since 1979. At the same time, support for the Centre and Liberal parties has dwindled, and they have both broken their all-time low records in the 1990s.

Thus, the Swedish party system went through several significant changes around 1990. New parties emerged, of which two proved to have lasting power. The dominant position of the Social Democrats was eroded, if not completely destroyed. The Moderates achieved permanent dominance in the non-socialist bloc, as the Centre and Liberal parties saw their support collapse. This, in turn, means that the party system had begun to change before 1990, when the issue of EC/EU accession was placed firmly on the political agenda with the surprise declaration by the Social Democratic government that it intended to apply for EC membership (Miles 1997a). In the following section, the development in the party system between 1994 and 1999 will be analysed, with the intent to establish whether the changes in the party system have proved to be permanent, and the extent to which this has been caused by the EU issue.

Developments in the Swedish party system 1994–99

Two months before the referendum on EU accession in November 1994, an election to the Swedish Riksdag was held. The Social Democrats recovered from the disaster of 1991 and went on to form a single party government. Of the four parties in the 1991–94 coalition government, the Moderate Party maintained its level of support from 1991, but the other three suffered significant losses; especially the Christian Democrats, who managed to hang on to their parliamentary status with a margin of some 3000 votes. The Green Party regained their parliamentary status after having lost it three years earlier, but New Democracy was annihilated. The Social Democratic minority government formed a parliamentary cooperation pact with the Centre Party in the spring of 1995, to carry its economic policies through parliament. In many ways, the development was a return to normality. The Social Democrats were back in the driving seat, and New Democracy, the most obnoxious of the new parties, turned out to be a temporary phenomenon.

But 1994 proved to be more of a temporary flashback than a return to normality. The election to the European Parliament in September 1995 suggested that the Swedish party system might never be quite the same again. The first Swedish MEPs had been appointed according to the parties' strength in the Riksdag, and taken their seats in January 1995. It had, however, been agreed that the Swedish delegation in the European Parliament should be made directly elected as soon as possible, and follow the general European election cycle from 1999 onwards. The lacklustre campaign was overshadowed by Prime Minister Ingvar Carlsson's announcement that he was going to resign in early 1996. There was little public interest in the election. The apathy could partly be explained by 'election fatigue', since it was the third election or referendum in a year. Still, the turnout of 41.6 per cent was much lower than expected. This was taken by many as evidence that EU membership had not been an instant success among the Swedish public. It was, furthermore, the lowest turnout in any nationwide Swedish election since the regional elections in 1922 (Widfeldt 1996b).

The headline 'DISASTER' of the Social Democratic tabloid *Aftonbladet* the day after the election signified the outcome for the governing party. A decline compared to the previous year's election had been expected, but 28.1 per cent, the lowest recorded by the party since the 1910s, was not. In absolute terms, this was a loss of a staggering 1.76 million votes compared to the Riksdag election, and in relative terms the loss was of over 17 percentage points. The other notable feature of the election was the success of the EU-critical Left and Green parties, who received 12.9 and 17.2 per cent of the vote, respectively. For both parties, this was their best ever result in a nationwide election, and they also improved on their absolute number of votes from 1994, which was no mean achievement considering the low turnout. To summarize, the 1995 European election had all the characteristics of a protest election: low turnout, poor result for the governing party and success for the anti-EU parties (Jahn and Widfeldt 1996).

An interesting novelty in the election was the introduction of a personal vote system. In short, the voters have the option to indicate preference for one of the candidates on their chosen party list. Candidates receiving personal preferences amounting to 8 per cent of the party's total votes were ranked above all other candidates on the party list, and among each other according to their respective number of votes. More than 50 per cent of the voters used their opportunity to indicate a candidate preference, but it did not affect the composition of the eventually elected candidates. The personal vote system was, however, considered a success (Widfeldt 1996b). Several candidates conducted personalized campaigns, and the system was made permanent for all future elections to the European and national parliaments, as well as to regional and local assemblies, but with the cut-off point reduced to 5 per cent.

The period between 1995 and the next Riksdag election in 1998 was characterized by increasing criticism against the Social Democratic government. The harsh remedies to reduce the national debt and fiscal deficit were heavily criticized, from within as well as outside the party. Göran Persson, who took over from Ingvar Carlsson as Prime Minister in 1996, had very low personal ratings in the opinion polls, and his party fared little better. Meanwhile, the Moderate leader Carl Bildt was able to build up a reputation as a statesman, due to his work as the EU mediator in the Bosnian conflict. At times, it looked as if the Moderates were threatening to take over as the country's biggest party. Even if this began to look increasingly unlikely as the election drew closer, it was apparent that the Social Democrats were in for a very difficult confrontation with the voters.

Indeed, the eventual result of 36.4 per cent was the lowest share of the vote obtained by the Social Democrats in a parliamentary election since 1921. A significant proportion of the lost votes went to the Left Party, who got 12 per cent. In fact, five of the seven parties broke some sort of a record in the 1998 election. Besides the Social Democrats, the People's Party Liberals and the Centre Party also suffered their worst ever results. The Left Party and the Christian Democrats, on the other hand, broke their all time high records in parliamentary elections. The popularity of the Left Party can, to a large extent, be attributed to discontent with the austerity policies of the Social Democratic government. The Christian Democratic surge came very late, and was only just picked up by the opinion polls before the election. Much of it appeared to be an effect of the very successful media appearances by party leader Alf Svensson. The election displayed various indicators of a decline in trust of the parties and politics in general. Most notable was the turnout of 81.4 per cent, which was the lowest in a parliamentary election since 1958 (Widfeldt 1998).

The European election in June 1999 underlined the developments of the previous year. The turnout of 38.8 per cent was 2.8 percentage points lower than in 1995, and the fourth lowest in the EU. The Social Democrats were further punished by the voters, and saw their number of MEPs reduced from seven to six. The Centre and Green parties lost one and two seats, respectively. There were gains for the Christian Democrats and the People's Party Liberals. In the former case, the 7.6 per cent and two seats was, in fact, a slight disappointment, after the very successful parliamentary election a year before. The People's Party Liberals broke a disastrous electoral trend, and gained two new seats. Much of this success can be attributed to their top candidate Ms Marit Paulsen, who had joined the party in November 1998. Previously a member of the Social Democrats, with a background in farming, she had already achieved a prominent position in the public debate, and her support for a 'Yes' vote in the 1994 referendum received much attention. She dominated, more or less, the 1999 campaign, and her down-to-earth appearance went down very well with the voters. The party's success was very much a 'Paulsen effect'. Indeed, simultaneous opinion polls about voter intentions for a possible parliamentary election showed less than half as much support for the People's Party Liberals as the 13.9 per cent gained in the EU election (*Dagens Nyheter*, 29 May 1999).

The Left Party made progress in terms of votes compared to 1995, but not sufficiently to gain new seats. Conversely, the Moderate Party kept their number of MEPs, despite a decline in votes. The Green Party lost two of the four seats won in 1995, although the result was still an improvement on the parliamentary election in 1998. Thus, there was a net loss for the two openly EU-critical parties. The Centre Party, which had been represented by one EU-critical and one EU-positive MEP between 1995 and 1999, lost one seat. After the personal votes had been counted, the remaining seat went to the EU-positive, former minister of agriculture, Karl Erik Olsson. Thus, with the lack of progress for the two most EU-critical parties, and the relative lack of success for EU-sceptical candidates in other parties, the outcome of the election was not a success for the EU critics. Nevertheless, the low turnout and the poor performance by the governing Social Democrats were both interpreted as indicators of the lack of popular support for EU membership.

The parliamentary and EU election results since 1994 are presented in Tables 5.1 and 5.2, respectively. To summarize, it could be argued that the Swedish party system has reached a new, if somewhat unstable, equilibrium. There are now seven parties in serious contention for seats in the Riksdag and European Parliament, compared to five before 1988. The Christian

Democrats and the Greens have proved to be more than transient phenomena, while New Democracy turned out to be an aberration. The Social Democrats had a very successful Riksdag election in 1994, but the results in the three subsequent elections, European and parliamentary, show that the party's support base is declining. Their position as the biggest party in the country is not under threat, however. With support from the Left and Green parties, they have continued as a single government, even after the disastrous 1998 election. In bloc terms, the advance of the Left Party has partly, but not in full, compensated for the Social Democratic loss in the socialist bloc. The Moderate Party has kept a firm grip on the position as the second biggest party in the country, and is as dominant as ever in the non-socialist bloc. Due to the weakness of the Centre Party and People's Party Liberals, the non-socialist bloc is still some way away from a majority position. It remains to be seen if the Liberal result in the 1999 EU election was the start of a more permanent recovery.

It is undeniable that the Swedish party system has undergone significant changes since the 1980s. Whether these changes have been caused by the EU accession or EU-related issues is less certain. The issue of EC/EU membership first began to surface in the 1988 election campaign, after having been, more or less, off the agenda since the early 1970s. This coincided with the entry into the Riksdag of the Green Party, but European issues were not dominant in the 1988 campaign, which was heavily focused on the environment. Thus, the breakthrough of the Green Party can hardly be attributed to its criticism of the EC/EU.

The same can be said of the breakthrough for the Christian Democrats and New Democracy in 1991. The Christian Democrats had shifted from a negative to a positive position on the EU in the late 1980s, but they have never been united on Europe, and it has never been a profile issue for the party. The temporary success of New Democracy was mostly due to the party's criticism of the political system and the established parties, and cannot be attributed to European-related issues.

The decline in support for the Social Democrats coincided, to some extent, with the road towards EU accession, but again, it is difficult to find arguments that link these two developments to each other. EU-related issues were not among the most frequently mentioned among voters who defected from the Social Democrats in 1991 (Gilljam and Holmberg 1993: 95). Whilst EU membership has been the source of much criticism and discontent after 1995, the Social Democrats have also suffered from the high unemployment figures and criticism against reductions in the welfare provisions. Thus, while the EU has not worked in their favour, it is not the only, possibly not even the major, reason behind the Social Democrats' difficulties.

David Arter (1999a), analysing the developments until 1994, describes Sweden as suffering from 'A mild case of Electoral Instability Syndrome'. It is indeed true that the traditional stability, verging on predictability, of the

Table 5.1.   Parliamentary elections in Sweden, 1994 and 1998

| | 1994 | | | | 1998 | | | |
Party	Votes	%	Seats	Change	Votes	%	Seats	Change
Left Party	342,988	6.2	22	+6	631,011	12.0	43	+21
Social Democrats	2,513,905	45.2	161	+23	1,914,426	36.4	131	−30
Centre Party	425,153	7.7	27	−4	269,762	5.1	18	−9
People's Party Liberals	399,556	7.2	26	−7	248,076	4.7	17	−9
Moderate Party	1,243,253	22.4	80	0	1,204,926	22.9	82	+2
Christian Democrats	225,974	4.1	15	−11	619,046	11.8	42	+27
Green Party	279,042	5.0	18	+18	236,699	4.5	16	−2
Others	125,669	2.2	0	0	137,176	2.6	0	0
Blank plus invalid votes	84,853				113,466			
Total votes	5,640,393				5,374,588			
Electorate	6,496,365				6,603,129			
Turnout		86.8				81.4		

Table 5.2.   EU elections in Sweden, 1995 and 1999

| | 1995 | | | 1999 | | | |
Party	Votes	%	Seats	Votes	%	Seats	Change
Left Party	346,764	12.9	3	400,073	15.8	3	0
Social Democrats	752,817	28.1	7	657,497	26.0	6	−1
Centre Party	192,077	7.2	2	151,442	6.0	1	−1
People's Party Liberals	129,376	4.8	1	350,339	13.9	3	+2
Moderate Party	621,568	23.2	5	524,755	20.7	5	0
Christian Democrats	105,173	3.9	0	193,354	7.6	2	+2
Green Party	462,092	17.2	4	239,946	9.5	2	−2
Others	73,284	2.7	0	12,031	0.5	0	0
Blank plus invalid votes	44,166			59,077			
Total votes	2,727,317			2,588,514			
Electorate	6,551,591			6,664,205			
Turnout		41.6			38.8		

Swedish party system is a thing of the past. At the end of the 1990s, however, there are signs that the party system has reached a new position of relative stability. This position can be described as a seven-party system, divided into two blocs, but with the Green Party as something of an outsider. The Social Democrats remain as the biggest party, but with a less secure position than before, and the Moderate Party dominates among the non-socialist parties. In its new shape, the Swedish party system is more fragmented than before. The fact that the Social Democratic government receives backing from the Left and Green parties could suggest that the system is also moving towards a higher degree of polarization. Against this, it could be argued that the pact is by no means certain to last until the 2002 election, and Göran Persson has not in the long term ruled out cross-bloc agreements, such as the one with the Centre Party between 1995 and 1997.

The internal situation within the Swedish parties

Even if the impact of the EU on the Swedish party system may so far have been somewhat limited, this does not mean that the Swedish parties are unaffected. Several major political parties face the threat of internal unrest, no matter what position it takes on any EU-related issue. In addition, the general level of EU scepticism among the Swedish public, as manifested in the EU elections and subsequent opinion polls, means that European issues constitute a potential threat to the legitimacy of the country's democratic system.

The Social Democratic Party (SAP) has been uncomfortable with European integration since the early 1970s. Party officials and activists have been deeply worried that the turmoil in their sister parties in Norway and Denmark in connection with the 1972 referendums might spread to the Swedish party, and for many years treated the issue as virtually non-existent. The SAP survived the 1994 referendum campaign remarkably intact, even though the party's voters were split right down the middle in terms of 'Yes' and 'No' votes (Holmberg 1996: 226f). This could, perhaps, at least in part, be explained by the fact that there was a 'feel-good factor' after the very successful election to the Riksdag two months before the referendum, but any such feel-good benefit was wiped away with the 1995 EU election, and has not been recovered since.

When Göran Persson took over as party leader and Prime Minister from Ingvar Carlsson in March 1996, the EMU was one of his most daunting challenges. His government was internally split on the issue, and the government's eventual decision was to adopt a 'wait and see' policy, and not join the EMU at its initial launch. This was preceded by a Commission of Inquiry, the so-called 'Calmfors Report', which presented its findings in November 1996. The recommendation was that Sweden would not join the EMU immediately, because it was yet too early to see what the EMU would develop into (SOU (1996b) – 1996: 158). In June 1997, the Executive Committee of the Social Democratic Party declared its intentions not to join the EMU from the outset. This was confirmed with a Riksdag decision in December of the same year. Persson has not ruled out EMU membership at a later stage, but has been treading very carefully. The cautious approach can, to a large extent, be explained by concern about party unrest, which is, by no means, a factor only relevant at the 'grass roots' level. A number of cabinet ministers, and the new EU commissioner from 1999, Margot Wall-ström, have publicly declared their support for EMU membership (*Göteborgs-Posten*, 20 July 1999). However, neither the government, nor the parliamentary group, have yet come to a unified standpoint.

While arguably the most urgent, the EMU is not the only EU-related issue which causes problems for the government. Göran Persson has to face up to the harsh realities of leading a minority government which is carefully guiding a reluctant country along the road towards further integration. Other difficult issues include the size of Sweden's budgetary contribution as part of full membership, where Foreign Secretary Anna Lindh has declared her ambitions to achieve a reduction, and the integration of defence policy. The fact that Persson's one-party government, severely weakened after the 1998 election, is dependent on the support from the EU-critical Left and Green parties to stay in office complicates the situation further.

The two core enthusiasts of Swedish EU membership, the conservative Moderate Party and the People's Party Liberals, have experienced very different fortunes since the 1994 referendum. Thus these two parties, who have been major components of the non-socialist opposition against the Social Democrats since the 1920s, and have participated in various coalition governments, can therefore no longer be regarded as equal partners. Clearly, the decline of the People's Party Liberals has been to a level which makes the party's political significance questionable, and its future is very uncertain despite the surprising success in the 1999 EU election.

The Moderates claim to be the European party *par preference* in Swedish politics. This is also reflected in the policy on the EMU. The party argues that the launch of the 'Euro' was a vital step in the right direction towards a freer single European market. With a common currency and free competition between enterprises, but also in terms of taxes and public service, favourable conditions will be created to give Europe the dynamism and prosperity it needs. On 17 March 1999, economic affairs spokesman Lars Tobisson claimed, in response to Foreign Secretary Anna Lindh's stated ambition to reduce Sweden's EU budgetary contribution, that it would have been SEK 2 billion a year lower if Sweden had joined the EMU from its beginning. Another high-profile issue of the Moderate Party is the ambition to secure the democratization of the former communist countries in eastern Europe. EU support to help consolidating the new democracies is considered essential. The party is also strongly in favour of the entry of the six countries currently negotiating for EU accession.[1]

The People's Party Liberals' misfortunes in elections and opinion polls have not triggered a reassessment of their EU-positive policies. In many respects, the party is close to the position of the Moderate Party. The Liberals advocate a Swedish EMU application before the end of 2001, preceded by a referendum in the second half of 2000. The pro-EMU position is justified by the argument that the absence of a common currency is the biggest obstacle to more trade. A common currency would also tie the countries closer to each other. However, EMU membership will have to be preceded by a referendum or parliamentary election; in this respect they are in agreement with the government.[2]

The official Centre Party line is that it supports Sweden's EU membership, but the 1996 party congress decided against joining the EMU (Centre Party 1999). The party is split on both counts. There are those who criticize EU membership as such, and there are also those who advocate joining the EMU. An example of the former is MEP Hans Lindqvist, who played a leading role in the 'No' campaign in the 1994 referendum and was voted into the European Parliament in 1995. Lindqvist was controversially put in third place on the party list for the EU election in 1999, and did not get enough personal votes to qualify for the only seat the party got in the election. Instead, the seat went to former minister of agriculture, Karl Erik Olsson. This was a victory for the pro-European faction in the party, as Olsson has for some years publicly argued in favour of joining the EMU (*Dagens Nyheter*, 7 February 1997).

The Christian Democrats favour EU membership officially, although the party leadership has to tread carefully in order not to evoke internal dissent. EU critics have new possible leading figures in Björn von der Esch, who was a member of parliament for the Moderates between 1991 and 1994, and newly elected MEP Lennart Sacrédeus. Von der Esch was expelled from the Moderate Party, and has been welcomed into the Christian Democrats, even though his presence could be a problem for the party leadership. Sacrédeus, who has firmly declared his opposition to EMU membership, launched a successful personal campaign, and despite being fifth on the party list, recorded enough personal votes to claim the party's second seat in the European Parliament.

The EMU is somewhat of a 'hot potato' for the Christian Democratic Party. So far, the party has come to a conclusion similar to that of the Social Democrats. The 1998 party congress argued that Sweden is not yet ready for EMU membership, and rejected a private congress motion which advocated joining directly. The issue will again be subject to debate at an extra party congress in 2000. There are signs, however, that the party leadership is moving towards a positive attitude. Even though party leader Alf Svensson had not yet declared his position in the Summer of 1999, there were reports that majorities in the party's national executive and parliamentary group were in favour of EMU membership (*Aftonbladet*, 27 June 1999).

The Left and Green parties have not changed their very EU-critical positions. Both want Sweden to leave the EU, and are firmly opposed to EMU membership. For the Left Party, there has been little reason to reassess its policies, after a series of very successful elections since Sweden's EU accession. The Green Party did not maintain its success from four years earlier in the 1999 EU election, but the result was, nevertheless, better than in the 1998 parliamentary election. The fact that several other green parties in Europe are EU-positive, for example the German and Finnish parties, suggests that there might be some room for diversity in the party. There was an attempt to launch a pro-EU Green Party list for the 1999 European election. It failed, as did an attempt at the party's extraordinary congress to remove the paragraph of leaving the EU from the election platform. Thus, while the Green Party remains predominantly EU-critical, it is of interest to note that some internal divisions have begun to surface. This was further underlined after the EU election, when five members of the Green Party with senior positions criticized other leading party figures for alleged unawareness of the implications of the Social Democratic foreign policy. The critics argued that the government's signing of the Cologne decision in June 1999, to give the EU military resources, was a threat to the Swedish non-alignment (*Dagens Nyheter*, 22 June 1999). This led to an internal debate, which ultimately concerned the future of the party's continuing support for the Social Democratic government.

A useful way of summarizing the debate among and within the Swedish parties is to use the 'Membership Diamond' (Miles 1997a) as a reference point. The Moderate and Liberal parties tend to focus on aspects that correlate to the Diamond's third 'point' (new challenges of economic interdependence), as they see participation in an integrated European market as central for the future of the Swedish economy. They also pay some attention to those issues associated with the fourth 'point' (security policy with a European identity), especially since they argue strongly for an expanded EU role in order to facilitate a peaceful stabilization of the new democracies in Eastern Europe (see Miles 1998b). The Green and Left parties also pay attention to 'point' four, but from a different angle, with emphasis on the consequences for Sweden's non-alignment. This issue, which was prominent in the debate up to the 1994 referendum, has been more in the background in the years following Sweden's entry into the EU. There is no reason, however, why this should continue to be so. New developments, such as the decision at the Cologne European Council meeting in 1999 (to strengthen the EU's role in 'crisis management'), will bring the issue of Swedish non-alignment back into the debate, as exemplified by the internal row in the Green Party.

EU critics also often refer to aspects associated with the first 'point' (a fragmenting, Europeanized Democracy) and argue that traditional Swedish democratic values will be compromised in the EU. This has been a recurring argument proffered by the Left Party and the Greens, as well as by EU critics in the Social Democratic and the Centre parties. The second point of the 'Membership Diamond' (declining corporatism) is also of relevance. The core components of Swedish corporatism – the centralized bargaining system on the labour market, interest group representation on the boards of public agencies, the policy-making role of commissions of inquiry with interest group representation, and the recurring summit meetings involving the government and the main interest organizations – are, to varying degrees, things of the past (Petersson 1994; Rothstein 1998). The Social

Democrats still accept some trade union funding, and retain some organizational union links, but are at pains to avoid any policy interference. Thus, aspects of Sweden's corporate model, which played a vital role in shaping the historical background behind Sweden's EU accession, have significantly declined in importance in common with the assertions underpinning 'point' two of the 'Miles Diamond'.

To sum up, the Diamond's third 'point' (new challenges of economic interdependence) has been the main source of controversy, within as well as between parties. In the near future, issues relating to the Diamond's fourth 'point' seem likely to increase in importance within the Swedish debate. Nevertheless, the first 'point' (democratic aspects) will continue to feature among the arguments put forward by EU critics, whilst the Diamond's second 'point' (declining corporatism) is largely important within debates of mainly historical significance. In short, it seems logical to argue that aspects of the 'Membership Diamond' are of value when analysing the context of arguments put forward by the Swedish political parties.

Conclusion: stability and change

In many ways, this account of the developments in the Swedish parties since 1994 is little more than a preliminary report. The most important issue since the EU accession, the EMU, has yet to be resolved by several parties. At the time of writing, it is not even totally certain whether the issue will be subject to a referendum or not. Therefore, any conclusions will have to be made with care. The party system in the 1990s has been less stable and more fragmented than before. At the same time, the limited changes after 1994 suggest that the party system may have reached a new position of relative stability. Despite electoral setbacks, the Social Democrats have managed to stay in power, as a single party government. Between 1994 and 1999, the party has governed for different spells supported by the Greens, the Left Party and the Centre Party. This suggests a loosening of the boundaries of the two ideological blocs, as neither the Greens nor the Centre Party could be described as belonging to the same bloc as the Social Democrats. On the other hand, it could suggest that the two most EU-positive parties, the People's Party Liberals and the Moderates, are being marginalized. In the long term, however, the Social Democratic leadership is likely to prefer a bargaining position with maximum freedom of movement, in order to carry through its economic policies and resolve several forthcoming issues related to European integration, such as defence integration. Thus, they are not likely to rule out future cooperation with any party.

Looking at the internal situation in the parties, the situation is a mix of flux and relative stability, similar to the state of the party system. Despite the exit demands by the Left and Green Parties, Sweden is likely to remain an EU member for the foreseeable future. This means that the EMU has taken over as the main conflict issue, within as well as among parties. The core EU enthusiasts, the Moderate Party and the People's Party Liberals, are both in favour of EMU membership, and appear virtually united in this respect. Conversely, the anti-EU Left and Green parties also appear united against the EMU. It remains to be seen whether the so far limited signs of dissension in the Green Party will develop into a more serious rift. If such a rift were to occur, it will not necessarily be about the EMU. The remaining parties are more or less split. The Social Democrats have delayed the decision, and while some leading party representatives have come out in favour of EMU membership, most leading figures have treated the issue with care. The Centre Party and the Christian Democrats have both relatively recently taken congress decisions against EMU membership, but in neither case has the issue been permanently resolved. In the Christian Democrats, there are signs that the top party levels are moving towards an EMU-positive position, but they will face stiff internal opposition if they are to make this the official party line. This is even more true of the Centre Party. If a referendum on the EMU is held in the next few years, the conflict lines and the strains on the parties look like being very similar to the EU membership referendum in 1994.

To conclude, the post-1994 development in Swedish parties, and their approach to the web of issues related to the European Union, is a mix of relative overall stability and constant change in detail. Exactly where this will lead Sweden after the turn of the millennium is very difficult to predict. What seems certain, however, is that European issues will continue to cause concern and internal unrest for many of the Swedish parties.

Notes

1.   www.moderat.se/ideer_asikter/fakta/31eu/html
2.   www.folkpartiet.se/fp/poliltik/eu.html

CHAPTER 6

Swedish Interest Groups and the EU

Michael Karlsson

Introduction

The aim of this chapter is to analyse Swedish interest groups and their experiences of the initial years of EU membership (1995–99). Utilizing the common basis outlined by Lee Miles in the Introduction, this chapter will use the conceptual framework of the 'Membership Diamond' (Miles 1997a; 1998b) and address four research questions. First, what are the main priorities of Swedish interest groups regarding European integration, and to what extent are these priorities in accordance with the general process of European integration? Since on the one hand Swedish industrial organiza-tions and trade unions historically have regarded liberal trade as a prerequisite of economic welfare (Dohlman 1989), they largely supported Swedish participation in the Single Market project. On the other hand, with increasing levels of economic interdependence, the integration process has also included general economic issues (such as a common currency and unemployment and taxation aspects) and thereby interfered with national arrangements specific to the Swedish economy. Given that this is the case, are the country's trade unions prepared to compromise on Swedish 'excep-tionalism' and is Swedish industry willing to accept increasing regulation at the European level? The first research question highlights the importance of the link between the Diamond's second and third points (declining corpor-atism and the new challenges of economic interdependence) to the understanding of Swedish priorities.

Second, to what degree have Swedish interest groups been 'European-ized'? Considering the significant internationalization of Sweden's economy, it would be reasonable to expect that much of the 'European-ization' of the country's interest groups took place prior to accession in 1995. However, although Swedish interest groups have, in some respects, been internationalized for a long time, this holds more for industrial rather than labour organizations (Elvander and Seim Elvander 1995). Conse-quently, as noted by Misgeld (1997), when the membership debate took off in the late 1980s the Swedish labour movement lacked a European strategy for the most part. It is therefore appropriate to see how EU membership has affected the 'Europeanization' of Swedish interest groups and to what degree the labour organizations have caught up and carried through essential organizational and procedural reforms in order to cope with circumstances arising from EU membership. Hence, the second research question's focus on the 'Europeanization' of Swedish interest groups emphasizes the explanatory power of the Membership Diamond's first and second 'points' (a fragmenting 'Europeanized' democracy and declining corporatism).

Third, have Swedish interest groups fully adjusted to EU membership or are they still to be regarded as 'newcomers' at the EU level? At least two aspects suggest that there might have been a considerable time dimension involved. In other words, conditions that have counterbalanced or delayed full membership from having a mere short-term impact on Swedish interest groups. The first aspect concerns the degree of internal unity and levels of support within the respective group's membership. In this case, there is reason to believe that the adjustment process has been delayed considerably among some of the trade unions since the EU membership itself is controversial within the labour movement (Bieler 1999; Esaiasson 1996). The second aspect concerns the fact that Sweden and the EU have different traditions with respect to interest articulation. Hence, while Swedish interest groups, at least up to the early 1990s, worked within a corporatist tradition (Micheletti 1995), they are now operating in a multi-level system of lobbying. Of course, as corporatism has declined in Sweden there is reason to believe that interest groups have gradually adapted to lobbying as a source and means of influence. It is quite likely that this will especially be the case in relation to industrial organizations, since they largely initiated the process of 'de-corporatization' in Sweden. The third research question stresses the conclusion made by Lee Miles (in Chapter 1) highlighting the relevance of 'two-level games' perspectives (Putnam 1988) to the 'Membership Diamond'. There is reason to believe that domestic conditions, such as lack of internal unity and member support within the labour movement (Level II), may severely restrict the government's choice of external bargaining strategies.

Fourth, what are the potential scenarios for future changes in Swedish EU policy to be influenced by, or reflect alterations in, the perspectives of interest groups? Of course, following the general decline of corporatism in Sweden, one would expect Swedish EU policy to be less influenced or restricted by interest groups. However, since it has been argued that a high degree of coordination at the national level is an essential precondition for success at the EU level, it seems important to ask explicitly if Swedish EU policy-making actually 'fits' into the general pattern of 'de-corporatization'? Furthermore, given the traditional strong ties between the LO and the Social Democratic Party ('the two branches of the Swedish labour movement'), it is possible that Social Democratic governments may be relatively more constrained than non-socialist governments. The fourth research question is also related to perspectives of 'two-level games', but focuses particularly on existing procedures for national coordination and how they affect the conditions for interest articulation in connection to Swedish EU policy-making.

The chapter will focus on the major Swedish interest groups within industry and labour. The industrial interests will be represented by the Swedish Employer's Confederation (SAF), which consists of 39 employer associations with 43,000 member companies; and the Federation of Swedish Industries (*Industriförbundet*), which is a cooperative organization for 7000 industries. The analysis of labour interests will include the Swedish Trade Union Confederation (LO), which has 19 affiliates representing 2.2 million blue-collar workers; the Swedish Confederation of Professional Employees (TCO), which includes 18 associations with 1.3 million white-collar workers; and the Swedish Confederation of Professional Associations (SACO), which consists of 26 associations embracing 460,000 members, mainly with university degrees.

Priorities towards European integration

What are the main priorities of Swedish interest groups regarding European integration and to what extent are these priorities in accordance with the general process of European integration? Of course, since the integration process affects economic and social conditions in general, the opinions of Swedish interest groups embrace considerably more than just the social dialogue. Besides the traditional concerns of the interest groups, EU membership has also brought about increasing pressure upon them to take positions on broader economic and political aspects of integration. Hence, this section will focus on the priorities of interest groups with respect to their traditional group concerns as well as items on the current EU agenda, such as EMU and the development of a common unemployment policy.

Industrial organizations

The main task of the Swedish industrial organizations is to facilitate the establishment, practice, ownership and development of competitive business in Sweden. Consequently, whilst unenthusiastic about European political integration, Swedish industry has largely supported EU integration that facilitates business, such as the development of a well-functioning Single Market and the establishment of a common currency. As regards the Single Market, Swedish industry has identified a number of obstacles to its successful implementation (Industriförbundet 1996a). First, EC competition law is generally believed by Swedish business to be too complicated and difficult to grasp, as well as the EU also seeming too bureaucratic. Second, competition is also perceived as being disturbed by political pressures over the control of state subsidies and by the European Commission's decisions to approve government subsidies within the steel and aviation sectors.

Third, it is claimed that EU regulations constrain competition within the sectors of transport, agriculture and public activities. As Swedish industrial organizations have paid attention to these problems, they have sometimes confronted the widespread protectionist tendencies common in some member states. Since Swedish industrial organizations are strong advocates of liberal trade, it has occasionally been somewhat of a 'cultural shock' to take part in the work of UNICE or ECOSOC. Another related aspect of protectionism concerns the fact that Sweden's trade with non-EU states in the mid-1990s increased more rapidly than the trade with other EU members. However, even though Swedish industry largely believes that EU membership has brought about a more protectionist trade policy, accession has, at the same time, allowed Sweden to enjoy the benefits accruing from the EU's larger negotiating strength, which should facilitate the opening up of important export markets outside the EU area (Industriförbundet 1996b).

As regards the EMU, the industrial organizations adopted a pro-membership position soon after Sweden became a full EU member in 1995. SAF decided in February 1995 to favour Swedish membership from the start of the EU's third stage of EMU in 1999. SAF argued that the EMU is a natural and desirable continuation of the integration process, and Sweden should join for reasons of economic efficiency (SAF 1997). In response to the government's decision that Sweden would not enter the third stage in January 1999, the Director-General of SAF has proposed that the government should pick a 'fast track' and aim at Swedish participation from 2001 – the year that Sweden also assumes the Presidency of the European Council (SAF, Press Release, 29 April 1998). *Industriförbundet* took up a definite position in February 1996, when it decided in favour of Swedish EMU participation from 1999. From the perspective of the Federation, participation in the 'Euro' should improve the conditions for growth and fresh industrialization in Sweden by lowering, for instance, transaction costs and interest rates. Accordingly, the government was called upon to decide in favour of Sweden's participation and to ensure that the economy fulfilled the conditions of EMU convergence as soon as possible. In order to increase further the competitiveness of the Swedish economy, the government was also urged to take structural measures with respect to wage-formation, nuclear power and taxes. However, should Sweden not be a member from the start in 1999, the Federation asked for an exchange rate arrangement in order to reduce speculation during the transitional period.

Finally, the Swedish industrial organizations have, in principle, shown considerable restraint with respect to increased economic and political integration in Europe (Industriförbundet et al. 1995). Although growing levels of economic interdependence often require some coordination of management responses, Swedish industry explicitly fears that a wide-ranging integration process will constrain the competitiveness of European industry by increasing regulation and bureaucracy. Consequently, the industrial organizations rejected the proposal of the Swedish government to include a separate chapter in the Amsterdam Treaty on a common employment policy. Instead, coordination efforts should focus on creating better competitive conditions by, for instance, facilitating a well-functioning Single Market, deregulating the labour market and by avoiding growth-impeding taxes. New regulations have, in general, been regarded as acceptable only when they make business easier, such as a common EU currency and/or a new 'European company' statute, which aim at simplifying the conditions for companies operating in several EU countries.

Trade unions

The priorities of the Swedish trade unions have, in many respects, been marked by a considerable continuity. Their strategies aimed at promoting the social and economic interests of their members did not change as a result of EU membership in 1995. Indeed, the EU policies of the Swedish trade unions have largely been about emphasizing the importance of balancing market forces by developing the social dimension of the Single European Market. Similarly, the trade unions have in general argued for a more active approach on the part of the Commission in, for instance, fighting unemployment and facilitating gender equality. However, when moving away from traditional trade union issues, it is not unusual to find considerable hesitation and deep splits within these organizations, as have been the case with respect to EMU.

As regards the Single Market, Swedish trade unions, whilst recognizing its potential in generating employment and growth, have stressed that it is most important that the EU develop a social dimension as a counterbalance. Consequently, the Confederation of Professional Employees (TCO) decided in January 1996 that the creation of a durable EU social dimension was the main priority within its EU policy (TCO 1996). From the perspective of TCO, a major obstacle to achieving this goal has so far been the lack of a strong social dialogue generating independent agreements – where the parties in the labour market take responsibility for, and guarantee, national implementation. To accomplish this, TCO argues, among other things, for a legal foundation enabling the sanctioning of parties who break central agreements, and for the European Council to relinquish decision-making by unanimity in order to strengthen the threat of legislation. Furthermore, since collective agreements cover large parts of the Swedish economy, the trade unions would, in general, like to see a formal confirmation in the TEU that such agreements can replace legislation when implementing EU rules at the national level.

In addition to the social dimension, Swedish trade unions have identified a number of other areas of direct interest to its members. For instance, there is a widespread view among these trade unions today that national efforts at fighting unemployment are not successful without the strengthening of the

EU's employment policy. To its satisfaction, TCO has concluded that the EU's objectives in this area are in accordance with trade union demands and Swedish traditions (such as the emphasis on an active labour market policy and education) (TCO 1996). As regards gender equality, the trade unions have, in principle, supported the intentions of the Commission and its gender equality programme for 1996–99. However, TCO has argued that the Commission's goals must be concrete in order to be able to evaluate possible progress. Still, the trade unions have found, in some instances, that Community law was useful in their efforts at promoting gender equality in Sweden.

A third area of interest concerns welfare issues. One particular problem that has been addressed concerns public finances, since tight fiscal management by governments can be undermined as member states are in competition with each other as regards tax incentives aimed at attracting foreign investments. To counteract such a development, TCO has argued for the establishment of minimum European rules governing taxation on business and capital. A fourth area of importance to Swedish trade unions deals with the terms of employment in a changing European labour market. Consequently, the trade unions have strongly supported the Commission's proposals on trade union cooperation within transnational companies and for EU regulation of the employment rights of part-time and time-limited workers.

Finally, as regards the EMU, the Swedish trade unions have been rather hesitant and split. On the one side, SACO concluded that Swedish EMU membership would be desirable for the long-term structural development of the Swedish economy (SACO 1997). From the perspective of SACO, the main advantage of EMU is that it brings stable market conditions, including low inflation and a stronger exchange rate, compared to the costs and risks of remaining outside. In addition, SACO preferred that Sweden's participation started from the beginning of the EMU's third stage in 1999 in order to ensure that the country took part in the formation of EMU's system of rules. On the other side, LO as well as TCO have decided so far to play a 'waiting game' with respect to Swedish EMU membership. The main reason for delaying a final decision originates in both cases from a fear that Sweden will relinquish its traditional economic and labour market policy which secured the country's welfare state.

The search for trade union unity has not been without complication. First, it should be noticed that 2 of the 19 individual member associations of LO have actually abandoned the central policy of the congress and taken an individual stand on the issue. The Swedish Metal Workers Confederation, whose members, to a significant degree, come from export oriented industry, decided in Spring 1997 in favour of EMU membership, while the Swedish Commerce Workers Confederation decided against. Second, although the TCO has not taken up a definite position on the issue so far, the Confederation did form a joint working group together with SACO and

SAF (two pro-membership organizations) in December 1997, in order to analyse the consequences of Sweden's decision not to join the EMU in 1999. In the group's final report, which was presented in February 1999, there was basic agreement between the three interest groups that Sweden would be substantially influenced by EMU even if it remained outside the 'Euro' and that the government was not doing enough to prepare companies and wage-earners for the changes resulting from EMU (SACO, SAF and TCO 1999).

The 'Europeanization' of Swedish interest groups

To what degree have Swedish interest groups been 'Europeanized'? It is assumed that 'Europeanization' can take place with respect to policy, organization and process. It should be evident from the previous section that the policies of Swedish interest groups have been considerably 'Europeanized' as regards their traditional concerns, but perhaps less so when considering matters concerning general economic and political integration. The focus of this section is on the organizational and procedural aspects of 'Europeanization'. In other words, to what degree have Swedish interest groups carried through any organizational changes in connection with Swedish EU membership? Since EU policy-making is often characterized as a multi-level process, it might be fruitful to distinguish between the 'Europeanization' of Swedish interest groups noticeable at the *European* and the *national* levels. Of course, both processes can be assumed to contribute to the fragmentation of Sweden's democratic norms as well as the country's declining corporatism – namely the Diamond's first and second 'points'.

The European level

The presence of Swedish interest groups at the European level is most obvious with respect to: (a) their participation in the Euro-groups, (b) the establishment of an office in Brussels and (c) their representation in formal and informal EU institutions within the Union's policy process (Karlsson 1999). In the first case, the 'Europeanization' of Swedish interest groups took place, to a considerable degree, prior to EU accession in 1995. Hence, SAF and *Industriförbundet* have long been members of UNICE (Union of Industrial and Employers' Confederations of Europe), and LO and TCO were among the founders of the ETUC (European Trade Union Congress) in 1973. The Euro-groups are, in general, highly valued by Swedish interest groups for their ability to supply information, provide contacts and carry out lobbying.

In addition, it is considered especially important to be a member of a Euro-group such as UNICE and the ETUC since they are represented within the EU's Social Dialogue process. This was, for instance, the main reason why SACO changed its European membership and joined the

ETUC in 1996. However, it would be too hasty to conclude that there has been a thorough 'Europeanization' of Swedish interest groups with respect to their participation in the Euro-groups. On the one hand, their participation in the Euro-groups was evident before Sweden became a full EU member, and it has increased even further since 1995. For instance, in 1996 SAF and *Industriförbundet* had about 50 representatives taking part in the working groups of UNICE (Industriförbundet 1996b). On the other hand, it should be remembered that any 'Europeanization' has taken place on the understanding that the national organizations have been allowed to maintain their 'sovereignty'. The Euro-groups have remained as confederations in which decisions on policy issues still require unanimity (Karlsson 1997).

As regards the Brussels offices, the 'Europeanization' of Swedish interest groups follows at least three basic patterns. First, their Brussels offices were, in general, established long before Swedish accession in 1995. Second, in accordance with broader patterns of internationalization, the industrial organizations were present in Brussels before the equivalent trade unions. Third, the interest groups have, in principle, preferred joint offices. The two industrial organizations – SAF and *Industriförbundet* – established, for instance, a common office in Brussels in the 1970s. The decision to increase their capacity to monitor and lobby the EC was mainly in response to the considerable increase in Swedish trade with EC countries that occurred since the mid-1960s. The presence in Brussels of Swedish interest groups entered a new phase in the 1980s, when the signing of the SEA brought about a tangible risk of increased trade barriers, perhaps making Swedish access to the EC markets more difficult. The SEA not only prompted the industrial organizations to expand their office, but it increased the pressure upon Swedish trade unions as well. Thus, the LO and TCO also established a common office in Brussels in the late 1980s.

Since Swedish accession in 1995, the two interest group offices have been further expanded and SACO has moved in together with the other two trade unions. At the same time, it is worth emphasizing that the main task of the two offices has remained much the same – the monitoring of the EU's legislative plans and future political developments so that these organizations can lobby successfully in the interest of their members. Related to this, the Brussels offices have sought to develop extensive networks of contacts, including representatives from Sweden, other interest groups and various EU institutions. These networks are used to receive information, to relay the positions of the interest groups and to build alliances.

Finally, as regards Swedish interest group representation within the EU's policy process, there have, of course, been significant changes in the degree of 'Europeanization' since 1995. First, Swedish interest groups have taken up their seats in ECOSOC (Economic and Social Committee) – the specific interest group institution of the EU. Sweden has, in all, 12 seats in ECOSOC, of which SAF, *Industriförbundet*, LO and TCO have one or two seats each. However, for a number of reasons some of the Swedish interest groups have been disappointed with ECOSOC. The Committee has, for instance, been criticized for only having a consultative status and for being too large (in all 222 seats) and cumbersome to work effectively. In addition, Swedish industrial representatives have disliked the fact that many of their European colleagues are appointed as a reward for long and loyal service rather than with the intention of them being proactive.

Second, EU membership has also opened the doors for Swedish direct or indirect representation in the so-called Comitology (the large number of advisory committees of the Commission). From the perspective of interest groups, one of the main advantages of these official advisory committees is that they enable them to have direct contact with civil servants in the Commission. Because of this, and in addition to the somewhat disappointing experiences of working in ECOSOC, Swedish interest groups soon expressed their aspirations of better utilizing the lobbying channels opened under Committology (Karlsson 1997).

The national level

The 'Europeanization' of Swedish interest groups is not only discernible at the European level, but has left considerable traces at the national level as well. This section focuses on two cases of 'Europeanization' in connection with the interest groups' internal decision-making processes on EU issues. Hence, the main offices in Stockholm have carried through organizational and procedural reforms with respect to: (a) the routine handling of EU issues, and (b) consensus-building and coordination arrangements on EU issues amongst the member associations.

In the former case, the governing organizational principle has changed considerably over the years (Karlsson 1997). Originally, the interest groups sought separate organizational solutions in response to the increasing need to cover developments within the European Community. These solutions could, for instance, mean that the offices instructed one or more of their employees to monitor current EC affairs on a full- or part-time basis. Of course, such solutions reflected a basic assumption that it was possible to separate national and international issues. However, after experiencing Swedish involvement in the EEA (European Economic Area) and EU membership, the interest groups have, one by one, reached the conclusion that EU issues can no longer be treated separately. Consequently, Swedish interest groups have ended up integrating EU issues into the activities of organizations based on functionality rather than territoriality. This means that an employee who, for instance, handles issues of education or environment does so irrespective of the territorial level. Since this principle can mean that a significant number of the employees are involved in the same policy process and, at the same time, some of the interest groups have established specific EU coordinators.

The second case of 'Europeanization' at the national level refers to the attempts of the interest groups to establish internal processes of consensus-building and coordination on EU issues. As will be clear from the next section, the problem of consensus-building and coordination has, in general, been a particular concern for the trade unions of LO and TCO. In order to cope with the split among and within the member associations they have both designed separate institutional and procedural mechanisms to facilitate coherence and a powerful presence in the external arena. The coordination process within LO is concentrated within a special EU committee. This is the forum in which the member associations put forward their opinions on EU issues, and, after exchanging views and some negotiation, propose recommendations with respect to the official positions of LO. The committee was set up prior to EU accession and played, for instance, a considerable role as regards the LO's evaluation of the outcome of the Swedish full membership negotiations. On the basis of the committee's evaluation, LO decided in June 1994 to refrain from taking a stand for or against Swedish EU membership in the forthcoming referendum (LO 1995).

To strengthen cooperation within the TCO, the TCO board has established a specific council for European issues (TCO 1996). In the council, TCO and the member associations cooperate together on EU issues as well as incorporating the activities within institutions such as ECOSOC and the ETUC. Furthermore, TCO has established a particular EUROCADRES council to look after the interests of its higher grade official members. A significant degree of coordination is also conducted within joint working groups. Returning to the 'Membership Diamond', the need to develop a particular process of consensus-building amongst, and within, the trade unions could be seen as a further confirmation of the fact that national consensus-seeking has become more difficult in Sweden. It seems also reasonable to expect that there should be a link between the two processes, with developments in the former process having implications for the latter.

Interest group adjustment to full EU membership

Have Swedish interest groups fully adjusted to EU membership or can they still be regarded as 'newcomers' at the EU level? This section will pay attention to two aspects that may have a decisive impact on the adjustment process. First, it is assumed that the adjustment may be extended considerably if there is evidence of internal splits and lack of membership support within Swedish interest groups. Since EU membership is, for instance, controversial within some of the trade unions, there is reason to believe that it will have a long-term impact on them. Moreover, given that interest group support may be of vital importance to the government occasionally, this may also lengthen the time dimension of Swedish adjustment at large.

Second, it is assumed that short-term adjustments may be delayed due to the fact that the EU has a rather different policy tradition with respect to interest articulation. Attention also needs to be paid to how interest groups have experienced the changeover from prior Swedish corporatist traditions to the multi-level lobbying system of the EU. By stressing the consequences of interest group opinion and corporate traditions for the adjustment process, these two aspects highlight the link between the domestic and the EU levels. Thus, from the perspective of 'two-level games', these two aspects could be seen as examples of how domestic conditions (Level II) restrict external behaviour.

Internal unity and membership support

The attitudes of Swedish interest groups towards EU membership have been marked by considerable continuity since the referendum in the Autumn of 1994. During the referendum campaign the major interest groups appeared to have somewhat different approaches towards Swedish membership, although not in a direct confrontation with each other (Esaias-son 1996). The business community was heavily engaged in the pro-membership camp and was the main sponsor behind one of their leading organizations *Stiftelsen Ja till Europa* (The Foundation Yes to Europe). The trade union movement, on the other hand, was more divided on the membership issue (cf. Bieler 1999). Consequently, the major trade unions – LO and TCO – as well as most of the individual member associations, took neither a stand for or against Swedish full membership nor proposed any recommendations to their members on how to vote in the ensuing referendum.

However, neutrality did not exclude activity during the referendum campaign. LO and TCO, for instance, conducted a comprehensive information campaign focusing on both the advantages and disadvantages of EU membership. Furthermore, many of the trade union leaders publicized their personal positions and views on the issue. Thus, it became apparent that there was overwhelming support for EU membership at the elite level within the trade union movement. For instance, the LO chairman and the trade union leaders from 16 of the LO's individual member associations argued publicly in favour of EU accession. Only two chairmen from the LO confederation openly opposed full membership.

The referendum in November 1994 revealed, with one clear exception, a similar pattern within the electorate. Consequently, as is shown in Table 6.1, there was strong support for EU membership amongst members of business organizations, the SACO and, to some extent, the TCO. However, as regards LO members, there was a significantly different pattern. A clear majority of LO members voted 'No' to membership, revealing a serious cleavage between the elite and member levels.

Many of the trends which became visible in the Autumn 1994 have

Table 6.1   Voting in the 1994 referendum on Swedish EU membership: divided into organizational affiliation (per cent)

	Yes	No	Blank	Total	Difference (Yes–No)	Total interviewed	Non-voters %
LO	37	61	2	100	−24	1253	17
TCO	59	39	2	100	+20	882	12
SACO	70	29	1	100	+41	252	10
Business organization	67	32	1	100	+35	96	20

Key: LO (Swedish Trade Union Confederation), TCO (Swedish Confederation of Professional Employees), SACO (Swedish Confederation of Professional Associations)
Source: Gilljam (1996):180

remained remarkably unchanged during the first five years of EU membership (1995–99). Interestingly, the same patterns also seem to repeat themselves with respect to Swedish EMU membership. The industrial organizations continue to favour EU membership strongly and have also taken up a pro-EMU position at an early stage, which seems to have firm support amongst the organization's mass membership. Opinion polls in 1998, for instance, indicated that no less than 89 per cent of Sweden's largest companies (Industriförbundet 1998a) and a 4 to 1 majority among the small and medium-sized enterprises were in favour of Swedish EMU membership (Industriförbundet 1998b). In a similar way, EU membership continues to cause deep splits amongst and within the trade union movement, and the same divisions also appear on the EMU issue. A closer look at developments at the member level reveals that support for Swedish EU membership, as well as for EMU participation, has been consistently rather low amongst trade union members (see Table 6.2). Scepticism is particularly strong amongst LO members, somewhat less apparent amongst TCO members, while rather weak amongst SACO's 'rank and file'. However, if a longer-term perspective is taken, there does appear to be a small change in the attitudes of LO and TCO members, with levels of support increasing steadily.

The pattern at the member level suggests that both LO and TCO should proceed rather cautiously on issues relating to EU membership and EMU participation, while SACO has significantly larger freedom of action. As regards Swedish EMU membership, the behaviour at the organizational level seems so far to be as expected. Hence, SACO was the first of the three trade unions to take a stand on the EMU issue, whilst LO, as well as most of the individual member associations, had still not decided on a definite position in early 1999. However, just as before the referendum in Autumn 1994, it is possible to detect an incipient positioning among some of the member associations and, once again, some of the earlier divisions are

Table 6.2   Public opinion attitudes towards Swedish membership of the EU and of EMU: divided into organizational affiliation 1997–98 (per cent, rounded values)

		November 1997			May 1998			November 1998		
		Favour	Oppose	No opinion	Favour	Oppose	No opinion	Favour	Oppose	No opinion
LO	EU	21	62	17	23	59	18	26	56	18
	EMU	18	57	25	22	52	26	25	44	31
TCO	EU	40	48	12	41	48	11	45	44	11
	EMU	26	49	25	32	42	25	39	37	24
SACO	EU	58	34	8	61	32	7	62	30	8
	EMU	36	39	25	45	35	20	50	29	21

Key: LO (Swedish Trade Union Confederation), TCO (Swedish Confederation of Professional Employees), SACO (Swedish Confederation of Professional Associations)
Source: SCB (1997–98)

reiterated. Hence, the Swedish Metal Workers Confederation has taken a firm pro-EMU membership stance, while the Swedish Commerce Workers Confederation publicly oppose Swedish participation in the 'Euro'.

Resembling the LO, the TCO has also decided to postpone taking a final, definite position. However, paralleling the less critical attitudes amongst its members, TCO has been somewhat more active in the domestic EMU debate so far. As mentioned earlier, TCO has taken part in a joint analysis with two pro-EMU membership interest groups. Yet, from a comparative perspective, underlying trends suggest that the two major trade unions – LO and TCO – are still more constrained on the EU and the EMU membership issues. Furthermore, there is reason to believe that this should have significant implications for governmental policy as well. Given the long-standing emphasis placed by government on having interest group support behind important policy decisions, combined with the traditional role of LO as one of the two 'branches' of the labour movement, it is quite likely that the inability of the major trade unions to provide strong support for governmental EU policy may lengthen considerably the time dimension of Swedish adjustment at large.

Adjusting to the EU's multi-level system of lobbying

The time dimension affecting the adjustment of Swedish interest groups to EU membership may also be influenced by their ability to adapt to normal methods of articulating interests within the EU – namely, by lobbying at the national as well as the European level. The fact that Sweden had a long tradition of corporatism up to the early 1990s may suggest that this adaptation has been problematic and considerably drawn-out in time. However, it is also possible that the interest groups are operating with different time dimensions. Since the industrial organizations initiated the process of 'de-corporatization' in Sweden in the early 1990s, it seems quite likely that the mantle of 'newcomer' should rather be ascribed to the trade unions. An examination of the time dimension produces at least two general conclusions.

First, although the Swedish interest groups were considerably 'Europeanized' by 1995 and were already familiar with the EU's multi-level governance, it is still appropriate to conclude that they have all experienced a learning process during the first years of EU membership. This learning process, which lengthens the time dimension, has two aspects. To begin with, the experience of participating in the EU's policy process reveals that interest groups initially had certain problems in locating the most effective channel for lobbying.

As mentioned earlier, the initial perceptions of Swedish interest groups towards the ECOSOC overestimated its importance as a means of influencing EU policy formulation. However, since some of the interest groups quickly concluded that it was necessary to focus more on the Comitology, it seems reasonable to argue that the period when Swedish interest groups could be deemed as 'EU newcomers' was rather short in time. Interestingly, some of the interest groups have suggested that the Swedish government acts more like an 'EU newcomer' since it is perceived to be somewhat surprised that these interest groups are so independent and active at the EU level. The second aspect of the learning process concerns the link between the European and the national levels. Although there is great awareness within the leaderships of Swedish interest groups that these two levels cannot be separated in practice, the major trade unions have found it necessary to remind their members of the impossibility for Sweden to carry out policies independently of events taking place at the European level. In the words of TCO, 'We have, above all, to learn that EU membership has made European policy a part of Swedish domestic policy' (author's translation) (TCO 1996: 13).

The second general conclusion with respect to the time dimension concerns the experiences of adapting to normal methods of articulating interests within the EU's policy process. Perhaps what is less surprising is that it seems as if the answer to whether the Swedish interest groups have adjusted or not is, to some extent, dependent upon the exact nature of the policy process. Consequently, their behavioural patterns reveal that, in cases where interest group participation has been more institutionalized, such as the Social Dialogue, the trade unions appear in general to have been more adaptable and have even shown some interest in extending ways of representing interests at the European level.

TCO has argued, for instance, in favour of strengthening the roles of both ECOSOC and the permanent committee of employment (TCO 1996). The industrial organizations, on the other hand, have been generally less interested in adapting to these institutionalized forms of interest articulation, since they are wary that these arrangements may constitute 'embryonic corporatism' at the European level. Of course, these rather different points of view also reflect how the interest groups evaluate the prospects for informal lobbying as their main strategy of influence. Finally, it should be emphasized that there has been a basic understanding between Swedish interest groups that EU membership should not be allowed, not even in the long term, to intrude upon their freedom to conclude collective agreements at the national level. This understanding was previously reached during Sweden's accession negotiations. It has found expression, for instance, in the practice of lobbying in which representatives from the Swedish govern-ment and the major interest groups within industry and labour have jointly approached the Commission in Brussels.

The interaction between the state and interest groups

What are the potential scenarios for future changes in Swedish EU policy to be influenced by, or reflect alterations in, the views of interest groups? Following the perspective of 'two-level games', there are strong incentives for governments to pay special attention to national coordination before acting internationally. This coordination usually implies that formal or informal channels of interaction are established through which domestic actors, such as interest groups, have an opportunity to communicate their preferences to political decision-makers. Depending on a number of factors, the coordination may include everything from mere consultation to actual decision-making. In the case of Sweden, special attention should be paid to how national coordination 'fits' into the general decline of corporatism since the early 1990s. Has the need for national coordination brought about a return of corporatism, or is it essentially carried out through consultative arrangements and more informal channels?

Formal interaction

During the accession negotiations, the Swedish government established a large number of reference groups to ensure that there was a consultation with, among others, the interest group community. However, after achiev-ing full membership in January 1995, many interest groups perceived that the existing structure of formal interaction with respect to EU issues was somewhat unclear. They have therefore requested the government to take the initiative on how future interaction with interest groups should be organized. LO and TCO have argued, for instance, that the pre-accession structure should be adapted to the post-membership situation (TCO 1996). Closer examination of the actual evolution of formal interaction between the government and interest groups since 1995 indicates at least three basic characteristics. First, the model of using reference groups, which was established during the accession negotiations, has largely remained unchan-ged, with, for instance, *Industriförbundet* represented in no fewer than 23 such reference groups in 1995 (Industriförbundet 1996b). Quite naturally, these groups were, in many cases, never dissolved in January 1995, but were simply connected to the newer EU working groups of the government.

Second, in parallel with the reference groups, a growing number of ministries have also established so-called 'three-party committees' (consultation committees which include representatives from the trade unions, the employers' confederation and the respective ministry). These committees developed incrementally and often as a response to lobbying by the major trade unions. Hence, three-party committees were established within the Ministries of Labour and Social Affairs in Spring 1995 after pressure from LO and TCO, and half a year later, the trade unions also gained regular consultative contact with the Ministry of Finance (TCO 1996). At the same time, they pushed for other ministries, such as the Ministries of Industry and Education, to adopt the model of three-party committees as well. The trade unions put forward three arguments in favour of this institutionalized form of interaction. They argued that it was required in order to: (a) ensure the sound and comprehensive preparation of Swedish EU policy; (b) to achieve, if possible, common positions between the government and the parties of the labour market; and (c) to facilitate the implementation of EU decisions in Sweden.

Third, although the reference groups, as well as the three-party committees, open up direct communication and allow interest groups to influence, it is important to emphasize that these formal interactions cannot be regarded as evidence of 'neo-corporatism' in Sweden. At first sight, these institutions seem to bear some resemblance to corporatism since they, for instance, only include a selection of the major interest groups representing industry and trade unions. However, there are also some notable differences compared to corporatism. The most obvious difference is related to the fact that these institutions only have consultative status – they have no authority to make compromises or decisions with respect to Swedish EU policy. Consequently, these interactions should be perceived as arenas for exchanging views and information, rather than as proper forums for negotiation with the government on Swedish positions.

Neither is there any serious interest among the involved parties to develop these meetings into decision-making bodies. The negative experiences of corporatism prevails and especially SAF, which initiated the process of 'de-corporatization' in Sweden in 1992, has consistently rejected any speculation suggesting that the three-party committees be given decision-making power. However, in one particular respect EU membership has actually brought about increased corporatism. This concerns the national committees which decide on the distribution of financial support awarded from the EU's Structural Funds. In this case, SAF has made an exception and joined the committees since industrial participation is required in order to receive support from the Funds. However, since this is obviously a minor exception to the general pattern of declining corporatism it does not, in any way, change the relevance of the 'Membership Diamond's' second 'point'. Furthermore, since a formal procedure for interest articulation within Swedish EU policy-making has been established, this can also be regarded as an example of the 'Europeanization' of Swedish democracy.

Informal interaction

In addition to formal interaction, there are also a number of informal channels for interest group influence on Swedish EU policy. The general pattern is that this informal communication tends to take place within more institutionalized elite contact and/or networks between the interest groups and the State (Karlsson 1997). After only six months of EU membership, the industrial organizations were able to discern a change in their informal interaction with the State administration. In their view, EU membership had brought about a significant increase in the frequency of interaction and there is now regular and almost daily exchanges of views and information between their own employees and the civil servants. The development was largely explained as being the result of, what they experienced as, the very short time-horizons within the EU. Besides this new lower-level interaction, interest groups also have the potential to lobby through existing contacts at the elite level. For example, the *Sällskapet Politik and Näringsliv* (Society, Politics and Industry), which includes members from *Industriförbundet* and the Swedish parliament, has in recent years arranged study trips to Brussels and a seminar for Swedish MEPs.

Another example of channels of interest group lobbying is the close financial and organizational links that exist between LO and the Social Democratic Party especially since, metaphorically speaking, their relationship is often characterized as 'the two branches of the Swedish labour movement'. The close bonds are, among other things, evident from the fact that the chairman of LO has also been traditionally a member of the executive committee of the Social Democratic Party. Another member from the LO 'family', who has been represented in the SAP committee in recent years is Göran Johnsson, the chairman of the Swedish Metal Workers Confederation. Finally, it should be added that Swedish interest groups have, in general, been less interested in using public-orientated strategies, such as opinion formation, to influence the government's EU policy. This has so far occurred mainly in connection with major decisions, such as the 1994 referendum on EU membership and the ongoing debate on a Swedish EMU membership.

Conclusions

The objective of this chapter was to analyse Swedish interest groups and their experiences of the first five years of EU membership (1995–99). The analysis used the conceptual framework of the 'Membership Diamond' and addressed the four research questions put forward in Chapter 1. First, what are the main priorities of Swedish interest groups regarding European integration and to what extent are these priorities in accordance with the general process of European integration? The comparison of industrial organizations and trade unions illustrates that their specific role as interest groups is clearly reflected in their priorities. In other words, their views are dependent on what is considered best for their members rather than for Sweden in general. Consequently, since the EU has in recent years put more emphasis on issues such as unemployment and gender equality, Swedish trade unions have been more attracted by the idea of European integration as a means of balancing 'market forces'. At the same time, there is evidence that Swedish industry fears that new regulation at the European level will cause problems for the successful implementation of the Single Market.

Second, to what degree have Swedish interest groups been 'Europeanized'? In general it is possible to speak of a far-reaching 'Europeanization' of Swedish interest groups with respect to their traditional concerns as well as their organization and processes for dealing with EU issues. A significant part of this 'Europeanization', however, took place prior to Swedish EU accession, such as their long-standing participation in the Euro-groups, the establishment of an office in Brussels, and the change of organizational principle for handling EU issues. Third, have Swedish interest groups fully adjusted to EU membership or are they still to be regarded as 'newcomers' at the EU level? The 'newcomers' epithet may be relevant to the extent that the interest groups initially experienced some problems in locating the most effective channel for lobbying. Otherwise it seems as if the adjustment process has been particularly problematic for the major trade unions, since there have been deep divisions amongst blue- and white-collar workers over EU membership.

Fourth, what are the potential scenarios for future changes in Swedish EU policy to be influenced by, or reflect alterations in, the perspectives of interest groups? As regards Swedish procedures dealing with EU issues, a system of consultative arrangements and more informal networks between the government and interest groups has developed. Although these channels cannot be seen as evidence of a return to corporatism in Sweden, they have, in fact, institutionalized several contacts through which Swedish EU policy may be influenced. Finally, by applying the conceptual framework of the 'Membership Diamond', such analysis does give a clearer picture of the role of interest groups in the making of Swedish EU policy. Particularly important was the dynamic between the Diamond's first and second points and the Level II aspect of Putnam's 'two-level games' perspective.

CHAPTER 7

Swedish Public Opinion and the EU

Rutger Lindahl

Introduction

The role of public opinion has, not least during the last decade, attracted great interest from analysts who study the process of European integration. In early works dealing with integration theory, their analytical focus was, however, primarily on the activities of integrationist elites and their significance to the EEC/EC policy process. In many of the 'founding' texts of functionalists and neo-functionalists, the relevance of mass attitudes was played down and/or even denied (Haas 1958; Haas and Schmitter 1964). This analytical position was later the subject of several critiques (for instance, Hoffmann 1966), but even though the focus of these critiques was still on the political elite, the importance of 'the popular base' for elite actions and of 'national consciousness' received greater attention. Indeed, neo-functional integration theory has been revised by many scholars over the years (see Haas 1971; Nye 1971) and one of the central elements of these revisions has been to reinstate the importance of public opinion within the process of European integration. In most cases, there is now a wider acceptance of the importance of mass attitudes. Joseph Nye comments, for example, that 'broad political opinion becomes more heavily involved as integration decisions make heavier incursions upon national sovereignty and the indentitive functions of the state' (Nye 1971: 89). Even if public opinion is not seen as the primary cause of European integration, it is now widely regarded as one of the key driving forces behind this process and must be considered in any analysis on the national as well as the regional level.

This chapter provides an overview of the development of Swedish public opinion on EU questions, principally focusing on the last decade. The question of the country's relationship with the EC (later the EU) during the 1980s slowly assumed a top-rank position in Swedish politics. It also moved from being an issue considered almost entirely by the Swedish political elite to one forming part of the general political discourse, involving progressively larger segments of the electorate. EU-related issues have successively moved on to the political 'A-list' during the 1990s where public opinion is often referred to by political and economic actors in Sweden. Public opinion trends now attract continuous interest from all kinds of organized interests and in the mass media, and the results of public opinion surveys are used by the politicians to legitimize their particular actions and/or for not acting at all. In the context of the 'Membership Diamond', which functions as a common conceptual framework for the analyses in this book, these aspects form part of its first 'point', which is concerned with the nuances of Swedish democracy and the role of public support for, and opposition to, the EU (see Chapter 1).

The empirical base for analyses of public opinion have gradually improved in both qualitative and quantitative terms, and there are several databases today offering rich opportunities for national and comparative studies. For regional comparisons, Eurobarometer is the most valuable resource, but in the case of Sweden, there are also several national data-bases. Assessments incorporated in this chapter will be based primarily on data from the National Election Studies, Department of Political Science at Göteborg University, the SOM (Society, Opinion, Mass media) Institute at Göteborg University and the Swedish Central Bureau of Statistics, Stockholm and Örebro.

Levels of public support for the EU

Support for the European Union can be analysed along many lines (Niedermayer 1995) and in this section these aspects will be evaluated using Eurobarometer data, which surveys general public support for EU membership over a long period. All three of the 1995 'intake' (Austria, Finland and Sweden) have a history of internal political conflict over EU membership and public opinion was also deeply divided on the issue. Even though the result of the referendum in each one of these countries approved EU membership, the roles of substantial and well organized opposition remain essential elements of EU-related political analyses today, especially since the Eurobarometer data shows that public opposition to the Union in the three new member states did not end on 1 January 1995. In 1998, Austria, Finland and Sweden occupy the last three positions in assessments of current EU support levels in the EU-15 (Eurobarometer No. 49). Figures 7.1a and 7.1b present results from Eurobarometer and the SOM Institute's surveys.

One possible explanation for these trends in public opinion can be found in the literature on 'social learning' (Niedermayer 1995). Using this approach, one hypothesis that could be used is as follows: namely, the longer the time duration of the country's EU membership, the higher the level of public support for EU membership will be (Wessels 1995a). The data on Sweden could indicate such a development amongst the country's voters. However, corresponding data from, for instance, Germany and the UK on the one hand and Greece, Spain and Portugal on the other do not support such a hypothesis. The duration of full membership cannot solely provide a sufficient explanation as to why the Swedish public is presently

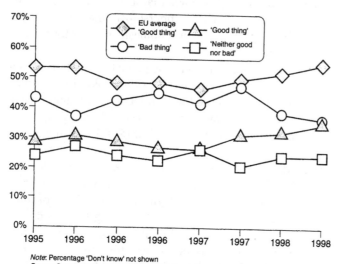

Note: Percentage 'Don't know' not shown
Source: Survey no. 49 – Trend Standard Eurobarometer 49 (data for Autumn 1998 (Eurobarometer 50) added by author)

Figure 7.1a   Support for EU membership in Sweden 1995–98

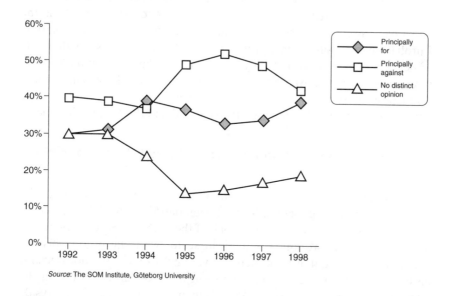

Source: The SOM Institute, Göteborg University

Figure 7.1b   Swedish opinion on EU membership 1992–98

moving in an EU-positive direction. One conclusion that can be drawn from current public opinion patterns in Sweden is that a substantial part of the electorate do not regard the issue of EU membership as finally settled. This fact will have a noticeable impact on Swedish domestic politics for the next two to five years at the very least.

Certainly, a majority of the Swedish electorate judge EU-related issues as being of high salience. Two thirds of the electorate answered a survey question by stating that they considered Swedish EU membership to be an 'important issue' in the 1998 parliamentary election and both proponents and opponents of full membership shared this view (SOM Institute Survey 1998).

Analyses of survey data since 1995 concerning the subjective level of information amongst Swedish voters indicate that the percentage of 'well informed' Swedes grew until 1997. However, the subjective level of information dropped drastically in 1998, especially amongst women. The subjective estimation of being 'uninformed' found amongst more than 60 per cent of the Swedish electorate is not satisfactory to anyone. One possible reason for this might be the intensified political debate on Economic and Monetary Union (EMU). In Sweden this debate was, and still is, kept on a technical level and has, thereby, added to the impression amongst the electorate that the EU is a complex and non-transparent organization, about which a great deal of information is needed in order to be able to understand how it works.

Given the results concerning the high issue salience of EU membership and the relatively low information level, it would be logical to assume that there would be a strong desire amongst the Swedish electorate for further information on the EU to be available. According to survey data from the late 1990s, Swedish voters do want to remedy their lack of information. Eurobarometer results from Spring 1997 and Autumn 1998 show that only 20 per cent of citizens were 'happy with' what they knew about the EU and more than 75 per cent wanted to learn 'a lot more' or at least 'some more'. The figures in Sweden were substantially higher than the EU-15 average and also higher than those for Austria, Finland and the UK, for instance.

Who is 'for' and who is 'against' Swedish membership of the EU?

When trying to answer the question 'What are the characteristics of a proponent and an opponent of Swedish membership of the EU?', it is easy to use general clichés. According to one of these, the average proponent is a middle-aged man, working in the private sector, with a fairly good income, living in a city in southern Sweden and voting for one of the non-socialist parties. In contrast, the average opponent is a woman, employed in the public sector, earning below average, living in a town or in the countryside anywhere in Sweden and voting for the Social Democratic Party or the Left

Party. How accurate are these stereotypes in practice? The analysis in this section focuses on the complications for political decision-making arising from existing differences amongst Swedish voters regarding their views on European integration. According to the 'Membership Diamond', these factors are primarily found in 'point' one, but the other three 'points' are also considered in the analyses (see Chapter 1).

Differences of opinion amongst Swedish citizens regarding EU membership have been recorded since these questions were introduced into opinion surveys (Lindahl and Nordlöf 1989; Petersson 1982; Todal Jenssen, Pesonen and Gilljam 1998). Men have always taken a more positive position than women have and the effect of the 'gender factor' is still notable in the late 1990s. In the 1998 SOM Institute survey, Swedish EU membership was supported by 46 per cent of men and only 30 per cent of women (see Figure 7.2). From the long series of Swedish election studies, we know that men show more interest than women do in politics generally, and especially in policy areas which could be labelled 'hard' (such as defence and foreign policy matters). In many cases, the opposite pattern is found in relation to 'soft', primarily domestic policy areas – for example, social welfare (Gilljam and Holmberg 1995; Petersson 1982). A possible explanation for the reported gender difference could be that EU issues, apart from being highly political, are also regarded as belonging primarily within the sphere of

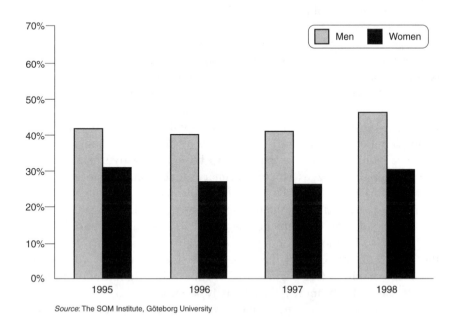

Source: The SOM Institute, Göteborg University

Figure 7.2 Support for EU membership in Sweden with regard to gender 1995–98

'foreign policy' and for this reason attract mainly the interest and support of men (Wessels 1995a: 109, 121f).

Since the decision by the government to seek full membership seemed rather abrupt and for many Swedes implied a break with the long tradition of neutrality/non-alignment and the abandonment of parts of the highly valued 'welfare society', it could be expected that older citizens would find it especially hard to support it. Younger citizens, who have not been affected over such a long time by Sweden's foreign policy tradition of 'non-alignment' nor had taken active part in the building of the 'welfare society' in the early post-war period, could, on the other hand, be expected to take a more positive position on EU membership. Analyses of data from the SOM Institute's 1995–98 surveys indicate that the 'age factor' does not have any noticeable effect. In all groups between 20 and 80 years of age, support for EU membership lies within the range of a few percentage points (in 1998 from 38 to 41 per cent). The same is the case for EU opposition (in 1998 from 41 to 44 per cent). Only amongst the youngest citizens (15–19 years of age) was the level of support remarkably lower (21 per cent in 1998), whilst EU opposition remains on the same level as that apparent in other age groups (43 per cent). Those who do not have a distinct opinion constitute more than one third of this age-group – namely 36 per cent (Lindahl 1999b).

In a previous comparative Nordic study of the results of the EU membership referendums in 1994, a number of hypotheses were tested (Pesonen, Todal Jenssen and Gilljam 1998: 23–34, 310–17). A majority of them were supported. Using the results from these 1994 studies, an extended 'socio/geographic centre–periphery hypotheses' can be tested, which includes a combination of social, economic, class and geographic factors (Galtung 1964; Ringdal and Valen 1998). This hypothesis considers whether citizens with good education, income levels above the average, working in the private sector and living in geographically central areas (which are defined as large towns or one of the three dominating city areas of Stockholm, Göteborg and Malmö) and thereby by definition belonging to the 'socio-economic centre' are expected to be more positive regarding EU membership than citizens with low (primary) education, income level below average, working in the public sector and living in geographically peripheral areas (which are defined as the northern parts of Sweden (in general) or in the countryside), and thereby belong to the 'socio-economic periphery'.

Using the education factor in the analysis gives a clear result. The higher the formal educational level, the more positive the attitude towards Swedish EU membership is (see Figure 7.3a). People with a good education are generally found to be more internationally oriented, have a better command of foreign languages and to be more open to international contacts and cooperation than people with lower levels of education.

Level of income is another factor that illustrates a well-known cleavage within the Swedish electorate. Results from a national opinion survey in

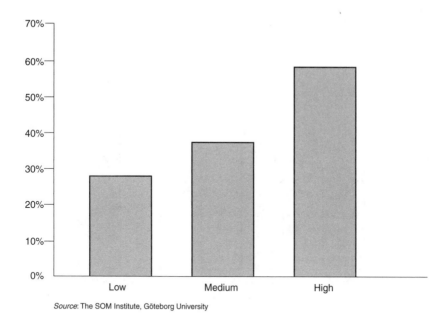

Source: The SOM Institute, Göteborg University

Figure 7.3a Support for EU membership in Sweden with regard to education (1998)

1998 show that citizens with higher income levels are considerably more pro-EU membership than citizens with lower levels of income (see Figure 7.3b). Higher levels of income are often, but not always, found in combination with higher levels of education and this combination probably stimulates the self-interest of people already enjoying sound economic resources and a good educational background to make the most out of what EU membership may offer in terms of increased business, career mobility and study opportunities (Pesonen, Todal Jenssen and Gilljam 1998: 31).

Turning to the question of whether employees in the private sector have a more EU-positive opinion than employees in the public sector, then there is no simple answer. Those employed by the state turn out to be slightly more pro-EU membership than those in the private sector. One possible explanation for this result is that state employees, even before EU accession, worked in an environment susceptible to international influences. For them, full membership was regarded as opening up new possibilities for international career mobility and securing jobs on the state level, rather than being interpreted as a threat. In the private sector, EU membership was perceived as, in part, facilitating expansion into new markets for companies and employees, but also as opening up domestic markets to greater competition, which might lead to the closing down of certain Swedish industries and rising unemployment. Hence, the results presented

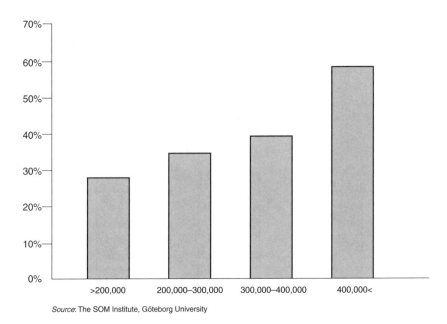

Source: The SOM Institute, Göteborg University

Figure 7.3b   Support for EU membership in Sweden with regard to income (1998)

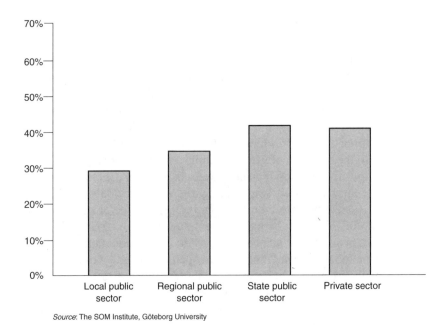

Source: The SOM Institute, Göteborg University

Figure 7.3c   Support for EU membership in Sweden with regard to employer (1998)

in Figure 7.3c should be read as suggesting a reformulating of the hypotheses.

In the reformulated hypothesis, state level employment should be treated as something different from traditional public sector employment. Public sector employment should preferably refer in the future to mainly the local and regional levels (at least with regard to EU issues). On these two levels, employment in the public sector is normally more closely connected to the basic public service functions of the Swedish welfare state. In the early days of the EU debates, the welfare system was expected by many Swedes to suffer greatly as a result of full membership due to increased public budgetary restrictions, tax limits and the large Swedish net contribution to the EU budget. It is therefore logical to argue that public sector employees on the local and regional levels are less enthusiastic about EU membership than their colleagues on the state level and in the private sector.

From the EU referendum study in 1994, it is clear that approval for Swedish full membership was secured due to voting patterns in the three dominating city regions of Stockholm, Göteborg and Malmö and in towns situated largely in the southern parts of the country. EU opposition was strongest in the northern and central parts of Sweden and in the countryside. As substantial financial support, from Swedish national and regional resources as well as from the EU's Structural Funds, has been distributed since 1995 mainly to regions where such opposition was most intense, it

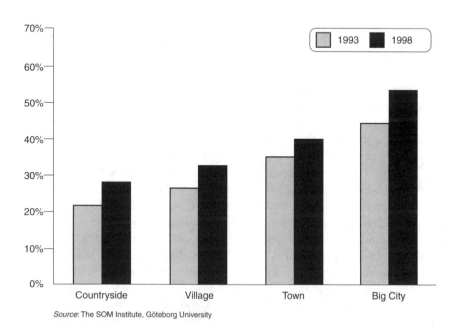

Source: The SOM Institute, Göteborg University

Figure 7.3d   Support for EU membership in Sweden with regard to residence (1993 and 1998)

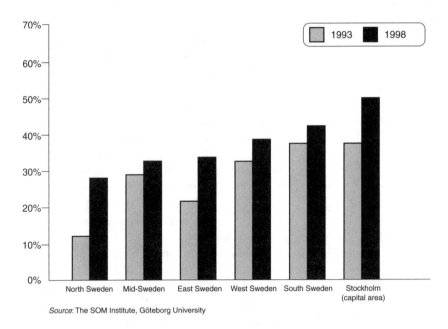

Source: The SOM Institute, Göteborg University

Figure 7.3e Support for EU membership in Sweden with regard to region (1993 and 1998)

could be expected that some increase in support levels for full membership might also occur. In Figures 7.3d and 7.3e, the results from national surveys in 1993 and 1998 are presented. As expected the general pattern has remained. Voters in the countryside and in the northern parts of Sweden are less supportive of EU membership than voters in towns and in the three big cities. There is, however, a noticeable rise in levels of support for EU membership over the five year period in question and the increase is strongest in the northernmost regions.

As regards the effect of the 'Left–Right dimension', then differences on EU questions, both between and within the political parties, have played an important role in creating fresh cleavages within the electorate. These results support the assertions of Lee Miles, that they have, at least to some extent, altered the basis for political decision-making and the functioning of the democratic system (see Chapter 1 and 'point' one of the Diamond).

The 'Left–Right dimension' in Swedish politics is closely linked to the socio-economic factors which have been analysed above (Gilljam and Holmberg 1995). In many countries, the process of European integration has been regarded, at least initially, as a socialist initiative strongly supported by a socialist federalist movement. This view received only marginal support in Sweden. The Swedish Social Democratic Party has been in office from the end of the war until 1976, from 1982 to 1991, and since 1994.

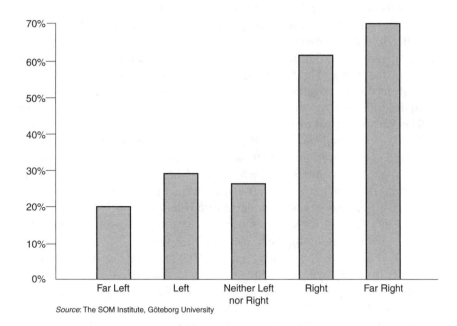

Source: The SOM Institute, Göteborg University

Figure 7.4 Support for EU membership in Sweden with regard to subjective 'Left–Right' (1998)

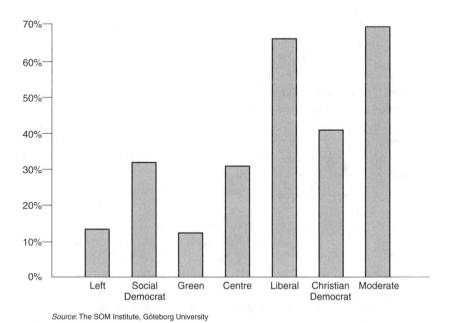

Source: The SOM Institute, Göteborg University

Figure 7.5 Support for EU membership in Sweden with regard to party preference (1998)

During the first period they carefully protected Sweden's policy of neutrality, which was, at this time, not perceived as compatible with EEC/EC
membership. The earliest signs of serious interest in Swedish participation
in European integration were found in the Conservative (now Moderate)
Party in the 1960s. The Communist Party (now the Left Party) warned
strongly at the time against moving Sweden closer to the EEC/EC. Results
from the opinion surveys in the 1960s indicate that the 'Left–Right' cleavage
in Swedish politics was evident early on in debates on EU membership (Kite
1996: 178–9; Lindahl and Nordlöf 1989: 162–4; Petersson 1982).

Indeed, the 'Left–Right dimension' is still apparent within Swedish public
opinion on EU membership. When asked about their subjective self-
placement on an ideological 'Left–Right' scale, opponents of Swedish EU
membership were dominant amongst those voters who position themselves
to the Left. Support for EU membership is strongest amongst those who
position themselves on the Right (see Figure 7.4).

If we analyse the positioning of the EU membership question with
reference to party sympathy, the 'Left–Right dimension' is, once again,
clearly visible. The Left Party holds the title as the strongest EU opponent.
The Green Party, which is somewhat difficult to place on this dimension,
also belongs to the strong EU opposition group. The common ground for
EU opposition focuses mainly on criticism of the Union's environmental
policy, concerns over the loss of national sovereignty and the uncritical
support of economic growth, combined with worries over the plans to
develop an EU 'common defence', the high cost for Swedish membership,
and that the EU's decision-making is too centralized and bureaucratic. The
Social Democratic Party is deeply divided. The Party's leadership strongly
supports EU membership but, at the same time, has been unwilling to take
a firm position on certain fundamental issues (like EMU), which have
prompted, from time to time, intense debates inside the Party. In the 1994
referendum, more than 50 per cent of the sympathizers of the Social
Democratic Party voted against EU membership (Holmberg 1996: 226). An
extraordinary party congress in Spring 2000 voted 'Yes' to Swedish membership of the 'Euro', but opinion polls show that a majority of party
sympathizers do not support this decision.

The leaderships of the Centre Party and the Christian Democratic Party
have also supported Swedish EU membership. Their parties' sympathizers
have, however, been deeply divided on the issue. During recent years, a
change to a more EU-positive position has been recorded among the
sympathizers of both parties. The Liberal and Moderate parties have been
the strongest groups of EU supporters since the 1960s. Within the Moderate
Party, there is, however, rather strong opposition from nationalistic conservative groups, who take similar positions towards European integration
as those found within, for instance, the British Conservative Party. Thus, in
any analyses, it is important to consider that all of the parties have to handle
substantial opposition from elements within their own 'rank and file' to their

official party policies relating to the EU (see Figure 7.5) – aspects which validate 'point' one of the 'Membership Diamond'.

Issues of great importance

Future trends in public opinion will, to a large degree, be linked to how certain fundamental issues of primary importance are played out in the Swedish debate. Changes in the balance of public opinion on one or two of these issues will have considerable consequences for the overall public opinion pattern.

National sovereignty

One of the fundamental visions behind European integration is the promotion of a 'European identity' amongst citizens, challenging the normal dominance of national identities, and also implying the transfer of national sovereignty to a supranational level in practice. For a mature and successful nation state, such as Sweden, this sort of change could be hard for its citizens to accept. One result from a comparative study of the EU membership referendums, held in Finland, Norway and Sweden in 1994, was that 'national sovereignty' was considered by the Swedish electorate to be of great importance when voting in the referendum (Oskarson and Ringdal 1998: 160–3). Very few, proponents as well as opponents, foresaw any improvement arising from EU accession in relation to 'national sovereignty'. The results indicate, however, that the proponents perceived that any loss of 'national sovereignty' (in terms of decision-making power) could be compensated by the improved possibility of influencing the EU (see Tables 7.1 and 7.2).

In later election studies and national opinion surveys, results indicate that the opinion patterns presented above still dominate amongst Swedish voters. When asked about whether they would support EU membership even if this means a reduction in political self-determination, the level of support declines amongst proponents as well as opponents. In 1998, results from a national survey indicated that support for EU membership is reduced by 18 percentage points and opposition is increased by 14 percentage points when such a formulated question is asked (compared to a question which only addresses their general attitude towards Swedish EU membership) (Lindahl 1999b). A 'deepening' of European integration towards a federal Europe also receives only weak support (Holmberg 1998: 270f).

All in all, analyses of recent survey data reveal that 'national identity' is still very strong amongst Swedish citizens and a corresponding 'European identity' remains weak. According to the latest Eurobarometer results (Eurobarometer No. 50, 1999), almost 60 per cent of Swedes see themselves as 'Swedish only', compared with an average for the EU-15 of 45 per cent for their own national identity. It can be concluded that concepts of 'national

Table 7.1   The arguments in favour of EU membership among EU-positive respondents (per cent). Argument groups are printed in bold type*

Democracy/Independence	**57**
Prevent the country from becoming isolated	37
Cooperation important/supranational institutions necessary	13
Secure national influence	8
Economy	**54**
Trade and industry, export, access to markets	27
Economy, economic growth	21
Labour market, unemployment	18
The EU's 'four freedoms'	2
Peace/Military security	**18**
Ensure peace	14
Security, defence	1
Environment	**7**
Environmental policy	6
Culture/Morality/Religion	**7**
We belong, we want to belong to Western Europe	0
Primary sector	**2**
Border control/Immigration	**1**
Welfare state	**1**
Other arguments	**10**
Proportion who mentioned at least one argument	*96*
Average number of arguments mentioned	*1.82*
Number of respondents with argument	762

*The table presents the percentage of respondents who mentioned the argument. Up to three arguments were recorded for each respondent. The table includes only persons with an opinion on the EU. The percentage which mentioned each type of argument, also the 'Average number of arguments mentioned', is based on respondents who mentioned at least one argument. Argument groups are printed in bold type, and the argument categories in normal type are the most frequent ones (at least 10 per cent of opponents or proponents).

Source: Oskarson, M. and Ringdal, K. in Todal Jenssen, Pesonen and Gilljam (1998) *To Join or Not to Join: Three Nordic referendums on membership in the European Union*, p. 152

identity' and 'national interest' will continue to be forceful factors in the moulding of public opinion probably for many years to come. Certainly, it will be several more years before Swedish citizens display greater acceptance of a 'European identity'.

Withdrawal from the European Union

Withdrawing from the EU is still presented by the Left Party and the Greens as a realistic alternative in Swedish domestic debates. In order to

Table 7.2 The arguments against EU membership among EU-negative respondents (per cent). Argument groups are printed in bold type*

Democracy/Independence	**53**
National sovereignty, independence	15
The EU is an undemocratic regime	26
Economy	**29**
Labour market, unemployment	10
Too expensive, too high contingent	10
Peace/Military security	**9**
Environment	**29**
Environmental policy	12
Food quality/medicines	20
Culture/Morality/Immigration	**3**
Primary sector	**4**
Agriculture	3
Fisheries, loss of sovereignty	0
Border control/Immigration	**19**
Weakened border control/more drugs	19
Welfare state	**11**
Other arguments	**13**
Uncertain future	9
Proportion who mentioned at least one argument	*86*
Average number of arguments mentioned	*2.05*
Number of respondents with argument	662

* See note to Table 7.1.

Source: Oskarson, M. and Ringdal, K. in Todal Jenssen, Pesonen and Gilljam (1998) *To Join or Not to Join: Three Nordic referendums on membership in the European Union*, p. 153

test public attitudes towards withdrawal, the SOM Institute's surveys have contained a question where voters are asked if they would like Sweden to leave the EU even if this meant a worsening of the country's economic situation. The reference to the potential risk of provoking a future economic recession is, like in the previous example, meant to stimulate the voter to reflect on consequences before answering the question.

The reason for referring to economic consequences is based largely on the fact that the change in its European policy by the Social Democratic government in Autumn 1990 was completed at a time when Sweden entered a period of economic recession and, consequently, the proponents of the policy change relied heavily on economic arguments to legitimize why the country should join the Union. Sweden's growing economic dependence on European markets – secured by the European Economic Area (EEA) – attracted substantial interest from the media during most of the 1990s and was also given high priority by those politicians and representatives of the export industries that supported Swedish EU accession.

Results from national surveys show that since 1995 there has been a small but stable majority in opposition to withdrawal if this worsened the economic situation. It is interesting to note that some of those who answered the general question on EU membership by stating that it was principally a bad thing, changed their minds and chose to support continued membership

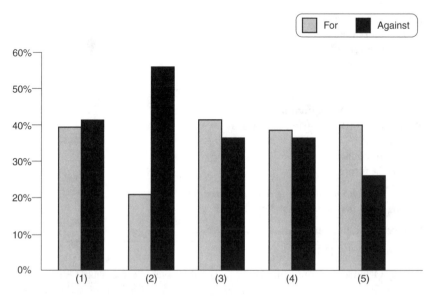

(1) General attitude to Swedish membership of the EU
(2) Attitude to Swedish EU membership 'if it means reduced political sovereignty'
(3) Attitude to Swedish withdrawal from the EU 'if it means worsened economy'
      (NB: those who have said 'no' to withdrawal are presented in the diagram as 'for' membership)
(4) Attitude to Swedish membership of the EMU
(5) Attitude to Swedish participation in prospective EU defence co-operation

The balance of opinion 1995–1998 (per cent positive responses–per cent negative responses; the index can vary between +100 and –100

	(1)	(2)	(3)	(4)	(5)
1995	−12	−42	−9	−39	−5
1996	−19	−43	−5	−28	+1
1997	−13	−47	−4	−20	+9
1998	−3	−35	−8	+4	+14

Negative balance of opinion indicates a majority preference for continued membership due to the formulation of the question

Source: The SOM Institute, Göteborg University

Figure 7.6   Attitudes to five questions concerning aspects of Swedish EU membership (Autumn 1998)

when confronted with the possibility of a worsened economic situation as one consequence of withdrawal from the EU (see Figure 7.6).

Economic and Monetary Union

A combination of the arguments apparent in the public debate on the two previously discussed questions are also evident in the increasingly intensified discussion on future Swedish participation in the EU's Economic and Monetary Union (EMU). Sweden's economy has been dependent on international trade and access to foreign markets for a long time and indeed, as Miles points out as part of 'point' three of the 'Membership Diamond', economic factors play a central role in the formation of Swedish public opinion on both EU membership and participation in the 'Euro'.

In the Swedish debate, those opposing Sweden's EMU membership argue that the country would lose the 'krona' – traditionally a strong symbol of 'national identity' – and control over financial and eventually fiscal policy. Those in favour of Swedish participation in EMU suggest that by staying outside, the country risks being marginalized and will consequently lose influence in other EU policy areas of 'national interest'. If this were the case, Sweden might also be less attractive to foreign investors (Calmfors *et al.* 1997). Given this potent mix of pro-EU arguments referring not just to matters of national sovereignty but also to the potential negative consequences for the economy, Swedish public opinion has gradually moved in a more EMU-positive direction (Hinnfors 1998). From a very EMU-negative position initially in 1995, public opinion in 1998/99 has altered to being slightly in favour of Swedish EMU membership (Lindahl 1999b). Opinion polls reported during Spring 1999 do, however, indicate that there is still a great deal of volatility in public opinion patterns, especially from a short-term perspective (see Figure 7.6).

The EMU issue has provoked an unusually intense and broad-ranging political debate, and as Miles argues as part of 'point' three of the 'Membership Diamond', one that affects the internal workings of Swedish political parties, trade unions and other organizations, forcing them to act with great caution. The Social Democratic government, backed by a majority in the parliament, decided in 1997 not to seek membership in the EMU from its start in January 1999 (see Chapter 9). The two major reasons that were given are interesting. First, the labour market situation needed to improve, including the lowering of unemployment, and the liberalizing of the wage negotiation system and job security laws. The second reason was that Swedish EMU membership must enjoy strong public support and, at this time, there was a large majority against Sweden participating, as well as the general public being rather dissatisfied with what had come out of EU membership so far.

In 1998, the European Commission judged that Sweden did not qualify to join the EMU in January 1999 as the country had not belonged to the

Exchange Rate Mechanism (ERM) for two years (see Chapter 9). In Sweden, many commentators perceived this as enabling the Commission to avoid a direct confrontation and also as a smooth way out of a political dilemma for the Swedish government.

The Riksdag decided that the final decision could only be taken after a referendum or after new elections to the Parliament. The Social Democrats decided to hold an extraordinary party congress in Spring 2000 with the EMU issue being the main item on the agenda. Indeed, other political parties and many organized interests have also decided to give this question high priority. The referendum will be preceded by an official information campaign on the 'Euro', and the probable effects for Sweden of joining or staying outside. All organized interests (whether they are for or against Sweden joining EMU), will be able to apply for financial support to fund their information campaigns. Many analysts consider an EMU referendum to be the last chance for those who want Sweden to leave the EU to propagate their case.

Even if the extraordinary SAP congress decides to support Swedish EMU membership, an EMU referendum will probably not take place until the government is sure there will be a stable majority in favour. The Persson government is expected to minimize the risk of losing office at the 2002 election by not moving too fast on this issue, especially as public opinion has turned more negative towards EMU membership.

On the EMU question, Swedish public opinion will not only be influenced by domestic political discussion, but also by the economic performance of the Euro-11 and developments in Britain and Denmark concerning their potential EMU membership. Public opinion is very volatile, so it is still too early to say whether Sweden should be seen as a 'Pre-in' rather than an 'Out' country.

Military non-alignment

Concepts like 'neutrality', 'military non-alignment' and 'international solidarity' play a central role in Swedish foreign and security policy (see Chapter 2) and from time to time this policy has been lively debated. Not surprisingly, the ending of the Cold War had a special stimulating effect on the Swedish domestic debates, with even NATO membership being seriously discussed. Once the Swedish Riksdag had affirmed in 1990 that EU membership was compatible with continued military non-alignment (Huldt 1994; Sundelius 1994), the main questions appearing in public circles related to the following: How far are the government and the people in Sweden willing to go when it comes to policy initiatives concerning the CFSP? Will the 'military non-alignment factor' continue to be important for the shaping of Swedish EU policy? What alternatives are acceptable to Sweden? These elements form central parts of the fourth 'point' of the Miles 'Membership Diamond'.

Those arguing against EU membership often make extensive use of arguments contesting the compatibility between military non-alignment and EU membership and a broad feature of their assertions is that Sweden will eventually have to accept membership of the Western European Union (WEU) and/or NATO. These EU sceptics also argue that the Union has ambitions of creating its own military capacity, which might turn it into a 'Fortress Europe' with aggressive capabilities and such developments would be detrimental to a new peaceful and stable security order covering all parts of Europe. The expansion of the Common Foreign and Security Policy (CFSP), as envisaged in the Maastricht Treaty, has frequently been used by opponents of EU membership in order to substantiate their argumentation. In contrast, the proponents of membership highlight the founding principles of European integration which aim to secure peace in Europe, and suggest that Sweden could not be forced to join any military alliance, especially since any developing EU 'common defence' would have to be based on a unanimous decision.

Analyses of public opinion at the time of the 1994 referendum indicated that 'peace' and 'military security' ranked very high amongst the preferences of proponents of Swedish EU membership (Oskarson and Ringdal 1998: 161) and full membership was perceived as promoting peace and security. Indeed, there were many EU sceptics who shared this view, but they qualified this by emphasizing that Sweden should not in any case join a military alliance or promote the development of a 'common defence' within the EU.

Nevertheless, Sweden, without any public debate, decided to join NATO's Partnership for Peace (PfP) initiative in 1994. Swedish armed forces have also participated in UN-sponsored peacekeeping missions to the former Yugoslavia and continued to do so even when the forces were placed under NATO command. These decisions were strongly supported by Swedish voters (Stütz 1999), even though the country's potential membership of NATO never attracted support from more than 20–25 per cent of the voters during public debates in the second half of the 1990s.

In addition, the 1996 Swedish–Finnish initiative proposing the incorporation of the 'Petersberg tasks' and the principles of conflict prevention and peacekeeping into the Amsterdam Treaty (see Miles 1998b) attracted substantial media and public interest in Sweden. The initiative was generally seen as a constructive alternative, providing Sweden and Finland with more time to consider future security policy options and avoiding unwanted confrontations with other member states over the interpretation of CFSP obligations.

Parallel to these developments it should be observed that an intense debate on defence issues started in the early 1990s, as a result of government plans to cut drastically the defence budget due to the ending of the Cold War, the reduced military threat to Sweden and the negative budgetary effects on finances caused by economic recession. A Government Commission report in 1994 on Sweden's non-alignment policy during the Cold War fuelled the debate by examining the rhetoric and deeds of Swedish governments during the 1950–60s (SOU (1994a) – 1994: 11). The Commission did not find any official documents indicating the existence of secret arrangements between the Swedish government and NATO, although there was some public discussion over whether the political and military elite expected that Sweden could fight an attacker alone, or if reliance on help from NATO constituted a fundamental factor in defence planning. For many, the results of this debate were summarized as being whether the EU could form an acceptable substitute for membership of a military alliance.

Results from the SOM Institute surveys show that support for Swedish participation in future EU defence cooperation has been rising since 1995. In 1998 it was supported by 40 per cent of Swedish citizens, with 26 per cent opposing such a development (see Figure 7.6). The result can be interpreted as support for a new defence policy where 'neutrality' is no longer the central element. Indeed, political commentators have argued that it is now probably only a question of 'political timing' as to when the change in policy formulation will be announced. One of the results of the Cologne summit in June 1999 was that the EU will take over some of the functions of the WEU, although Sweden, together with the other non-aligned EU member states, succeeded in preventing the formal merger of the EU and the WEU. Regardless of this, the EU's extended role in conflict prevention and peacekeeping (including also peace-enforcement) prompted the Greens and, to some extent, the Left Party, to criticize vehemently the Persson government for not using its veto. Yet no further or intense public debate on this theme ensued.

This can be partly explained if the Swedish public's interpretation of the concept of 'EU defence cooperation' is clarified. In a 1998 national survey, voters were given four alternative interpretations to choose from. One fifth of the respondents preferred the most far-reaching alternative, which included full participation in all forms of EU security and defence cooperation. Surprisingly, only 8 per cent did not want Sweden to participate in any kind of security or defence cooperation. As many as 27 per cent of the respondents did not state any distinct opinion on this question.

When answering the more generally formulated question on future defence cooperation discussed earlier, 26 per cent stated that they were opposed to this kind of cooperation. The reason behind the different opinion patterns is probably the addition of an extra option, according to which Sweden should only participate in conflict prevention and peace-keeping missions. This alternative was chosen by almost half of the electorate. The result is hardly surprising as it is in accordance with Sweden's existing policy, which allows room for an active foreign and security policy without including the collective defence commitment, which is the cornerstone of defence alliances like NATO. Given these results, it would seem that aspects of the fourth 'point' of the 'Membership Diamond' are confirmed.

Is EU membership 'good' or 'bad' for Sweden?

Swedes are, according to Eurobarometer surveys (see Figure 7.7 and Table 7.3), the most discontented citizens in the EU-15, with dissatisfaction with the impact of EU membership remaining high. The next section focuses on Swedish attitudes towards the consequences of EU membership, with the aim of adding further nuances to this evaluation of public opinion trends.

Two general tendencies are notable regarding recent developments in Swedish public opinion on the EU. First, a much larger percentage of the Swedish electorate today, when compared to a couple of years ago, are able and willing to express not only a general attitude regarding the Swedish EU membership, but also more detailed views concerning its effect on different sectors of society. Second, these attitudes are, in many cases, still rather volatile and easily affected by wider opinion and mass media reports about the Union.

Among the results from Eurobarometer, it is interesting to note that support for the EU seems to be related to perceptions of whether their respective country has benefited (or not) from EU membership. Among the eight countries where the EU support is over 50 per cent (not presented in Table 7.3), seven occupy the top positions when referring to their citizens'

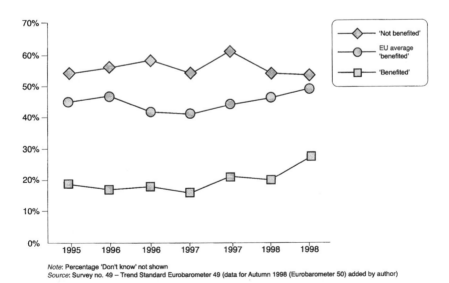

Note: Percentage 'Don't know' not shown
Source: Survey no. 49 – Trend Standard Eurobarometer 49 (data for Autumn 1998 (Eurobarometer 50) added by author)

Figure 7.7 Benefits from EU membership in Sweden 1995–98

Table 7.3   Benefits from EU membership (per cent by country, 1998)

Country	Benefited	Not benefited	Index	Don't know
Ireland	85	5	+80	10
Greece	76	17	+59	7
Denmark	70	20	+50	10
Luxembourg	69	14	+55	17
Netherlands	67	22	+45	11
Portugal	67	18	+49	15
Spain	58	25	+33	18
France	53	27	+26	20
Italy	51	27	+24	22
Belgium	44	32	+12	24
Austria	41	34	+7	25
Germany	39	36	+3	25
Finland	39	44	−5	17
Great Britain	37	42	−5	21
Sweden	27	53	−26	20

Note: The index presented in the table is calculated by reducing the percentage 'Benefited' by the percentage 'Not-benefited'

Source: Eurobarometer No. 50, 1999

subjective view on whether their country has benefited from EU membership (presented in Table 7.3). In Sweden, the citizens are the least supportive and the most discontented as regards the perceived benefits accruing from joining the Union. One explanation is that domestic debates over the last couple of years have, to some extent, focused on Sweden as a major net contributor to the EU budget. In combination with the effects of the government's extensive austerity programmes, this may have a strong negative effect on public attitudes concerning how EU membership has impacted on Sweden so far. Issues central to the 1994 referendum campaigns, such as the high hopes of increased economic growth, more jobs, lower food prices, greater financial support from the EU's Structural Funds, have simply not been met in the eyes of many Swedish citizens.

Data from surveys carried out by the SOM Institute provide a base for deeper analyses. During the 1994 referendum campaign, voters were asked about their expectations regarding the consequences of Swedish EU membership. Out of nine policy areas, four were, by a majority of the voters, expected to generate positive outcomes and five to generate negative (see Table 7.4).

When the electorate was polled again in 1997, three new policy areas had been added. The 1997 results indicated that there were still four policy areas where the balance of opinion was on the positive side. But only two of these were the same as in 1994. In two politically central policy areas, the 'national

Table 7.4 Answer to the question of whether Swedish membership of the EU so far has meant 'Improvement', 'Neither improvement nor deterioration', 'Deterioration' or 'No opinion' (per cent 1994, 1997 and 1998)

| Subject-area | Effect of Sweden's membership of the EU | | | | | | | | | | | | | | |
| | Improvement | | | Neither/nor | | | Deterioration | | | No opinion | | | Index | | |
	1994	1997	1998	1994	1997	1998	1994	1997	1998	1994	1997	1998	1994	1997	1998
Environment	25	12	10	34	62	52	41	26	21	–	–	17	–16	–14	–11
Economy	55	16	15	24	48	38	21	36	35	–	–	12	+34	–20	–20
Employment	42	10	12	32	61	49	26	29	36	–	–	13	+16	–19	–24
Agriculture	33	27	16	28	37	25	39	36	42	–	–	17	–6	–9	–26
Social welfare	7	3	3	42	66	58	51	31	21	–	–	18	–44	–28	–18
Equality	13	6	5	50	80	64	37	14	13	–	–	18	–24	–8	–8
Military security	48	20	17	32	70	51	20	10	11	–	–	21	+28	+10	+6
National sovereignty	5	3	2	24	44	34	71	53	51	–	–	13	–66	–50	–49
Possibility to influence the EU	57	34	31	23	42	30	20	24	25	–	–	14	+37	+10	+6
Food prices	–	35	36	–	41	34	–	24	20	–	–	10	–	+11	+16
Crime fighting	–	7	10	–	52	43	–	41	33	–	–	14	–	–34	–23
Business competition possibilities	–	43	32	–	46	37	–	11	11	–	–	20	–	+32	+21
Higher education and research	–	–	28	–	–	45	–	–	4	–	–	23	–	–	+24

Notes: In the 1997 study the following subject areas were added: 'Food prices', 'Crime fighting' and 'Business competition possibilities'. In the 1998 study, the alternative answer 'No opinion' was added, as was also the subject area 'Higher education and research'. The index is calculated as the percentage for 'Improvement' minus the percentage for 'Deterioration'.

Source: The SOM Institute, Göteborg University, 1994, 1997 and 1998

economy' and 'employment', public opinion had changed from being rather positive to quite negative. As regards the effect of EU membership on Sweden's military security, there was a positive balance of opinion on both occasions; however, the level of opinion in 1997 was not as positive as it was in 1994. Similar results are found regarding the possibilities to influence EU decisions.

The balance of opinion concerning the impact of EU membership on food prices and the conditions for Swedish companies' competitive market positions were found to be positive, while the consequences for effective crime fighting was perceived to be influenced in a negative way. Lower food prices were high on the proponents' list of positive consequences arising from EU membership in 1994. In the years immediately after Swedish accession, this promise was regarded by a majority of the citizens as not being fulfilled. In 1997, and even more so in 1998, the balance of opinion had changed in an EU-positive direction. Yet, even in 1998, 8 out of 13 policy areas showed a negative balance of opinion. With this in mind, it is somewhat surprising to find that the overall view of Swedish EU membership has become more positive in the last three years.

When searching for adequate explanations for these results, it is important to note that a very high percentage of the people who have been asked these questions chose the alternative 'neither positive nor negative consequences'. This could mean that they, for some reason, do not want to 'take sides' with either of the two major groups, that they do not feel qualified to judge or that they have not experienced any positive or negative consequences that can be clearly associated with EU membership. In its 1998 survey, the SOM Institute tried to clarify the picture somewhat by adding the answer alternative 'I do not have any decided opinion'. This, however, resulted in only minor changes in the general pattern of public opinion. The percentage of the electorate that holds no decided opinion varies, depending on the policy area, between 9 and 23 per cent and this must be regarded as normal. The 'neither/nor' alternative still, in most cases, attracts the largest number of answers.

Regarding EU membership, the most forceful factor behind the opinion pattern turns out to be the fundamental attitude of the people (see Table 7.5). Where a majority of the proponents experience positive effects accruing from EU membership, the opponents find negative ones (and vice versa). In five cases, the two groups are in agreement with each other. In four of them the balance of opinion is negative for both groups (agriculture, social welfare, national sovereignty and crime fighting) and in one case (higher education and research) it is positive. The greatest differences of opinion between the two groups are found regarding the attitude towards Sweden's ability/possibility to influence the EU (85 units) and the effects of EU membership on the economy (72 units). The strength of the influence of these underlying attitudes on Swedish EU membership is illustrated by the fact that statistical data indicate that food prices have lowered, in some cases

Table 7.5 Answer to the question of whether Swedish membership of the EU so far has meant 'Improvement', 'Neither improvement nor deterioration', 'Deterioration' or 'No opinion', distributed with reference to basic attitude concerning Sweden's membership of the EU (Index 1994, 1997 and 1998)

| | *Attitude to Sweden's membership in the EU* | | | | | |
| | *Primarily for* | | | *Primarily against* | | |
Subject-area	*1994*	*1997*	*1998*	*1994*	*1997*	*1998*
Environment	+13	+4	+4	−49	−29	−27
Economy	+75	+23	+19	−10	−51	−53
Employment	+53	+4	+8	−29	−38	−36
Agriculture	+22	+18	−5	−33	−28	−49
Social welfare	−21	−10	−4	−69	−44	−35
Equality	−5	+1	+1	−48	−17	−18
Military security	+51	+36	+27	+4	−5	−9
National sovereignty	−46	−36	−38	−87	−65	−65
Possibility to influence the EU	+70	+58	+53	±0	−21	−32
Food prices	–	+45	+49	–	−11	−8
Crime fighting	–	−15	−1	–	−50	−42
Business competition possibilities	–	+64	+51	–	+12	−2
Higher education and research	–	–	+42	–	–	+10

Notes: In the 1997 study the following subject areas were added: 'Food prices', 'Crime fighting' and 'Business competition possibilities'. In the 1998 study, the subject area 'Higher education and research' was added. The Index is calculated as the percentage for 'Improvement' minus the percentage for 'Deterioration'.

Source: The SOM Institute, Göteborg University, 1994, 1997 and 1998

by large amounts, since the accession and yet, the EU opponents claim that the Union's effect is still negative (Lindahl 1998).

Long-term trends and decisive moments

Although there seems to be little change in the general trends in public opinion during the last four years, there are, as this chapter has demonstrated, at least a few signs of reconsideration among Swedish citizens. In particular, events of special importance are due to take place over the next couple of years that may have an impact on future long-term trends in Swedish public opinion.

For the first time, Sweden in 1999 held European direct elections at the same time as the other EU member states (see Chapter 5). Many were hopeful that this event would stimulate interest not only for the European Parliament but also for a number of current policy issues of strategic importance, especially since the previous direct election to the European Parliament in 1995 (see Chapter 5) had recorded an all time low voter turnout (41.6 per cent), a poor outcome for the Social Democrats but good results for the anti-EU Left Party and Greens, and led to Swedish EP representation of 22 MEPs that was split evenly between pro- and anti-membership (11 each).

The outcome of the 1999 European direct election sent a 'shock-wave' through the Swedish political system since only 38 per cent of the electorate turned out to vote. This could be regarded as an illustration of not only a general problem of legitimacy for the European Parliament but also for the democratic foundation of the EU. In Sweden, all political parties were well aware of the risk of a low turnout and made great efforts to stimulate the political debate on the EU in order to convince the electorate to vote. They had, for example, recruited well known candidates and made an early start of their campaign activities. Yet, the result clearly demonstrated that they had not been very successful (see Chapter 5).

With the Social Democrats and the Greens doing badly, the Moderates and Centre Party modestly, and the Left Party improving somewhat (see Chapter 5), two parties could be named as clear winners. The Christian Democratic Party, which in the 1995 election did not qualify for the allocation of seats, received almost eight per cent of the votes and two seats. The pro-EU Liberals, whose top candidate was a 'grass roots' politician (Marit Paulsen), trebled their share of the vote and also their number of seats compared to the European election in 1995. In the 1999–2004 European Parliament, there will be seven anti-EU or EU-critical Swedish representatives, but 15 MEPs who are clearly pro-full membership, suggesting that the balance has swung in favour of the pro-EU forces. Unfortunately, however, the European election of 1999 did not provide a good test of the possibilities for a change in the fundamental divide concerning public opinion on Sweden's EU membership. Too many of the electorate chose not to vote. This basic problem will have to be tackled more intensively by the political parties in the near future. An EMU decision, in a referendum or in the next parliamentary elections, will provide the next opportunity.

Conclusions

Sweden's EU membership remains an open question for a large part of the electorate even though it is five years since accession and the country's political parties all have to cope with internal cleavages on EU-related issues. It is questionable whether Swedish society has settled down and accepted full membership, especially since public opinion surveys still indicate, for instance, that there is a distinct cleavage between those who belong to the 'socio-economic centre' and those from the 'periphery'. There is also a clear 'Left–Right' dimension in the opinion patterns.

The basic public opinion pattern has been quite stable for a long time, although there has been a swing within public opinion towards a more EU-positive position during the last few years. Noteworthy are the results concerning public opinion on EMU membership and participation in EU defence cooperation, which are elements identified as important in shaping Swedish attitudes within the 'Membership Diamond' (see Chapter 1).

Clearly, there remains much to be done to convince the average Swede of the (especially long-term) benefits arising from EU membership. More voters are dissatisfied than satisfied with what Sweden has gained from full membership so far. Over half of the investigated policy areas record a negative balance of public opinion. It is also important to observe, however, that a majority of the citizens in several cases state that they have not experienced any noticeable effect resulting from EU membership.

Aspects of the 'Membership Diamond' are borne out by Swedish public opinion trends. According to the results of public opinion surveys, it is reasonable to interpret that rising economic interdependence (the Diamond's third 'point'), the risk of being politically marginalized and growing sympathy with enhanced security policy cooperation (the Diamond's fourth 'point') are factors that work in favour of 'deepening' Sweden's relations with the Union. Any negative effects arising from full membership on national sovereignty and the country's democratic traditions, plus public opposition to the strengthening of federalist tendencies within the EU (all aspects of the Diamond's first 'point') in combination with fundamental cleavages between, as well as within, Swedish political parties and interest groups (the latter being central to the Diamond's second 'point') work in the opposite direction. The friction between these factors reflected in the divisions within public opinion has forced Swedish governments and political parties to act with great caution and follow a 'mixed' approach to European integration. In order to find a way out of this dilemma, and to facilitate greater constructive use of Swedish full membership, an answer to the fundamental question of 'continued EU membership or withdrawal from the Union' must be found.

Sweden can, quite obviously, still be regarded as a new member of the European Union and the instability within Swedish public opinion reflects this. After all, five years of EU membership is not a long time. The European direct election in June 1999 did not provide a clear-cut answer to the fundamental question of continued Swedish full membership. The next likely opportunity to solve this problem, once and for all, will be the referendum on EMU membership. This assumes there will be a referendum. The governing Social Democrats will most probably, and judging from their poor performance at the 1999 European election, be very careful and not unnecessarily challenge anti-EU opinion inside the SAP. Hence, the next major test of the strengths of the proponents and the opponents of Swedish EU membership may be postponed until, or after, the next parliamentary election in Autumn of 2002. A daring prognosis for the next five years goes in favour of the proponents since concerns over increased economic and political marginalization will, more than likely, prevail over fears surrounding 'national sovereignty'. Under this scenario, Sweden will be, in many ways, more 'Europeanized' in 2005, but will, most probably, still be unwilling to accept a 'Federal Europe', remaining the home of many active critics of the Union and its policies.

PART III

Policies

Swedish Industrial Policy and Research and Technological Development: the Case of European Defence Equipment

Ulrika Mörth[1]

Introduction

In 1995 Sweden joined the European Union. In what ways has membership changed Sweden's industrial and research and technological development (RTD) policies? This is, to be sure, a difficult question to answer. Being part of the European Union has pervasive consequences for the Swedish state, for the relationship between state and society, for the organization of government and for different policy areas. The national political agendas tend to merge into a European agenda. The borders between internal and external policies are diffuse. Hence, it is important to study the transformation of governance that is taking place. However, these changes are not easy to study. A traditional approach would entail a study in which an attempt is made to try and measure in what ways a national policy has been affected by the European Union. It can then be ascertained the extent to which a respective national policy 'fits' the equivalent policy of the European Union and under what circumstances there is a 'misfit'. Pressure for national adaptation is thus high when there is a mismatch between the national policy and the policy within the European Union.

This author argues that although such studies have their merits, they also give the impression that Europeanization is a one-sided process. Europeanization is not only about a process in which national policies should be adapted; it is also a process where both actors and interests are formed. This author's view of the linkages between the domestic Swedish processes and Europeanization differs from the editor's 'point' one of the 'Membership Diamond'. 'Europeanization creates both actors and interests. It changes what government officials think and say as well as what they do' (Jacobsson and Mörth 1998: 4). Taking part in the work of the European Union makes what is referred to as 'Swedish' more important. The institutions within the EU want to know what Sweden thinks about all sorts of questions. This means that the demand for national positions and actors increases in the European Union. You could argue that governments are continually pressed into discussions with others, 'both to discover and to promote their ideas, even though this is learned in conjunction with others. It can therefore be said that the nation-state is at the same time being diluted and recreated through the process of Europeanization' (ibid.: 34). Thus, transformation and embeddedness cover my understanding of the process of Europeanization. Indeed, it is multi-level governance (Kohler-Koch 1996; Marks *et al.* 1996).

Furthermore, it is important to bear in mind that national adaptation to the European Union is a process and partly takes place before formal entry into the Union. This is obvious, for instance, in the case of Swedish agricultural policy, which was reformed before Sweden actually became a formal EU member. We have to study these so-called anticipated adaptations towards the European Union.

A further complication in measuring the EU's impact on national policy concerns the fact that EU membership has not been a prerequisite for taking part in various policy areas within the European Union. Sweden has been called the 'reluctant European', an epithet reflecting the fact that the Swedish government and parliament carried on an inconclusive discussion of the politically sensitive question of Swedish membership of the EU for 30 years. When particular areas of policy are examined, however, Swedish policy towards the European Union is revealed to be more varied than the official EU policy. This is especially true for the field of research and technological development. Sweden has been part of the formation of a European technology community for some time. In fact, when EUREKA (the European Research Coordinating Agency) started in the mid-1980s the Swedish government was very active in the initial phases of the new collaboration. The Swedish decision to join EUREKA was important during a time when EU membership was not on the political agenda and when the process of creating an internal market, the EES (the European Economic Space) process was going on. It was obvious to the decision-makers that being part of that economic process also included active participation in various projects of European RTD collaboration. Before EUREKA, Sweden had also been part of COST (Coopération européenne dans le domaine de la récherche scientifique et technique), that had started at the beginning of the 1970s. Furthermore, as a non-EU member, Sweden also participated on a programme-by-programme basis in the EU's framework for research and technological development. Swedish participation in individual EU programmes therefore started in 1987.

So, has the country's EU membership affected Sweden's RTD policy? The answer is both yes and no. Membership has, of course, entailed a more direct Swedish influence on the EU's RTD policy, especially concerning the framework programmes. The Swedish government is now represented in the formal institutional set-up and can take part in all policy areas and formal decision-making processes. On the other hand, it can be argued that Sweden's RTD policy has been Europeanized for quite some time and that this policy does not differ in any crucial way from the RTD policies of other European countries. A convergence of national RTD policies during the 1980s has been analysed from a policy diffusion perspective in which the OECD functioned as a harmonizing agent (Mörth 1998a).

This chapter addresses RTD and industrial issues and how these issues are linked to security and defence matters. Indeed, to separate between these two types of issues can be characterized as a 'line in water'. When EUREKA was launched in 1985, the programme was the first European response to the SDI (Strategic Defence Initiative) programme of the United States. Due to the political sensitivities at the time EUREKA was designated as a civilian programme, although everyone realized that it was difficult to make a distinction between various types of technologies (Mörth 1996). During the mid-1980s it was obvious that the threat of SDI was not primarily a military threat to Europe – it was an industrial and a commercial threat.

The European research and technological development activities and the emerging information society have become part of the very future of Europe. Since the founding of the European Communities in 1957, technology policy has aimed at improving the worldwide competitive position of European industry, especially towards the US. However, the need to address the issue of European competitiveness seems to be more on the European agenda in the 1990s than it was in the early years of the EC.

The 'line in water' and European 'soft power'

The future of the European defence industry is on the political agenda, nationally as well as internationally. Defence budgets are falling and national defence policies move in a more European and international orientated direction. New security threats are identified that require new tasks (see Chapter 2). Furthermore, technological change alters the ways defence development and production is done. Technologies of civilian origin are becoming more important even for defence purposes. Major national industrial restructuring took place during the 1980s and thus before the events in Eastern Europe and the former Soviet Union. This was due to the creation of the internal market and the Single European Act (SEA) in 1986/87.

It is quite clear that the European governments long ago began to realize that the strategy of national champions within the field of high technology would not be sufficient (Sandholtz 1992). By engaging in European projects the governments increased their capability but they also lost some of their national autonomy. This dilemma is more complex than ever. The knowledge-based power structure is not only about technical innovations – it is about the information society and the future of the welfare state. In addition, the end of the Cold War has opened up commercialization of the defence industry. Thus, there seem to be very few national policy areas that are 'sacred' from a process of Europeanization.

The European Union is active in the ongoing process of liberalization of various policy areas, the so-called new competition policy areas (Cini and McGowan 1998). The revitalization of the European integration process in the 1980s and the creation of the internal market meant that competition policy was seen as a European-level response to the industrial downturn that had swept the region over the previous decade.

The rationale behind the EU's effort to liberalize the defence industrial sector is, of course, to strengthen Europe's competitiveness towards the US. In 1993, when the Delors Commission presented the White Paper on 'Growth, Competitiveness and Employment', it was clear that the EU's technology policy would become 'a very different animal' (Peterson and Sharp 1998: 114). By the late 1990s, the EU's technology policy had a far clearer and more widely accepted rationale than ever before. Thus, the 1990s are characterized by the building up of Europe's structural base of civilian power – so-called 'soft power' (Nye 1990; Nye and Owens 1996).

It is obvious that there are potential synergy effects between the defence-related RTD projects and EU's framework programme. To link these RTD activities is, however, a politically sensitive issue. In April 1997 the Commission presented a proposal for the fifth framework programme (F5P) for research and technological development (1998–2002, see European Commission 1997a – COM(97) 142). A significant part of the framework programme pertained to dual-use technology.[2] However, the Commission's formal proposal for the fifth framework programme made no mention of whether dual-use technology should be part of the programme or not, although this matter had been mentioned in an early internal draft and had been raised by several member governments. Hence, the suggestion to take into account dual-use considerations within the framework programme proved to be very controversial – both inside DG XII and the Cresson cabinet, but also amongst the member states.

One reason for this controversy is, of course, the fact that defence industrial issues require cross-border competence and do not fit into the traditional distinction between economic/RTD/industrial and defence/security issues. Thus, to incorporate defence, industrial and RTD issues within the framework programme would jeopardize the civilian character of the first EU pillar (Mörth 1998b).

At the European level, the European Commission has repeatedly emphasized the linkage between defence-related industry and the European technological and economic base. Against this background, it is not surprising that the Commission has presented several Communications during the 1990s that proclaim a deregulation of the defence industry. The Commission's arguments for the necessary national deregulation and the need for a European regulatory framework are based on both economic and security factors – namely on both the first and second pillars. Most of the arguments about restructuring the European defence industrial market centre on Article 223[3] of the Treaty of Rome. This Article allows governments to exempt defence firms from EU rules on mergers, monopolies and procurement. Article 223 is thus a major obstacle to a unified defence equipment market. The question of a reinterpretation of Article 223 is politically sensitive since this could imply that defence equipment would be subject to the regulations of the internal market. This means that national governments would also be limited in their efforts to support the national defence industry.

In January 1996 the Commission presented a COM document, 'The challenges facing the European defence-related industry: a contribution for action at European level', which raised the issue of incorporating dual-use technology into the framework programme (see European Commission 1996 – COM(96) 10). The Commission argued that it was necessary to consider how, and to what extent, increased civil defence synergies could be promoted at the European level with the aim of optimizing the overall use of research and development. The Communication called for a more proactive and consistent European approach to the defence industry. It showed the Commission's ambition to pursue a more comprehensive industrial policy – an action plan – that not only included the civilian industry in Europe but also the defence-related industry. The document has been the subject of heated debate within the Commission and the European Parliament, and between the member states.

The tension between an economic and a security perspective on defence equipment, evident in the Communication from 1996, was toned down in a Communication in November 1997 (see European Commission 1997b – COM(97) 583 Final). Interestingly, the perspective of this document is a rather pragmatic view of the defence industry and the market for defence products. The Communication is very clear on the dual nature of the defence industry and does not pursue one perspective, but two – a community and a CFSP perspective. Clearly, this Communication entails a combination of the first and second pillar instruments. A European defence equipment policy would be linked to Community policies (industry, trade, customs, the regions, competition, innovation and research) and CFSP measures – it would be a pillar one and a half. The Communication is under consideration within the Council. It has not yet reached a common position, but a proposal to a common position is discussed within the working group POLARM (Ad Hoc Working Party on a European Armaments Policy, September 1999).

To sum up, there have been many initiatives from the European Commission during the 1990s. The question of the economic side of a European defence identity was already discussed in Maastricht I but was dropped during the early phase (Törnquist 1996). Even earlier, the problems with the procurement of defence equipment were discussed during the 1970s as well (ibid.). These issues are still very controversial but they are no longer a hidden dimension in the European integration process. Furthermore, the role of the European Union, especially the role of the European Commission, within the field of defence equipment is not self-evident. Basically there are three options for a European defence equipment policy (de Vestel 1998).

The first vision is to maintain the status quo: that is, to follow the course of informal market integration, restricting political intervention to just a few initiatives. This means a weak European framework. At the present time, it appears that this option is only considered as a last resort. The second option, presented by the European Commission and the European Parliament, is a federal policy. The idea is to create a single market for defence equipment based on the model of a civil single market (Mörth 1998b). However, between the status quo and a federal Europe there is a third option – a regime for Europe (de Vestel 1998). This regime for Europe consists of many organizations and regulating concepts, such as the EU, the WEU and NATO. Although the future role of the WEU is unclear, it is very likely that its subsidiary organs will play a major role within a European regulatory framework.

Thus, the foreign and security implications of defence equipment require a role for NATO and the WEU and the internal market aspects give the EU an obvious regulating function. It is also obvious that the research programmes within NATO, its work on standardization (interoperability) and the ambitions to create a defence market will be part of this European cooperation. Indeed, the organizational framework for the integration of defence equipment in Europe is complex. The process of national deregulation and European regulation entails many different actors and regulatory concepts. Although it is obvious that the EU, the WEU and NATO complement each other, it is also clear that they are rivals. There are competing conceptualizations of how this market will be regulated and organized. It should also be noted that there are often unclear authority relations between these organizations, especially concerning the new multinational and multifunctional forces. Competencies are also overlapping.

Table 8.1 shows how two integration processes intersect in the field of defence equipment. Indeed, they are based on different logics in the international system – anarchy and interdependence. This is an instance where 'points' three and four of Miles' Membership Diamond (the New Challenges of Economic Interdependence and Swedish Security Policy with a European Identity) can be said to influence Sweden's stance towards the EU.

The Swedish discourse: from self-sufficiency to mutual interdependence

The end of the Cold War has put the European governments in a dilemma – one that placed them between an emphasis on national security interests

Table 8.1 Two integration processes within the defence equipment sector

Defence frame – Anarchy	Market frame – Interdependence
Dynamics: the end of the Cold War, military interoperability.	**Dynamics**: internationalization of high tech industry, internal market.
Prime Issues: Petersberg tasks, CJTF*, PFP – A European Security and Defence Identity (ESDI).	**Prime issues**: a European defence equipment market – An Aerospace and Defence Company (EADC).
Prime Actors: NATO, WEU, EU (second pillar).	**Prime Actors**: EU (first pillar), WEAG/WEAO**, Industry.

* Combined Joint Task Forces
** Western European Armaments Group/Western European Armaments Organization

on the one hand, and the internationalization of economy and technology on the other. A closer relationship between civilian and defence-related industry is needed for reasons of economic competitiveness. A strong European defence industry is also an important foundation for a European security and defence identity (ESDI). The tension between security and economic interests is not a new phenomenon. The case of the restructuring of civilian industry from the 1970s to the mid-1980s – from a national champion's strategy to a European technology community – showed that governments were fearful about losing control over strategic technology (Mörth 1996; Peterson 1992; Sandholtz 1992).

This national dilemma is evident for the Swedish government and the restructuring of the defence industry. There is a conflict between protecting national security interests on the one hand (the non-aligned strategy), and maintaining access to high technology on the other. Potential military resources are to be found in international and civilian commercial markets. This means that the government must seek high technology through the international market over which the government has very limited control. The defence industry is embedded economically and technologically at the international and global level, but the respective firms are, at the same time, dependent on national political decisions and regulations (Sally 1996).

The Swedish government's handling of this dilemma between national political requirements and an increasing process of internationalization and commercialization of the defence industry has resulted in a shift from a self-sufficiency perspective to one that emphasizes mutual interdependence. According to the self-sufficiency perspective increased international cooperation leads to more dependence. This means that national vulnerability is increasing. The political decision-makers, therefore, strive to achieve independence and autonomy within a policy area. The government's perspective on international cooperation is clearly based on the logic of anarchy. Thus, this means that it is difficult to combine the internationalization of the defence industry and national security interests, especially concerning security of supply of strategic goods and *matériel*. In the government's defence resolution (Defence Bill 1991/92: 102) it is stated that 'It is, furthermore, essential that cooperation within the defence equipment area must be structured in a way that takes Swedish security policy into consideration'[4] (p. 78). The issue of defence equipment is thus framed in a domestic and national context. International cooperation is important but must be congruent with national security interests.

In the mid-1990s the Swedish government presented a different view of the increasing cooperation within the defence equipment sector and national defence and security policy. The argumentation was no longer based on the logic of anarchy, but on that of interdependence. International cooperation within defence equipment was not presented as a threat but as an opportunity. The government even went further and argued that the international defence equipment cooperation is a prerequisite for the survival of the Swedish national defence and the national defence industry. A small country could no longer develop 'leading edge' technology. The Swedish government argued that increased participation in European cooperation could increase national autonomy within defence equipment. Furthermore, Swedish participation in different international fora creates 'prerequisites for the ability to affect the direction of an emerging Swedish defence policy' (Defence Bill 1995/96: 12, p. 136). The defence equipment policy is thus framed into a European and international context. Another way of putting it is that the government used to focus on Sweden's dependence on the external environment but has shifted its focus to how Sweden can participate and influence this external environment.

This means that the government will be active in the emerging European defence equipment collaboration. The basic notion is that no country, including Sweden, can be self-sufficient and rely on 'National Champions'. Furthermore, this offensive European strategy will reduce the asymmetrical dependence on American high technology (Mörth and Sundelius 1993). As the Swedish defence minister, Björn von Sydow, has stated, 'We have an interest in being independent and not to be dependent on US aeroplane manufacturers and the US Congress to decide which defence materials we may export' (*Göteborgsposten*, June 12 1998).

The Swedish government stresses that European cooperation will be based on mutual interdependence. It is stated that the end of the Cold War has opened up cooperation based on mutual interdependence. In the report from the defence planning group (Swedish: *försvarsberedningen*) for the defence decision in 1998 it is stated that increased Swedish integration in different international settings is the most promising solution:

> The rapid restructuration of the international defence industry sector during the last few years and the increasing competition within this sector strongly underlines the need for state authorities as well as industry in Sweden to increase their international cooperation within the defence industry. If this

does not happen, we risk a severe reduction of Swedish industrial capacity within this sector and we may end up being dependent on external suppliers in a way that is both wide-ranging and one-sided (Government Report Ds 1998: 9).

European collaboration is essential in order to maintain national technological capacity. In the Government Bill presented in the Spring of 1999 (Defence Bill 1998/99: 74), it is stated that 'Our future industrial capacity will have a structure where mutual industrial dependencies across national borders will be an important factor' (ibid.: 116). This means that the Swedish defence industry must be part of the ongoing process of internationalization and Europeanization. 'To enable Swedish defence industry to work successfully for its interests in a European restructuring, industry itself has to offer technological competence and concrete plans for renewal in important areas of defence *matériel*, while the government has to create positive conditions as well as incentives for industry' (Defence Bill 1998/99: 74, p. 117). This reasoning brings to mind 'point' three of Miles' 'Membership Diamond' (new challenges of economic interdependence). The Swedish government attempts to profit economically from being able to participate in political processes within the EU.

A crucial issue is, of course, what is meant by mutual interdependence. In a letter of intent (LoI), signed by six defence ministers[5] in June 1998, it is stated that the governments accepted mutual interdependence and they further stated that 'this will include obtaining commitments, some of which may be legally binding, from each of the participants involved either in the constitution of a Transnational Defence Company, or in the jointly determined abandonment of activities by a company located within the territory of one or more of the other Participants' (LoI: 3). Thus, the Swedish government recognizes officially that national self-sufficiency is no longer realistic. The future for the problem of security of supply in a crisis (or war) must therefore rest on mutual interdependence. It is also obvious that cooperation based on mutual dependency means that there will be centres of excellence with a single source structure. The delicate political problem is, of course, for the government to identify those strategic competencies that must be kept in Sweden and to negotiate terms of contracts for, amongst other things, European alliances and mergers. Furthermore, an important constraining factor on Sweden's participation in European collaboration is the strategy of non-alignment. Thus, a tricky task is to establish credible political commitments without being part of a more formal arrangement (see pp. 136–7 on LoI).

Low profile on a high level

The Swedish government takes active part in the ongoing restructuring of the defence industry and the process towards increased European cooperation within defence equipment.[6] As an EU member, Sweden takes part in the work on the formation of a European regulatory framework for defence equipment that is occurring within the EU. However, Swedish official reactions to the communications from the European Commission are rare. According to the documents from POLARM, there are many national disagreements. One such disagreement concerns the role of the European Commission and thus the supranational character of a common policy on defence equipment (POLARM 11/98). The Swedish government has not yet presented any written positions within POLARM (May 1999). The government's position concerning the character of European cooperation within the field of defence equipment is rather imprecise other than the government's stated preference that such cooperation should be built on an intergovernmental basis (Defence Bill 1998/99: 74).

Since 1997 Sweden cooperates fully within WEAG. It is sometimes stated that Sweden has observer status within WEAG, but the fact is that WEAG is not treaty-based. It is instead based on mutual understanding between the participants. The formal linkage between WEAG and the WEU is weak but informally this linkage is very strong. In Erfurt in 1997, an agreement – the so-called European partnership for defence equipment – made it possible for non-aligned countries like Sweden, Finland and Austria to take part in the work of WEAG. The Swedish NAD (Conference of National Representatives) in WEAG also participates within CNAD (Conference of National Representatives) in NATO. Furthermore, as part of PfP (Partnership for Peace) Sweden takes active part in the ongoing process of interoperability within NATO's new crisis management tasks.

There is also activity outside the three organizations of the EU, the WEU and NATO. The overall purpose of the LoI initiative is to create a European Defence and Aerospace Company (EADC). The Swedish Defence Minister, Björn von Sydow, stated after the agreement that Sweden 'must make sure that we can import defence *matériel*' (*Svenska Dagbladet*, 7 July 1998). Increased European cooperation creates an opportunity for Sweden to maintain the high level of its technology.

The letter of intent can be interpreted as a way for the governments to take away the initiative from the Commission and as a means of getting around the problems within POLARM (where all countries are represented). The governments seem to have taken a lead in the process, but it was, in fact, industry and the European Commission that put defence equipment on the political agenda and forced the governments to react. The work of the six governments in LoI is carried out in six working groups (security of supply, export procedures, security of information, technical information, RTD, harmonization of military requirements). They are expected to present reports in the Summer of 1999. Sweden heads the important group on research and technological development. Although Sweden joined this process at a rather late stage, the Swedish government managed to get its representative to chair this working group. Sweden is not a small state in this field. Indeed, Sweden has the fifth largest defence industrial sector in Europe after the UK, France, Germany and Italy. The

Swedish government clearly regards this work as highly important. This is shown by the fact that the Swedish chairman is the Head of an independent Swedish Agency.

Indeed, Swedish participation within the LoI framework is important considering the fact that the other participants within the groups also participate within NATO and WEAG. In the RTD group, for instance, the participants are also part of WEAG's panel II, WEAO and within those parts within NATO that deal with RTD. Sweden's participation in European and defence-related RTD activities is mainly regulated by the so-called SOCRATE (A System of Cooperation for Research and Technology in Europe) by which Sweden can participate in the EUCLID and THALES projects. Thus, Sweden's participation within RTD does not cover all RTD activities within WEAG and WEAO. The SOCRATE agreement was reached in the Autumn of 1998. It created some domestic turbulence due to the fact that the agreement was reached with an international organization (the WEU), and that involves certain aspects of international law. These aspects were only considered at a late stage in this rather quick political process. The agreement involved, among other things, changes in the law on immunity and privileges in certain cases. The agreement entails that the 'Research Cell' within WEAO can enter into research contracts, which are to be accepted by the so-called NAD representatives.

The SOCRATE agreement is, of course, a rather small part of Swedish expenditure on research and development. In fact, the bulk of Swedish research and development is national. Furthermore, Sweden is not participating in any project within SOCRATE so far (May 1999). However, in the long run the potential is, of course, huge and the SOCRATE agreement shows the Swedish government's determination to be more European-oriented in its defence-related RTD activities.

As discussed on pp. 130–2, a formal linkage between civilian and defence-related RTD is politically controversial within the EU. In practice, however, the borders between defence and civilian RTD are diffuse, both at the European level and nationally. New types of networks are created 'to link military and civil R&D organizations, embracing government, industrial and, possibly, academic institutions' (Hagelin 1997: 237). The Swedish government's position is that these two RTD spheres should be more closely linked. In fact, in one of the Swedish position papers on the fifth framework programme on research and development it was stated:

> Global disarmament means that the competence developed within the defence industry can increasingly be applied in other areas. Development is also enhanced by convergent requirements on defence and civil systems. The FP should stimulate 'Dual use' – technologies.[7]

However, this Swedish policy did not seem to be known by several of my interviewees (Mörth 1998b). One of them suggested that this could be explained by the fact that the Swedish position is the result of a patchwork among several ministries in which the Ministry of Education puts the pieces of the puzzle together. It is possible that this explanation is also relevant for other countries and their position papers. My empirical findings suggest that people (both in Brussels and in the capitals of member states), who have very little knowledge of the security and defence implications of the increased importance of dual-use technology handle the civilian RTD issues. In the Swedish case, they are simply handled by different people and ministries (Mörth 1998b).

The Swedish competence on these issues in Brussels used to be divided between the representation office (which deals with civilian RTD issues) and the embassy (which is responsible for the contacts with the WEU and NATO). Thus the complexity of the defence equipment issue, the fact that it concerns 'civilian' as well as defence-related issues, has caused some domestic coordination problems. In 1997 the Swedish government decided to establish a new position at the Swedish embassy in Brussels. The new position was described as a counsellor for total defence (*'totalförsvarsrådgivare'*), responsible for 'international issues that touch upon both military and civilian defence' (Government Paper 1997/98: 29, p. 12). An important reason behind the establishment of this new position was thus to reduce the coordination problem between the civilian and the defence-related spheres.

The fact that the issue of defence equipment concerns economic and defence-related aspects entails that different parts of the Swedish government and agencies are active in different parts of the EU and other European bodies. They are embedded in various transnational networks. The defence-related ministry and agencies are active in the EU's second pillar and the WEU, and those parts of NATO that are open for Swedish participation. Issues that are related to the EU's internal market and other community issues activate a different range of Swedish ministries and state agencies. The result is national fragmentation. At the same time, the Swedish government is expected to present national positions on issues that require consideration from many perspectives.

What is needed from the government's viewpoint is therefore an increased effort to coordinate the transnational activities by the ministries, agencies and industry. This is not an easy task. A question that was noted by the special group that prepared Swedish accession to the WEAG was how to coordinate the defence equipment issue. Who 'owns' the question and who are the other parties involved? This is not always clear-cut because the distinctions between the respective authorities of the agencies are, for obvious reasons, seldom distinct. Thus, there are political and bureaucratic rivalries on how to frame the issue of defence equipment. The complexity of the issue of defence equipment also suggests that administrators and other decision-makers are uncertain as to how they should handle these issues. One illustration of this complexity is the fact that parallel to the LoI initiative in June the six industry ministers also reached a common position in July 1998. The questions that are related to the creation of a European

Aerospace and Defence Company are, to a very large extent, community issues and are linked to the internal market.

One important issue is the difficulty to create European companies or *societas europea*. This does not only affect the defence industry, but also other industrial sectors. The Commission presented a proposal for a European Company Statute in the beginning of the 1970s. National differences concerning social, legal conditions and tax differences have, however, prevented the adoption of a supranational legal form. The creation of a European Company Statute would require deregulation of national company rules. It would also put pressure on tax harmonization.

Another factor behind the difficulty for the Swedish government to present so-called national positions within the sector of defence equipment is the dominance of experts and administrators. For instance, WEAG is a transbureaucratic cooperation that interests national procurement agencies in particular. Indeed, the highly technical and complex empirical fields involve experts rather than politicians. The Commission's communications on the formation of a European regulatory framework for defence equipment are in line with the general notion of how European governance moves towards a more regulative state which creates an increased need for experts and expertise knowledge.

A market-led process?

The overall impression is that the process towards a European regulatory framework is market-led. Swedish defence firms are active in this European process, especially Saab, which is one of the participants in a would-be European Aerospace and Defence Company. Swedish defence firms, as well as those from other countries, are seeking agreement-based cooperation, joint ventures, mergers and acquisitions. Cooperation has mostly been agreement-based, but this process of Europeanization has somewhat changed from the mid-to-late 1990s. British Aerospace has 35 per cent of the shares in Saab and the British company Alvis owns Hägglunds.

Business leaders make few official statements concerning the political part of the cooperation, such as on the role of the EU, WEAG and NATO. The Association of Swedish Defence Industries has, however, been very active in pursuing a more European-oriented defence industry policy. It has since 1997 participated in EDIG (European Defence Industry Group), which takes active part of the work within WEAG. From an industrial perspective, political commitments are seen as important for industry in a situation which is dominated by the uncertainty of a regulatory framework, nationally as well as at the European level. By recognizing a more European dimension in the defence equipment policy, the Swedish government seems to be prepared to change some of the national rules and its role as a 'gatekeeper' within this policy area.

Proceeding towards a European regulatory framework will, of course, entail domestic changes, especially concerning the domestic rules that regulate the defence industrial sector. The so-called Swedish 'acquisition model' will change. Today the Swedish defence industry must get political permission for its various activities, for instance, in manufacturing equipment, forming alliances with other firms or exporting defence equipment. The European Commission will also examine mergers or other deals if the affair has any implications for the civilian sector. The national rules not only function as a control mechanism for the government towards domestic industry: they also function as an important instrument to control foreign industry's influence over Swedish firms.

One important rationale behind this political will to deregulate the national defence industrial framework is, of course, the fact that potential military resources – especially high technology ones – are to be found in international and civilian commercial markets. This means that states, in order to maintain access to high technology, must seek it through the international market. The Swedish government seems to be well aware of the need for creating a more European regulatory framework, but also of the fact that the national deregulation entails risks. Market-led integration does not necessarily converge with national political considerations. Two different logics influence companies and states, respectively. 'Mutual industrial dependence is primarily created based on industrial considerations, but for states mutual interdependence is grounded in the security policies of the states concerned' (Defence Bill 1998/99: 74, p. 119).

A prerogative for the government is, for instance, to see that the international activities of defence firms do not lead to one-sided dependencies. The government has an interest in the ownership structure of strategic assets, such as production and research and technological development. This could be a rather difficult task since the government at the same time pushes the idea that the defence industry should survive on commercial grounds. In the Government Bill of Spring 1999, it stated that 'The responsibility for the restructuring of defence industry primarily rests on the companies themselves' (ibid.: p. 116). It is also clear that defence firms are an important base for national security and defence policy. The government's new policy of 'reconstitution' – to make it possible to acquire defence *matériel* in a changing political situation, requires strategic competence on the part of internationalized Swedish companies.

An important track concerning the work on the possible creation of a European Aerospace and Defence Company is carried out by European industry. The Swedish company Saab is one of the participants. In March 1998 the company partners presented a proposal, which was classified. In October 1998 the six partners submitted a report to the European governments. According to newspaper articles this report indicates that substantial disagreements still cloud the restructuring of the European aerospace industry. Differences exist on the scope of the business with regard to regional aircraft and ballistic missiles. It is quite clear that the implementation of the planned EADC will follow step-by-step and not happen as a single-step merger. However, there is still no route map for the implementation of EADC (March 1999). A politically sensitive issue concerns the government's rights in the new company. The partners seem to agree that governmental interests should be secured by guaranteeing universal limits on voting rights rather than prior approval by the governments of particular share acquisitions.

A related question concerns intellectual property rights. These rights should be owned by the companies, and not by the governments. The report also discussed coordinating tax and procurement issues. It is stated in the report that the companies are ready to enter into dialogue with governments on all these points. As long as there is no European Company statute, it is, of course, difficult to create a European company. Until such a statute is decided it is likely that a European company will be a multinational holding company with national subsidiaries. Furthermore, there also seems to be a discrepancy between the politicians' vision of a strong Europe *vis-à-vis* the US and the international conditions in which European defence companies work. The creation of a large European company is perhaps not the best option from the perspective of economic competitiveness. Thus, transatlantic consolidation is as attractive as European industrial consolidation.

Swedish decision-makers often state that there is no contradiction between the notion of building a stronger European defence industrial base and the fact that the US is a major player within this policy field. In the Defence Bill of Spring 1999, it is stated that 'European cooperation within defence industry should be fashioned in such a way as not to affect negatively transatlantic relations within this area' (Defence Bill 1998/99: 74, p. 125). Indeed, within certain technology fields there are no alternatives to the US as a partner (ibid.). This means that there is a tension between the European collaboration on the one hand, and dependence on US technology on the other. Sweden is dependent on US technology, but it is, at the same time, anxious to participate in the creation of a strong European defence industrial base *vis-à-vis* the US.

Being a good European: an informal and decoupled strategy

How has the Swedish government handled the fact that the sector of defence equipment concerns multiple issues and actors? First of all, the government has established several different coordinating groups that cross ministerial boundaries. On top of this, there is also a special EU coordinator within each ministry. Indeed, EU issues are often horizontal in character and seldom follow the vertical structure of the government. Work within the framework of the LoI entailed that national representatives took part in the six working groups. A national steering group was established which, amongst others, consisted of the Swedish participants in these six working groups. Swedish industry also took part in this national coordination work. The overall impression of these special national coordination groups is that they do not seem to be very productive.[8]

Thus, the government tries to coordinate the transnational activities nationally by establishing various coordinating groups. Furthermore, since the issue of defence equipment is not only turbulent but also politically sensitive, the government must handle this issue delicately. It has tried to 'informalize' participation in international cooperation, and it has also partly 'decoupled' industrial aspects from the defence aspects of the defence equipment issue due to the strategy of non-alignment.

'Informalizing'

The Amsterdam Treaty and the strengthening of EU's defence capacity in Cologne in Spring 1999 caused some domestic political debate. The government has no interest in starting a domestic debate on the Swedish relationship with the WEU and NATO. One way of dealing with this politically sensitive issue is to handle the sector of defence equipment informally by avoiding any formal commitments that can in any way be interpreted as jeopardizing the strategy of non-alignment. It is obvious that the government has prioritized the intergovernmental and informal work of the LoI initiative. Furthermore, Swedish participation within the loose and legally weak cooperation of WEAG and the government's interest of taking part in JACO[9] suggests that informal, loose and ad hoc based cooperation is preferred to more formal arrangements. However, the SOCRATE agreement is a formal international agreement and was approved by the Swedish parliament, even if the political and security potential of these European defence-related RTD projects was not really discussed in the Riksdag or in the Swedish media. The agreement was presented as an international RTD agreement and was thus 'depoliticized'. Also, because the policy sector is heavily dominated by military and other experts, administrators and industrial representatives, an impression is created of a lack of clarity when it comes to political accountability. These officials are part of a dense transnational network. There is therefore risk of a gap between power and responsibility.

This is not a purely Swedish phenomenon. The general empirical observation on the governance processes in the EU is the existence of various transnational networks. So, one important way to participate in the European integration process is to take active part in various transnational and informal networks. Furthermore, these networks can help Swedish decision-makers to navigate in a complex policy sector and, at the same time, avoid making any formal commitments concerning Swedish security policy. Studies of the European Union and other types of transnational cooperation emphasize the importance of informal networks as a way of building trusting and intimate relationships (Haas 1992; Verdun 1999). Supportive networks are organized according to sectorial aspects (Héritier 1999).

The rather ambiguous and unclear policy of the Swedish government can be explained by the existence of these transnational and informal cooperation arrangements. To be unclear and ambiguous is thus a way to take part in the complex process without excluding any path that cooperation may take. The various initiatives and ongoing events within this policy field require political flexibility and room for manoeuvre. Indeed, the complexity of the issue of defence equipment, the competition between the EU, the WEU, NATO and the future of a European security and defence identity require an ambiguous strategy. The trick is to maintain some ambiguity while, at the same time, being able to move forward in the policy-making process (Sahlin-Andersson 1998).

This means that Swedish actors and interests are formed in the process – in the meeting within various networks and institutional arrangements. A new form of cooperation is created – a change from a national regulatory framework to a European regulatory framework. Hence, it is difficult to 'measure' Europeanization with the yardstick of 'fit' or 'misfit'. Such an analysis requires an identification of what already exists, primarily within the EU. My empirical analysis shows, however, that the legal framework and the political process at the European level represents a 'work in motion'.

'Decoupling'

As discussed above, the issue of defence equipment concerns both market and defence-related aspects. Indeed, Table 8.2 shows that the subject of defence equipment raises different issues depending on how you frame the issue – for example, from an industrial or a defence-orientated perspective.

The complexity of this issue is often perceived as a national coordination problem. However, separating the market aspects from the defence-related aspects can also be regarded as creating an opportunity in the political handling of this delicate issue. It gives the government more room for manoeuvre.

The basic notion is that the political decision-makers perceive a tension between the need to uphold the strategy of non-alignment on the one hand, and the necessity to attend to practical activity on the other. The issues are complex and are part of a process that cannot really be politically controlled. The dilemma for the government is that it must maintain political support for its non-alignment strategy, and at the same time be a flexible European partner within a turbulent political process. In the organizational literature, it is argued that a common way of dealing with inconsistent

Table 8.2   Parallel issues within the field of defence equipment[10]

Issue	What's at stake?
Defence industry	National competence in high technology.
	Competitive aspects.
	EU's internal market.
	National deregulations.
	Regulations at the European/international level.
Defence policy	National sovereignty.
	The non-aligned strategy.
	National security interests.
	Crisis management tasks.
	A common European defence identity/policy.

demands is to differentiate between the informal and the formal organization. This lack of congruence between the formal and vertical structure of an organization and its work activities is called 'decoupling' (Brunsson 1989). It can be argued that the Swedish government's emphasis on informal channels in the European cooperation partly supports this theory of how decision-makers handle inconsistent and complex demands. Another example of 'decoupling' is to separate between issues. Hence, by framing the defence equipment issue as an industrial issue, the emphasis is on the importance of national capacity in high technology and avoids questions of sovereignty and on the direction of Sweden's security policy.

This author's empirical analysis suggests that the government sometimes links the European defence equipment cooperation to Sweden's security and defence policy; for instance, the importance of taking part in European defence equipment collaboration in order to participate in European crisis management tasks. However, the linkage is rather imprecise and does not say anything about how increased participation in European defence equipment collaboration and crisis management tasks will affect Swedish security policy. The main argument for taking part in this European cooperation is that it strengthens the national capacity within the field of defence technology. What is needed is to strengthen the national and European defence and industrial base. Thus, the issue of defence equipment is often framed as an industry issue and not primarily as a defence issue. The foundation of the political argument of this point is industrial strength rather than defence policy.

Paradoxically, the Swedish Ministry of Defence seems to take the lead in the ongoing process of incorporating defence industry policy into the more civilian and commercial-based industry policy (Sandström 1997).

To sum up, this chapter has analysed Swedish participation in a historically formative moment in the process of European integration. It illustrates a process in which there are multiple actors, issues and political levels. Indeed, this is a case of multi-level governance. The intersection of the two logics in the international system – anarchy and interdependence – activates companies and governments; industrial issues and defence issues; the company level, the governmental level and the European level. The complexity among, and interactions between, these actors, issues and levels makes this a fascinating field of study. This author's research on these issues concerns the consequences for Sweden as part of this formative process.

Notes

1. The author would like to thank the Swedish Council for Research in the Humanities and Social Sciences (HSFR) for financing the research incorporated in this chapter.
2. Dual-use refers to technology that can be used for both civilian and military purposes.
3. In the Amsterdam Treaty, the new number of the article is Article 296.
4. All translations from Swedish are by the author.
5. Defence ministers from Germany, France, United Kingdom, Italy, Spain and Sweden.
6. There is also a Nordic dimension to European cooperation in the defence industry. A Memorandum of Understanding was signed in 1994 between the Nordic countries with the aim of finding common objects for procurement.
7. See http://www.cordis.lu/fifth/src/ms-se l.html.
8. Please note that the author has yet to be able to analyse the work of the working groups within the framework of LoI due to the fact that their work has been secret.
9. In January 1997 the Joint Armaments Co-operation Organization (JACO or OCCAR – the French abbreviation) was created to act as a joint programme office on behalf of France, Germany, the United Kingdom and Italy.
10. Figure 8.2 draws on a model by Jacobsson (1987).

CHAPTER 9

Swedish Monetary Policy: On the Road to EMU?

Mats Kinnwall

Introduction

In September 1992 the Swedish krona was subject to massive attack by speculators. The Swedish Central Bank, the Riksbank, defended the peg by hiking the instrumental interest rate upwards to 500 per cent. However, the Riksbank only managed to ward off the speculative attacks temporarily. Pressure on the krona remained and the Riksbank was forced to admit defeat finally in November 1992 and allowed the krona to float freely.

The events of Autumn 1992 not only constituted the end of an economic policy doctrine that had lasted for decades, in which a fixed exchange rate was the pillar of Swedish monetary policy, but these events also paved the way for discussion of future Swedish EMU membership. After all, the first steps towards closer Swedish relations with the EC had already been taken in 1990–91, when the Swedish parliament had approved the government's decision to apply for full EC (later EU) membership.

According to the Maastricht Treaty, EMU is one of the most vital components of further EU integration. Hence, once the decision to apply for EU membership had been taken, Sweden started to reflect upon the EMU question as well. Indeed, EMU-related matters are the most obvious illustration of the third 'point' of the 'Membership Diamond', describing how Sweden as an EU state (at least in a formal sense) also has to reform its political institutions. Sweden has no 'opt-out' and, hence, is obliged to join EMU formally when qualified. However, soon after the referendum in 1994, many politicians declared that the EMU issue should be decided by the Swedish parliament.

The EMU question also places pressure on Sweden to become further Europeanized (in line with aspects of 'point' one of the 'Membership Diamond'). In order to qualify as a full EU member, Sweden reformed its constitution, especially the legislative framework governing the Riksbank. In short, the Riksbank has become more independent relative to the Swedish political system.

The aim of this chapter is to evaluate those factors vital to Sweden's decision on whether or not to join the 'Euro'. One conclusion that may be drawn is that many of the commonly used arguments in favour of Swedish EMU membership have lost some of their persuasive power since Sweden seems to be able to stand on her own two feet from an economic perspective. Inflation is under control, the business cycle outlook is benign, interest rates have come down substantially and there are no severe threats to public finances. The economic arguments are not overwhelmingly in favour of imminent Swedish EMU entry. Since Swedish public opinion – which at present seems very EMU-negative (see Chapter 7) – is crucial in shaping governmental attitudes towards EMU, the EMU proponents will probably have to rely, for the most part, on political arguments in order to convince the Swedish public of the merits of joining the 'Euro'.

Approaching EMU: a lengthy process

While the speculative attacks on the krona were the 'trigger' prompting Sweden's consideration of potential EMU membership, the process actually started much earlier and dates back to the 1970s. These years were a disappointing decade for the Swedish economy (see Figure 9.1). Growth stagnated relative to competitors, whilst wage and price inflation (relative to Germany) never seemed to settle down after the oil crises. In an effort to restore competitiveness, Sweden devalued its currency on two occasions in 1977 after the collapse of the 'Snake connection'. However, these efforts turned out to be in vain since the underlying factors behind the country's deteriorating competitiveness were never dealt with properly. An expansive fiscal policy (both cyclical and structural), combined with an accommodating monetary policy and a change in the balance of power between the forces operating in the labour market in favour of the trade unions, spurred on inflation. Eventually, the second oil crisis in 1979 triggered a new round of 'cost crises' which led to devaluations in 1981 and 1982.

While the devaluations of 1977 and 1981 were completely 'defensive', and aimed at restoring lost competitiveness, the 1982 devaluation was not! Admittedly, the traditional signs of an 'overvalued' currency were there: an accumulated current account deficit as well as wage and price inflation that had been higher than in the 'anchor' economy (Germany) for several years. However, the 1982 devaluation was partly 'offensive' and an essential ingredient in the new Social Democratic government's strategy aimed at 'kick-starting' the economy. Yet, Swedish politicians learnt something from the failures of the 1970s. Other important new ingredients in the policy mix were fiscal prudence and restrictive, mostly informal, wage policies.

To start with, this new policy – 'the third way' – was quite successful, though monetary policy was too accommodating. Average GDP growth in 1983–87 was 2.7 per cent, substantially higher than in the 1970s, whilst the inflation path followed a sharply downward slope. However, labour costs that were relatively stable immediately after the devaluation started to climb. Hence, the real exchange rate was slowly, but continuously, creeping upwards.

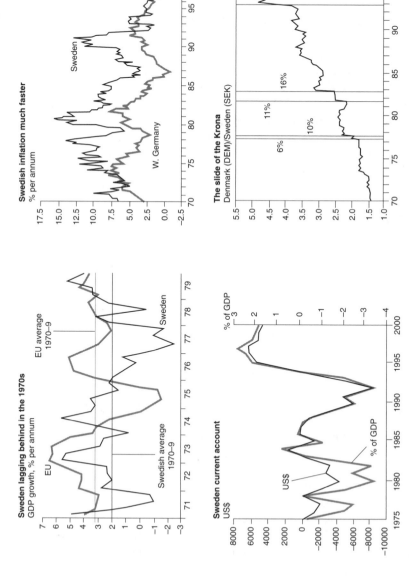

Figure 9.1 Sweden's economic performance 1970–98

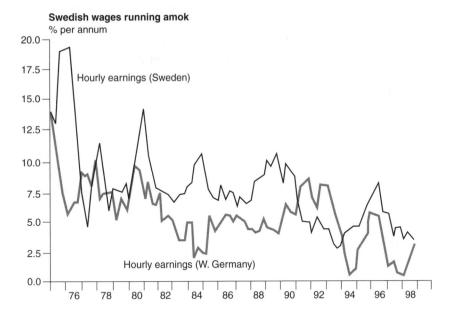

Figure 9.2 Swedish wage inflation 1975–98

In 1987 and 1988 it became more and more obvious that 'the third way' would not succeed since price and wage inflation had started to accelerate dramatically (see Figure 9.2) and, at the same time, the real economy lost momentum. From 1990 all of the main economic indicators began to move in the wrong direction and things went 'pear-shaped' at a horrific and rapid pace. Inflation reached double-digit numbers and in 1991 the economy experienced a recession that lasted for almost three years.

In an attempt to restore confidence in the krona and limit inflationary expectations, the government declared in its 1991 budget proposal that 'fighting inflation' was the overall objective for Swedish fiscal policy (see Ministry of Finance/Riksdagen 1991) and unilaterally 'pegged' the currency to the ECU in the Spring of 1991. However, the 'ECU peg' should also be interpreted in the light of changing attitudes towards the EU. In December 1990, the Riksdag had already decided that Sweden would apply for EU membership. This decision was followed up in the government's 1991 budget proposal (see Ministry of Finance/Riksdagen 1991) in which the Social Democratic government declared its ambition to apply for EU membership, once a comprehensive evaluation of aspects relating to Sweden's foreign and security policies has been completed.

Credibility is the key

The main reason why 'the third way' turned out to be a 'dead end' was the lack of credibility in the low inflation, fixed exchange rate regime. A fixed exchange rate in an environment characterized by high inflation expectations and a recently deregulated capital market triggered massive foreign borrowing. As the capital market completely lost confidence, a sudden outflow of foreign assets forced the Riksbank to raise the interest rate dramatically in order to defend the krona in the Autumn of 1992. The rebalancing of portfolios after the crash also contributed to the sharp and prolonged depreciation of the krona, the collapse in private sector balance sheets and the erosion of public finances during the first years of the float. In these respects, the Swedish situation in the late 1980s was a clear parallel to that prevailing in Asia in the late 1990s.

One factor explaining the lack of confidence in the krona was the failure on the part of the Swedish government to maintain fiscal discipline. The budget did not produce a surplus until 1987, despite the booming economy, implying that the structural budget deficit was huge. Capital and credit markets in Sweden had traditionally been regulated strictly, facilitating low real interest rates. Yet, in an economy with deregulated capital markets, the Swedish government's expansive fiscal policy would probably have implied higher interest rates and, hence, even worse public finances.

The spending spree in the household sector was further fuelled by the credit expansion in the wake of the massive deregulation of the Swedish credit market. Real estate prices accelerated to unsustainably high levels, supported by rising inflationary expectations. Another factor was the monetary policy regime in itself. The booming economy put greater (and appreciating) pressure on the Swedish krona and in order to defend the currency's 'peg', the Riksbank contributed to further credit and money expansion.

The Riksbank's dilemma in the 1980s clearly illustrates the 'pros' and 'cons' of joining a monetary union. On the one hand, a central bank can 'borrow and import credibility' and, hence, bring down interest rates. On the other hand, there is a risk that the country in question may join any arrangement with the 'wrong' real exchange rate or experience an appreciating drift in the equilibrium real exchange rate after entering the monetary union. That, in turn, tends to lead to excessive credit creation with potential bubble effects. This is a good description, for instance, of the current Irish situation.

Though the bubble of the 1980s and early 1990s was bound to collapse sooner or later, the final blow resulted from two shocks, one domestic and one external. In 1990 a major tax reform prompted a sudden increase in after-tax real interest rates. The reform, in combination with a world-wide increase in real interest rates, pulled the rug from under the Swedishreal estate market as borrowing became more expensive and the bubble burst. Collapsing house prices and a sudden and dramatic rise in unemployment depressed consumer spending, ensuring that a recession was inevitable.

Since the Swedish government budget was extremely sensitive to fluctuations in the business cycle, the recession triggered a dramatic deterioration in the government's fiscal position. The tax reform in itself contributed to this deteriorating situation for the government since the reform relied upon a shift from direct taxes to value added tax (VAT). Hence, as consumption decreased and the construction industry collapsed, VAT revenues fell sharply. Government financial balances went from a surplus of 4.0 per cent in 1990 to a 7.5 per cent deficit in 1992. The worsening of the government's fiscal position, combined with the prospect of essential fiscal tightening ahead on the part of government, reinforced the downward spiral in the household sector. Furthermore, it eroded the already faltering confidence in the fixed exchange rate – the only remaining pillar of Sweden's economic policy framework. The Swedish economy continued its free fall after the fixed exchange rate regime collapsed in December 1992, and so did the international markets' confidence in the krona. The Swedish currency depreciated by 25 per cent during the first four months after the currency was allowed to float.

Fiscal policy convergence and yet credibility problems

EMU entry: the only option?

Despite the dramatic initial weakening of the krona, many analysts considered that it would only be a matter of time before the fixed exchange rate regime would be re-established. After all, Sweden had maintained a fixed exchange rate for decades! What possible anchor for monetary policy could there be except for a fixed exchange rate? However, immediately after the collapse, the Riksbank adopted an inflation target of two per cent with a tolerance interval of ± one percentage point. While the target was to be officially implemented by 1 January 1995, the declared inflation target in reality became the Riksbank's new nominal target by 1993.

In the beginning, Sweden paid a very high price for its past sins, in terms of wide interest rate margins and a volatile exchange rate. The idea that Sweden would ever be able to restore market confidence in its economic policy on its own seemed totally unrealistic. Hence, there were widespread doubts about whether the inflation target would survive. According to this line of reasoning, the Riksbank would never be able to defend its inflation target in the long run because of weaknesses in the budget process and the Riksbank's lack of political independence. Fiscal excesses and a malfunctioning labour market would, sooner or later, spark off inflation. Political pressure would prevent the Riksbank from 'pricking the inflation bubble' through the tightening of monetary policy and investors on the financial markets would realize this and put a large risk premium on Swedish bonds and the krona. Hence, the costs of pursuing an independent monetary policy would, sooner or later, prove to be intolerably high.

At the same time, it became increasingly obvious that unilateral exchange rate pegs were vulnerable and the costs of defending them (when subject to attack) were very high. The Swedish experience and the collapse of the ERM system in 1992–93 were just two examples that these systems do not guarantee economic stability and are not robust to speculative attacks. The breakdown of currency regimes amongst the 'Asian tiger' economies in 1997 confirmed the weakness of unilateral pegs. The bad experience of a unilaterally fixed exchange rate was one reason why Sweden refused to join the 'broad band ERM' after Sweden became an EU member in 1995. It is probably also one reason why Sweden prefers to stay outside the ERM2 mechanism prescribed for EMU 'outsiders' under the present system.

In accordance with the reasoning behind the third 'point' of the 'Membership Diamond', EMU membership appeared to be one alternative left for Sweden, given that the 'fixed-but-adjustable-peg' system was largely discredited and there was an initial lack of credibility or belief in the longer-term viability of Sweden's existing inflation target.

The 'bumpy road' to credibility

After the initial turbulence settled, the new nominal target for monetary policy was relatively well received by the financial markets. The spread of the bond yield to Germany narrowed from 300 basis points after the float to just over 100 basis points in the Summer of 1993. The krona recovered somewhat from the initial collapse. However, as the gravity of the fiscal deterioration became clear and the financial markets started to bet on the Swedish state defaulting, international confidence in Swedish economic policy vanished. The public deficit continued to rise and the bond yield spread widened to 500 basis points. On 24 April 1995, the value of the krona reached a record low of 5.4 against the D-Mark, 36 per cent below its value in November 1992.

At that time, if not earlier, the government recognized that it needed to take extraordinary measures to restore market confidence. It declared its ambition to fulfil the Maastricht criteria for fiscal prudence and accelerated the reconstruction of public finances. Adopting the Maastricht criteria for fiscal stabilization was, however, not entirely a result of acute crisis politics. It also reflected an attempt by the government to prepare Sweden for future EMU entry, if and when that day should come. The start of a process of reforming the laws governing the Riksbank can also be seen as a step towards Sweden preparing for a future EMU membership, in line with 'point' three of the 'Membership Diamond'. Whatever the objective, the fiscal restoration programme paid off in terms of a slow narrowing of bond yield spreads and a strengthening of the krona.

Despite the recession, the Riksbank started to tighten monetary policy in mid-1994. One of the factors triggering this sequence of interest rate 'hikes' was probably developments on the bond and currency markets, which were widely interpreted as signs of rising inflation expectations. Additional factors included the relatively generous wage agreements and rising household inflation expectations in the medium-term perspective. All these signals could be perceived as amounting to a lack of confidence in Sweden's inflation target.

Even though an inflationary spurt never materialized, the Riksbank continued to act cautiously and waited for market confidence to return, before initiating a sequence of significant repo rate cuts. Once started, the Riksbank cut the repo rate by almost five percentage points within less than a year (from 8.91 per cent to 4.1 per cent). It turned out that even this drastic move was well in line with the inflation target. Inflation followed the repo rate down and has been well below the target for most of the 1995–99 period. Hence, credibility in the inflation target appears to have been gradually established despite the fact that the government has maintained its 'wait-and-see' strategy on joining the 'Euro'.

The krona's stabilization and the narrowing of yield spreads beginning in mid-1995 proved that it was possible, albeit to a limited degree, for a small country to earn credibility and support for its monetary policy. The self-imposed 'strait-jacket' in the form of a commitment to fulfil the Maastricht criteria for fiscal policy actually worked. The simultaneous rise in inflation after the depreciation proved to be much smaller than expected, ensuring that the inflation target gained credibility as well. Hence, the argument that staying outside EMU would impose intolerably high interest rates and a volatile krona has gradually been less persuasive in public debates.

Does this relatively benign development indicate that there is, after all, an alternative way for Sweden other than to join the EU's monetary union and 'borrow credibility' from the European Central Bank (ECB)?

The Calmfors Commission's report

By Swedish standards, the process leading up to EU membership in 1995 was extremely short. The country became a full EU member only about four to five years after the debate was initiated. The relative speed by which EU accession was achieved created a widespread feeling in Sweden that EU membership was forced upon the Swedish people by the 'elite', especially the politicians. Indeed, the high degree of EU scepticism amongst the public after the 1994 referendum and the very low turnouts in the direct elections to the European Parliament in 1995 and 1999 (see Chapter 5) are indicative that this may still be the case.

The EMU project, with its focus on price stability and the perceived neglect of unemployment, was considered the most obvious symbol of the existing 'neo-liberal' ideology driving EU integration. Opponents of Swedish full membership of EMU do not accept that Sweden should adopt this ideology and reform its political institutions in line with the obligations arising from EU, and especially EMU, membership (see 'points' one and three of the 'Membership Diamond'). One complicating factor for this line of reasoning was, and still is, the fact that the Riksbank also pursues a monetary policy focusing on price stability whilst the Swedish government stresses fiscal prudence. Hence, it is difficult to argue that monetary or fiscal policy outside EMU would be directed any more (than at present) towards 'growth and employment' priorities.

Since Swedish public opinion towards EMU continues to be split and volatile, the governing Social Democrats decided not to risk upsetting the SAP's sympathizers and voters by pushing hard for Swedish EMU membership. Instead, the government insisted on the need to investigate whether there were aspects of EMU that might collide with 'Swedish values' such as low unemployment and Swedish traditions of 'transparency'. Once again, aspects of 'point' one of the 'Membership Diamond' seem to be at work here. In order to prepare the ground for a firm and secure decision (in favour) of Swedish EMU entry, the government appointed a group of experts, the so-called Calmfors Commission, to investigate thoroughly the consequences for Sweden of entering and/or staying out of the 'Euro'.

The conclusion of the Calmfors Commission in its final report (Calmfors *et al.* 1997) was that, on balance, the political arguments are largely in favour of EMU membership, whilst the economic arguments, at least for the time being, speak out against. The most important political argument supporting Swedish EMU membership was, according to the Calmfors Commission, that entry would increase Sweden's influence within the European Union. In particular, the Commission considered a number of important questions. First, it addressed the so-called 'integration argument'. According to the Commission, economic integration within the EU has never been considered as an objective in itself but rather as a prerequisite for political integration. Therefore, the EMU project could be interpreted as an important step in facilitating such political integration, even though the Commission did not rule out the fact that substantial integration might occur even without EMU. Second, the Calmfors report considered issues relating to the creation of the European Central Bank (ECB) and concluded that existing EU arrangements allowed for political control and accountability over the ECB; however, this was not yet at a sufficient level to satisfy the concerns of the Commission.

Third, the Calmfors report also mentioned aspects relating to legitimacy and, more specifically, the need to gain public approval as the basis of any decision on Swedish participation in the 'Euro'. It appears that the experiences of the 1994 EU membership campaign made a lasting impression on the Calmfors Commission as well: verifying elements of the first 'point' of the 'Membership Diamond'.

As for the economic arguments, the Commission concluded that the common currency will bring efficiency gains, but that these gains are probably limited and difficult to estimate accurately. The Commission regarded other structural factors, rather than a common currency, as more important in influencing levels of economic efficiency. Regarding the credibility arguments, the Commission concluded that EMU membership would probably imply greater credibility *given the (then) prevailing Riksbank legislation*. However, any reform strengthening the Riksbank's independence would, according to the Calmfors report, be an equally good alternative. It is worth noting that the relevant legislation has been changed since the report's publication, in a way that guarantees the Riksbank's independence to be at least as strong as that of the ECB.

The Commission also considered the implications of EMU membership to be ambiguous in relation to macro economic stability aspects. The main objection to Sweden entering the EMU (at the time the report was published) was the poor situation of the Swedish labour market. There was, according to the Calmfors report, no reason to expect that the unemployment rate would in the long run depend upon the country's currency regime. However, any volatility in Swedish productivity, output and employment levels would probably be higher if Sweden adopted a common currency rather than if Sweden retained the krona. Thus, any negative shocks after Swedish EMU entry might provoke a rise in unemployment from an already unacceptably high level. Hence, the Commission concluded that Sweden should not enter EMU unless the situation on the labour market improved. This argument is especially relevant since cyclical increases in unemployment tend to lead to a permanently higher rate of unemployment.

When all these arguments were weighed together, the Calmfors Commission finally ended up recommending that Sweden should not enter EMU in the first wave in 1999. This 'wait-and-see' attitude also became the policy of the Social Democratic government, whilst the Liberals and Moderates pushed for EMU membership as soon as possible. Indeed, this 'wait-and-see' strategy is consistent with Sweden's traditionally cautious policy on EU issues and development, associated with the 'Membership Diamond's' first 'point'. In other words, 'Do not join and try to influence but stay out and see how things turn out'.

Where do we stand today?

When the current (June 1999) situation in the Swedish labour market is compared with that prevailing when the Calmfors report was published, then what is immediately noticeable is how remarkable the decline in unemployment has been. The June 1999 figure for 'open' unemployment was just below five per cent compared to around nine per cent in late 1996. The total rate of unemployment (including people in labour market programmes) has fallen from around thirteen per cent in 1996 to below nine per cent. Hence, the main objections raised by the Commission against EMU entry have become less relevant. Yet, the situation is still fragile. It remains to be seen whether the improvements in the Swedish labour market will last without spurring on inflation and thus provoking substantial 'belt-tightening' to stave off these inflationary tendencies by the Riksbank.

According to the Calmfors Commission at least, the political costs of 'staying out' of EMU and the comparable gains in economic efficiency accruing from EMU entry should be greater, the more EU countries that go on to join the 'Euro'. Indeed, while the Commission assumed that only a limited (small) number of countries should and would join the third stage of EMU in 1999, it turned out that a vast majority of the EU countries actually went on to participate in the 'Euro' from the beginning. At least in theory, and on balance, this factor should weigh in favour of Swedish EMU membership. However, in practice, this aspect has not been as influential as first appears, especially since Denmark and the UK also remain outside the 'Euro'.

The costs of 'staying out' of EMU – low so far

A common pro-EMU argument that appears in the country's political debates has been that 'staying out' of EMU will damage the public's interests via higher interest rates. In the Winter of 1999, when the government issued statements that were widely interpreted as signals of a more pro-EMU position on the part of the Persson administration, Swedish yield spreads narrowed and the krona strengthened. Thus, EMU proponents interpreted these events on the financial markets as reflecting the *expectation* that Sweden would soon join EMU. Indeed, there might be something in this argument, especially when it comes to the krona, but it is definitely not the whole story. For instance, the ten-year yield spread versus Germany bottomed out at below 20 basis points in the Summer of 1998, long before impending Swedish EMU membership was discounted on financial markets. Looking further back, the ten-year yield spread in relation to Germany has been at or below 0.5 percentage point since early 1998. Another indication of Sweden's strength is that the Riksbank was able to cut the repo rate below the ECB's refi rate in March 1999.

In addition, the krona has continued to fluctuate, reflecting economic changes in Sweden and in the world economy. Nevertheless, this is what should be expected from a floating exchange rate. For instance, the krona weakened considerably in connection with the global financial crisis of Autumn 1998. This did not, however, reflect any lack of confidence in Swedish economic policy on the part of the international financial markets, but rather a general flight from small illiquid markets into liquidity. The weakening of the krona operated in a 'textbook' fashion – namely as a cushion against an international downturn, and thus, mitigating any potential negative impact on the Swedish economy.

The minimal real costs of a floating exchange rate

The most appropriate and relevant evaluation of the floating regime so far would be to compare the *actual* Swedish achievement with the *hypothetical* outcome should Sweden have retained the peg. Of course, this comparison is impossible to make. Hence, we have to rely on cross-section comparisons, which are unreliable in several respects. One important deficiency of this method is that countries are starting from different points and positions in the business cycle. The Swedish cyclical downturn in the 1990s, for instance, was much deeper than in many of the EMU countries. Hence, it could be expected that Sweden would have followed a different route for several years compared to countries like France, Germany and Spain, where the cyclical downturn was much less pronounced.

Average fixed capital formation in Sweden since the currency crisis has been close to the EMU average and above the average of the 'core' EMU states (France, Germany and Italy) (see Figure 9.3) . The average GDP growth rate has also been in line with the EMU average and even above the 'core' EMU average. Although difficult to estimate, there are no clear indications that any exchange rate volatility has hampered Swedish investment or growth. Hence, it seems relatively safe and reasonable to argue that volatility on financial markets is not a major argument for joining EMU at the moment.

Sweden has earned, not borrowed, credibility

It has taken considerable time and effort for Sweden to restore market confidence in its monetary and fiscal policy. Anyway, it is fair to say that Sweden has not *borrowed* but *earned* credibility during recent years, riding on the back of fiscal consolidation and low inflation. Today, most political forces regard the EU's 'Growth and Stability Pact' as a sound and integrated part of fiscal policy and this element of the Union's EMU concept has been accepted by all political parties except the Left Party and some 'left-wing' Social Democrats. From the perspective of the second research theme proposed by Lee Miles (in Chapter 1), there seems to be clear evidence that Sweden has been 'Europeanized'.

Moreover, recent developments and the general outlook for the next few years do not lend support to arguments that suggest that Sweden, if outside EMU, will lag behind in terms of economic growth. On the contrary, Sweden has faired well compared to the 'core' states of Europe and there are reasons to expect that this relatively good performance will continue. Public finances are in good shape; indeed, a lot better than those in the 'core' of EMU, which bodes well for optimism within Swedish households. The 'Euro's' weakness since the beginning of EMU in January 1999 has also encouraged some Euro-sceptics to suggest that Sweden can stand on her own two feet, outside EMU.

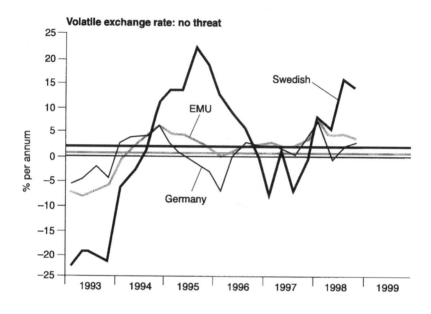

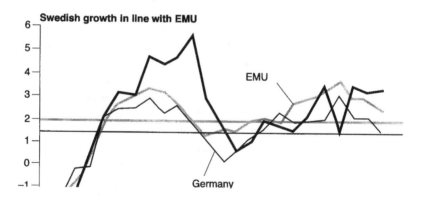

Figure 9.3   Swedish growth and exchange rate patterns

Thus far, Sweden's 'earned credibility' and relatively good economic performance in terms of growth and employment have not had any major impact on the political debate surrounding Swedish EMU entry. Swedes are too used to regarding their economy as lagging behind and perceiving the country's labour market as inflexible. However, if and when it becomes self-evident to the politicians that Sweden can manage on her own, then the nature of the political debate in Sweden on EMU will probably change as well.

Structural differences are important

The Swedish economy is gradually transforming itself from a traditional manufacturing and commodity-based economy. Nowadays, the economy appears to have a comparative advantage in the growing 'high-tech' sectors, such as information technology (IT) and pharmaceuticals (see Figure 9.4). This makes the Swedish economy less vulnerable in relative terms to competition from low-cost producers in Eastern Europe and South East Asia compared to many 'core' EMU economies. In this respect Sweden has more in common with countries like the UK and even the US than with the 'core' EMU states.

An important factor behind the development of these new 'growth-

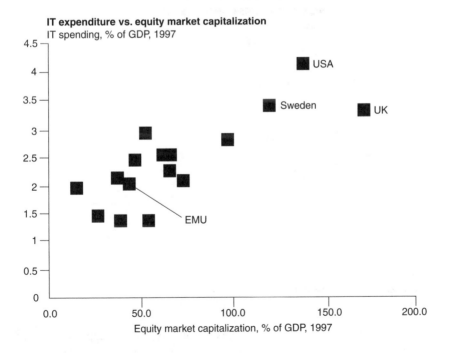

Figure 9.4 Equity market capitalization

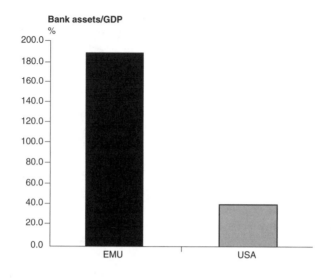

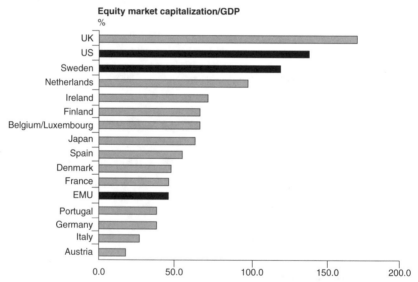

Figure 9.5   Bank assets and equity markets

enhancing' sectors in Sweden has probably been capital market deregulation. Compared with many EMU economies, Sweden has developed a more 'modern' capital market structure, with a high degree of equity market capitalization and large household mutual fund assets (see Figures 9.4 and 9.5). New sectors are almost by definition more risky than established sectors. Since banks are often more 'conservative' in their credit policies, those capital markets dominated by banks might be less efficient in allocating capital to emerging sectors. Though EMU in itself will gradually contribute to the formation of a more efficient capital market in core 'Euroland' as well, a high equity market share will probably help Sweden keep its 'comparative advantage' in this field for quite a while.

However, there are other factors that might hamper Swedish growth relative to the existing EMU countries. One important factor is the tax system. Sweden has the highest tax burden on labour income within the EU. Lower marginal taxes on mobile human and physical capital will, most likely, be an essential 'growth-enhancing' factor in an emerging high-tech economy. EMU membership would probably speed up Swedish tax harmonization with EU standards. The prospects for Swedish tax reform, even while the country remains outside EMU are, however, rather promising. There is a strong political desire within the Persson government to cut taxes on labour, as well as on capital and wealth, within its present term of office; that is before 2002.

The different trends within 'Euroland'

Thus far, it is safe to say that the costs for Sweden of 'staying out' of EMU have been small. On the other hand, the EMU has only existed for less than two years. Nevertheless, what is already apparent is the existing tensions between the 'Euroland' countries, such as in relation to differences in economic growth and the fiscal positions of respective governments. For instance, while German growth for 1999 was ± 1.5 per cent, the Irish economy grew by more than 9 per cent. Even more importantly, the German growth differential when compared with a large country like Spain might be as wide as two percentage points per year for the next few years. These differences will certainly have implications for patterns in real exchange rates within 'Euroland' and put a strain on certain EMU states' monetary policy. In short, no single, common ECB monetary policy can be designed to suit all EMU countries.

Due to the different economic structures of the EMU countries and their varying positions in terms of economic development, there are reasons to expect internal tensions to remain within 'Euroland' for the foreseeable future. These aspects are relevant to Sweden's EMU entry as well, since the country is different in terms of the structure of its economy, prospects for growth and its fiscal position, when compared to 'core' EMU countries. Sweden's relatively good future growth prospects will, most likely, lead to an appreciation of the krona. Based on historical relationships, there is also a risk that the convergence rate for the krona will be set too low (making the krona too weak), which may lead to 'overheating' of the Swedish economy in the next few years.

At this point in time, it is meaningless to evaluate the consequences of 'staying out' of EMU since the future costs (and benefits) of staying out are very hard to foresee and the net benefits of joining the 'Euro' are uncertain. Simultaneously, the costs of leaving EMU unilaterally (once joined) are probably very high, perhaps prohibitively so. Hence, there is a 'value in waiting', in the sense that there might be very good reasons for being extra careful before taking the decision to enter EMU.

Sweden and EMU: membership in 2004?

Since the Social Democratic Party's leadership are afraid of splitting the SAP internally on the EMU issue, they have been as equally reluctant to push public opinion forward on the EMU issue or even to show their cards. On the contrary, instead of the government trying to persuade public opinion and influence it in favour of EMU membership, it has been the divisions within Swedish public opinion that have dictated the Persson government's position on EMU. This strategy also probably reflects a genuine uncertainty amongst leading Social Democrats on whether EMU is a good thing or not. Hence, from a tactical perspective, the government's existing 'wait-and-see' stance is a wise strategy. If the 'Euro' turns out to be a success, then Swedish public opinion may swing in favour, thus giving the Social Democrats the basis to push for Swedish EMU membership. However, if the EMU project runs into too much trouble, they have justified their existing policy and have additional reasons to argue for remaining outside the 'Euro'.

In January 1999, when Swedish public opinion became more positive towards the 'Euro', the Persson government announced what was widely perceived as a timetable for Swedish EMU membership. First, an extraordinary party congress intended to, and did, take a (Yes) decision in Spring 2000. Second, and on the basis of the SAP's approval, the government could then move forward to holding a referendum in Autumn 2000 on Swedish EMU entry, paving the way for parliamentary approval for Sweden to join the 'Euro'. According to this timetable, Sweden might become a full EMU member as early as 1 January 2001, at the same time as when the common currency is to be fully introduced. A natural step on this road to EMU would be to tie the krona to ERM2. It is unlikely that Sweden would be refused to join EMU on the ERM criteria. Still, if Sweden finally decides to apply, an ERM2 link for a year or so would secure EMU membership.

However, Swedish public opinion on EMU had, to some extent, swung back in the negative direction since Winter 1999. One reason was that the 'Europhoria', created in the wake of the launch of the EMU's third stage in January 1999, subsided. Another factor was that the corruption scandal of the European Commission in 1999 restored some of the Swedish public's negative feelings and suspicions about the Union in general. Most Swedes, whether they are for or against EU, are proud of the democratic openness of their country's political system and the scandal involving the Commission tended to highlight the lack of democratic accountability present in the Union today. Indeed, the reaction of the Swedish public to events in 1999 highlight that the assertions made by Miles as part of the first 'point' of his 'Membership Diamond' are as relevant as ever.

It has also become clear that the economic growth outlook for Sweden in the next few years is more favourable than that of many of the EMU countries. Although Swedish interest rates will probably stay higher than interest rates within EMU, this does not signal a lack of credibility but rather that the Swedish economy is steaming ahead. The relatively favourable economic development in the UK also probably affects the Persson government's view on the need for rapid EMU entry since it appears that it is not just Sweden as an 'EMU outsider' that can manage successfully without EMU.

Given this background, it came as no surprise that the Social Democrats in May 1999 seemed to have second thoughts on the EMU issue and it now appears as if the Persson government has changed its mind, at least in terms of the provisional political timetable for Swedish EMU entry. Though still unclear, a much more likely scenario than holding a referendum in Autumn 2000 now appears to be that any final decision will be postponed until after the next general election in September 2002. EMU membership in 2004 at the earliest is, thus, now the most likely scenario.

Unless there is a political earthquake in Sweden, it is impossible to imagine the country entering EMU against the will of the Social Democrats since it is fair to say that the current political landscape largely dictates that it is ruling Social Democrats that will decide on the issue. Hence, if the Social Democrats make up their minds and go for EMU membership, they should have few problems securing a parliamentary majority behind government policy. The crucial thing will be public opinion (see Chapter 7). It appears unlikely that public opinion will swing massively in favour of a 'Yes' to EMU, especially if the economic forecasts for Sweden prove to be correct; Sweden can 'manage best on her own'. It is, therefore, highly probable that the Social Democrats will stick to their 'wait-and-see' strategy for at least the next few years.

The Calmfors Commission in 1996 concluded that the political arguments have been the main driving force behind the creation of EMU and related political arguments will also be crucial to Sweden's decision on participating in the 'Euro'. In the longer-term perspective, the most vital political question will be whether Sweden can continue to be an EU member without joining the EMU as well. Will it be possible for Sweden in the long run to stay in the EU but outside EMU, despite the fact that Sweden has ratified the Maastricht Treaty and fulfils the convergence criteria? Probably not!

Sweden, EMU and the 'Membership Diamond': concluding remarks

The Swedish decision in 1994 to enter the Union had far reaching implications for Sweden's monetary and fiscal policy framework. The Riksbank Law, regulating the Riksbank's relationship towards Sweden's political system, has, to some extent, been 'Europeanized' and is evidence of the 'Europeanization' process apparent in 'point' one of the 'Membership Diamond' and considered as part of this book's second research theme (see Chapter 1). This reform was implemented in 1999. In some respects, the new Riksbank Law actually guarantees that the Swedish Central Bank has greater political independence than the equivalent legislation regulating the ECB. Furthermore, the Riksbank is as devoted to the goal of price stability as is the ECB. By 1995, Swedish fiscal policy was formally directed towards fiscal prudence in line with the EU's 'Growth and Stability Pact'. The country's fiscal position is currently better than that of most EMU countries and there are no major threats to fiscal stability in the foreseeable future.

This brief survey of Swedish monetary policy does verify the 'Membership Diamond' advocated by Lee Miles. The EMU issue, which makes up the mainstay of the third 'point' of his 'Membership Diamond', is the main political issue driving Sweden towards a closer relationship with the EU and acting as a catalyst for institutional reform of the country's political and financial institutions. Equally, the EMU question is responsible for maintaining some elements of political division within and amongst the major political parties and within public opinion as indicated by the first 'point' of the 'Membership Diamond'. In addition, the prospect of EMU has attracted the attention of Sweden's major interest groups and financial institutions, consolidating elements of the Diamond's second 'point'.

In the longer term, the question of Swedish EMU membership will have to be finally dealt with. Abandoning Sweden's national currency will, of course, imply a significant institutional change and may be evidence that, in this policy area, Sweden has yet to become fully adjusted to the demands of being an EU member state (see the third research theme outlined in Chapter 1). It seems unlikely that Sweden can remain as a full EU member without adopting the common currency in the very long run. Sweden will probably become a member of EMU, but more likely later than sooner.

What remains to be seen is whether the EU project will continue to be mainly the subject of interest to Sweden's political and economic elite or if public opinion will finally move in a more EU-friendly direction (the fourth research theme outlined in Chapter 1). Such a shift – if it occurs – will not be imminent. Certainly, the 1999 direct elections to the European Parliament (see Chapter 5) suggest that the Swedish electorate does not care about the EU and it is hard to argue that the EU has gained significantly in popularity since Sweden became a full member in 1995. Since Swedish economic trends are likely to be favourable compared to the EMU average for the next few years, it seems unlikely that economic factors will persuade the Swedish public opinion to become more EU or EMU friendly. Hence, in order to influence public opinion positively, the proponents of EMU will have to rely on other arguments rather than just the economic costs of 'staying outside the Euro'. In the end, the political benefits of 'going in' might perhaps be enough to convince Swedish public opinion.

CHAPTER 10

Swedish Environmental Policy

Katarina Molin and Rüdiger K. W. Wurzel[1]

Introduction

Sweden has long played an extremely active role in international environmental politics and has acquired a reputation for being an 'environmental leader' state (see, for example, Andersen and Liefferink 1997; Kronsell 1997; Liefferink and Andersen 1998a; 1998b; Lundquist 1997; 1998; Molin 1999). The United Nations (UN) Conference on the Human Environment in Stockholm in June 1972 was initiated by the Swedish government which wanted to draw attention to transnational pollution issues such as acid rain (see, for instance, Wurzel 1993: 180). More recent Swedish international environmental policy initiatives have included important proposals for the Convention on Long-Range Transboundary Air Pollution (LRTAP), the protection of the Baltic Sea, the implementation of the principle of sustainable development and renewed efforts to tackle the problem of acidification within the UN Economic Commission for Europe (ECE) as well as on the EU level.

Three main factors help to explain why Sweden became an environmental leader state. First, Sweden, which is one of Western Europe's largest countries, suffers from relatively high 'ecological vulnerability'. The country is adversely affected by acid rain in particular as a result of strong prevailing winds and its geographical location but also as a result of the relatively low 'buffer capacity' of its soils against acidifying substances (that is, mainly sulphur dioxide and nitrogen oxides). Because much (air) pollution is imported from other states, the effectiveness of domestic pollution abatement measures crucially depends on action taken in neighbouring states and/or on the international level. Second, as in a number of other policy fields, Sweden has traditionally presented its domestic (environmental) policy solutions as a model for others to follow (see Liefferink and Andersen 1998a). Third, prior to the economic crises of the 1990s, there was a relatively broad consensus amongst Swedish policy-makers that stringent domestic environmental standards could help both to protect the environment and improve economic competitiveness. Put simply, this concept of 'ecological modernization' (for instance, Hajer 1995; Weale 1992) presumes that stringent 'environmental policy pays', at least when a long-term perspective is taken. This is for two main reasons: first, preventative action is often less costly than curative or clean up measures; second, progressive domestic environmental measures may give indigenous corporate actors a 'first mover advantage' *vis-à-vis* their foreign competitors. This is because such actors often manufacture products (for which there is domestic demand) at an earlier stage compared to those countries which adopt stringent environmental standards only after a certain time lag.

The concept of ecological modernization closely resembles certain aspects of the concept of sustainable development, which was popularized by the 1987 Brundtland Report (Brundtland Report 1987), and has played a central role in Swedish environmental policy even before EU membership.

However, the harsher economic climate of the 1990s forced advocates of ecological modernization on to the defensive which, until then, seemed to complement the wider 'Swedish project' of a comprehensive welfare state that tried to ensure a high standard of living (including an unspoilt environment and protection from health hazards) for all citizens (see also Kronsell 1997: 54). Some environmental issues also contributed towards the gradual erosion of Swedish consensual politics and corporatism well before the emerging crises of the welfare state. The most important example of this is the controversy surrounding the use of nuclear energy which led to the emergence of new political actors such as the Green Party (*Miljöpartiet – de Gröna*) and triggered a marked increase in public support for environmental groups that make use of unconventional methods to influence environmental policy-making (see Jahn 1992). This corroborates aspects of 'points' one and two of the 'Membership Diamond' as defined by Lee Miles in Chapter 1.

Since the referendum in 1980, Sweden has been committed to phasing out nuclear energy. However, society remains split on the need, and, even more so, the timing of this move, which is not affected by EU membership as member states are free to decide on whether to use nuclear energy. In fact, almost half of the EU's member states have either never made use of this type of energy source or are now committed to the phasing out of nuclear power. Sweden (and Austria) nevertheless insisted on a (legally non-binding) declaration, which was attached to the Accession Treaty stating that the right to choose its sources of energy would not be affected by EU membership. On the other hand, EU membership had a major impact on lesser politicized environmental issues, such as product standards (for example, emission limits for cars) which must be approximated in such a way as to ensure the free movement of goods within the Single European Market (SEM).

The 'Europeanization' of Swedish environmental policy-making is therefore most advanced with regard to product standards especially since most of these were already covered by provisions of the European Economic Area (EEA) agreement. This is one of the reasons why the Swedish government has lobbied hard to achieve the widening of the so-called 'environmental guarantee' in Article 100A (SEA), which allows member state governments – under certain circumstances – to adopt nationally more stringent standards. It also insisted on transitional arrangements which allowed Sweden to keep its stricter national standards for a number of (primarily chemical) products while EU standards would be reviewed within a period of four years.

This chapter starts with a brief assessment of some of the core features of the domestic environmental policy system, which was well developed long before Sweden joined the EU. This is followed by an analysis of the accession negotiations and the review process before scrutinizing the environmental priorities of the Swedish government during the negotiations of the Amsterdam Treaty. The next part outlines the Swedish government's wider strategy towards EU environmental policy while examining a number of core issues (for example, acid rain and car emissions) which were of high priority for domestic actors. However, attention will be drawn to the fact that Sweden, as all so-called environmental leader states, has shown certain 'weak spots' (Wurzel forthcoming). The conclusion argues that the 'Europeanization' of Swedish environmental policy and policy actors has taken place unevenly and varies from issue to issue as well as from actor to actor. Overall there is little difference between elite and public demands when it comes to the pursuit of a more progressive EU environmental policy. However, while the government and most officials remain convinced that the protection of the domestic and wider European environment is best served through Swedish EU membership, this view is not shared by many environmentalists who still fear that the EU exerts downward pressures on the country's relatively high domestic standards.

Core features of contemporary Swedish environmental policy

Early Swedish pollution control measures can be traced to the nineteenth century or even further back in history. However, as in most highly industrialized liberal democracies, modern day environmental policy has come about only since the late 1960s (see Lundquist 1997; Weale 1992).

Core actors

Following the upsurge of environmental awareness since the late 1960s, Sweden has adopted a number of core guiding principles, a wide range of pollution control measures and built up highly differentiated administrative capacities to counter pollution problems. Public environmental awareness has remained very high up to now (Eurobarometer 1995) and some five per cent of Swedish citizens belonged to an environmental group in the mid-1990s (Lundquist 1997: 55).

The most important core central governmental actors in the environmental field include the Ministry of Environment, the Swedish Environmental

Protection Agency (SEPA) and the National Chemicals Inspectorate (KEMI). The Ministry of Environment was not established until 1987. It is a relatively small ministry with a staff of approximately 150 civil servants. Initially, its international division dealt with EU environmental policy issues; a separate EU unit has only existed since the 1990s. SEPA was already established in 1967. In the late 1990s, SEPA had a staff of some 480 civil servants. It is an independent and influential agency which was, more recently, given the task of formulating sectoral plans and programmes (Lundquist 1997: 50).

The fact that a separate environmental agency deals exclusively with chemicals is unusual in comparison to most member states and illustrates the importance that Sweden attributed to chemicals. Some 150 civil servants worked for KEMI in the late 1990s. Sweden's chemical policy, which is based on the substitution principle (which states that chemical substances must be substituted with less harmful substances whenever possible) and the precautionary principle, is one of the most stringent in the world (Kronsell 1997: 54). It is therefore no surprise that for a number of Swedish regulations on chemicals in particular, transitional arrangements had to be found during the accession negotiations because they were perceived by, amongst others, the Commission as a barrier to trade under the EU Treaty. The agreed solution foresaw a four year transition period (rather than the three year transitional period as the Commission had proposed) during which Sweden was allowed to keep its stricter national standards while the EU reviewed its legislation with the aim of trying to raise its standards (the so-called review process).

The most important environmental non-governmental organizations (NGOs) are the Swedish Society for Nature Conservation (SNF – *Naturskyddsföreningen*), the World Wide Fund for Nature (WWF) and Greenpeace Sweden which, in the mid-1990s, had memberships of 200,000, 150,000 and 110,000 respectively (Lundquist 1997: 55). More unconventional and/or grass roots oriented groups such as the Swedish Anti Nuclear Movement (*Folkkampanjen mot Kärnkraft*) and Friends of the Earth Sweden (FoE – *Jordens Vänner*) mustered merely 3000 and 1600 members. Most Swedish environmental NGOs (including Greenpeace and FoE) strongly opposed EU membership out of fear that it would lead to a lowering of national standards. However, proponents of EU membership in the two biggest groups, SNF and WWF, narrowly gained the upper hand, though both were split internally. By the late 1990s, the scepticism of Sweden's environmentalists *vis-à-vis* the EU had not waned significantly (interview information from senior FoE and SFN campaigners in February 1998 and July 1999 respectively).

Swedish industry, on the other hand, strongly supported EU membership overall. In fact the (then) chairperson of Volvo, Pehr Gyllenhammar, played an influential role within the Roundtable of European Industrialists, which pushed hard for the creation of a SEM (without trade barriers) even before Sweden had joined the EU (Moravcsik 1991: 44; Sandholtz and Zysman 1989). In the environmental field, the 'level playing field' argument played a certain role for the highly export oriented Swedish industry, which has to comply with some of the most stringent domestic environmental laws in the world (OECD 1996: 21). This can partly be seen from the fact that it did not use the review process to lobby for the raising of EU environmental standards in those cases where Swedish laws were more stringent.

Instead, the Swedish industry umbrella group, *Industriförbundet*, has often taken a similar line as industry's European umbrella group UNICE which, on the other hand, often exhibits a certain 'north–south' split when it comes to environmental issues. So far, Sweden's industry considers the EU's impact on domestic environmental policy as very limited (written communication from *Industriförbundet* dated July 1999). However, it is too early to judge fully and to what degree, if any, EU environmental policy will exert adaptation pressures on Swedish industrial and other policy actors. All new member states are usually given an unofficial period of grace before the Commission starts legal proceedings in cases where they fail to implement EU environmental legislation correctly. EU directives which may trigger infringement procedures against Sweden include the environmental impact assessment (EIA) directive, the bathing water directive and the nitrates directive.

Environmental issues have long been important to all political parties in Sweden, although to varying degrees. The only highly divisive issue of major significance concerns the phasing out of nuclear power, although this has remained largely an issue of domestic politics. Since the 1998 election, the Social Democratic Party (SAP) minority government has relied upon the support of the Green Party and Left Party – both of which are opposed to both the use of nuclear power and EU membership. This illustrates the importance of 'point' one of the 'Membership Diamond' as defined by Lee Miles in Chapter 1 (see also Miles 1998b: 341). However, the adoption of market instruments and cost-effective environmental policy measures, which was strongly fostered by the Bildt government during the early 1990s, has continued under various SAP administrations. In order to comprehend the recent shift from 'command and control' environmental regulation (see Dryzek 1997: 82) towards the wider adoption of market instruments (such as environmental taxes, tradable permits and eco-labels) and an emphasis on cost-effectiveness, it is necessary to assess briefly the development of the core environmental policy principles and measures.

Core environmental policy principles and measures

In the 1970s and 1980s, Swedish environmental policy was based largely on a media centred (that is air, water and soil) problem-solving approach. It also relied heavily upon (end-of-pipe) emission limits that were gradually tightened as the best available technology (BAT) advanced (see also

Lundquist 1997). Since the late 1980s, a shift towards a more integrated approach occurred which aims to take into account pollution control in the round. More recently there has also been a greater stress on cost-effective measures which are derived from environmental quality objectives (EQOs) rather than the BAT. This policy shift can largely be explained by the fact that as domestic environmental policy measures gradually became more stringent they increasingly yielded smaller margins of return. Put simply, the cost of clearing up the remaining pollution is increasingly becoming more expensive, at least for some issues. However, domestic policy-makers also became more cost-conscious when Sweden was hit by economic recession in the early 1990s. Importantly, the recent shift in Swedish environmental policy towards cost-effective EQO-derived policy measures fits in well with similar trends on the EU level (see Héritier *et al.* 1996).

However, some of Sweden's core environmental policy principles have not been accepted or fully implemented within EU environmental policy. The following four action-guiding core environmental principles form part of modern day Swedish environmental policy: the principle of integrated pollution control, the precautionary principle, the substitution principle and the principle of sustainable development (see also Ministry of the Environment 1997; SEPA 1993). All of these principles are enshrined within the EU Treaties, although their implementation is far from perfect to say the least. The only exception is the substitution principle, which was unacceptable to some member state governments despite heavy lobbying by the Swedish government during the Intergovernmental Conference (IGC) which negotiated the Amsterdam Treaty (see Molin 1999).

The accession negotiations and review process

Environmental issues played a central role during the accession negotiations and the subsequent referendum campaign. The Swedish government was determined to be seen by its electorate as acting tough with regard to defending stricter national standards. The fact that public environmental awareness was very high in Sweden, Finland and Austria (as well as Norway which did not later join) put the applicant states into a strong bargaining position. The Commission and existing member states were well aware that a 'Yes' vote in the referendum on EU membership would depend, to a considerable degree, on whether Sweden and the other applicant states would be allowed to keep their more stringent national environmental standards. Clearly, this illustrates the analytical usefulness of international relations' two-level games as identified in Putnam's seminal work (Putnam 1988). However, full EU membership requires a degree of transnational involvement of Swedish core policy actors (including societal actors) in EU environmental policy-making which goes beyond traditional international relations.

Cooperation between the applicant states was very close during the early phase of the accession negotiations in particular, although this eased somewhat towards the final stage which was taken up with bilateral negotiations with the Commission on country specific issues. However, no attempt was made to keep alive this alliance once Sweden had become a full member. The last year of the review process saw the reactivation of closer cooperation between Swedish, Austrian and Finnish officials who again tried to come up with a common strategy with regard to those issues on which the EU had failed to raise its common standards. However, Swedish officials cooperate more closely with their Finnish and Danish counterparts on environmental issues within the Nordic Council.

Semi-permanent alliances do not exist within the Environmental Council where they are viewed with suspicion. Instead, cooperation must be established on an issue by issue basis, despite the fact that the EU's environmental leader states (the old 'green trio', Denmark, Germany and the Netherlands, as well as the newcomers Austria, Finland and Sweden, are traditionally grouped into this category) often find themselves taking up similar negotiating positions on a relatively wide range of environmental issues (see Liefferink and Andersen 1998a; 1998b). Swedish officials have undertaken considerable efforts to avoid antagonizing the southern member state governments. Attempts have been made on several occasions to help bridge the North–South split which often opens up within the Environmental Council. They have sought to establish closer contacts with their counterparts in southern member states while trying to convince them that ambitious environmental standards and economic prosperity are not mutually exclusive (interview with a Swedish official in January 1998).

The most controversial environmental issues for Sweden during the accession negotiations and review process concerned chemical products (see also Barnes 1996) and transport pollution abatement measures. In the Swedish case, more than 70 (categories of) chemical substances were covered under the review process. In the majority of cases, EU environmental standards were raised by the end of 1998.

However, the EU failed to adopt the more stringent Swedish restrictions for arsenic, pentachlorophenol (PCP) organotin compounds and cadmium (see KEMI 1997). The derogations for Sweden (as well as Austria and Finland) therefore had to be extended until 2002, although the legal status of the new derogations remains disputed (see *EWWE* of 8 June 1999: 1). The EU's failure to adopt more stringent restrictions on the use of cadmium (in, for example, batteries, plastics and fertilizers) was hotly disputed in particular and has attracted considerable public and media attention. Sweden's KEMI insists that there is conclusive scientific evidence that cadmium, which is non-degradable and accumulates in soil (especially when the soil is affected by acid rain), can cause kidney damage, particularly for risk groups such as diabetics and the elderly (KEMI 1997: 4). The DG for Industry (DGIII), which was the Commission's lead department for chemical substances during the review process, has so far blocked attempts by DGXI (Environment) to press for tighter regulations (*ENDS Daily* of 2 August 1999). It therefore remains to be seen whether Sweden will eventually have to follow Finland which has already lowered its standards to bring them in line with EU legislation. So far, Sweden has taken a tough stance mainly because much is at stake politically. In the run up to the 1995 referendum the Swedish government stated categorically that domestic environmental standards would not be lowered as a result of EU membership.

Efforts by the British (1998) and German (1999) EU Presidencies to place a review of the EU's chemicals policy on to the Environmental Council's agenda were strongly supported by the Swedish government. A Swedish Environmental Ministry official responsible for chemicals was seconded to the German Federal Environmental Ministry (*Bundesministerium Für Umwelt*) for a few weeks during the German Presidency following secondments of Swedish officials to Britain and Austria during their respective EU Presidencies. Swedish policy-makers are optimistic that their expertise with regard to chemical regulations will allow them to influence decisively the review of the EU's chemicals policy. It will also present them with an opportunity to make a renewed push for the introduction of the substitution principle on the EU level. The review of the EU's chemicals policy, which will continue into the Swedish EU Presidency in 2001, is likely to constitute a high profile issue for the new Environmental Commissioner, Margot Wallström, whose actions will be closely watched in her native Sweden. This issue shows that major reforms within EU environmental policy are time consuming and need early attention by those who want to leave an imprint on the EU's policy output – a fact which Swedish policy-makers have grasped quickly. However, it also illustrates that five years of EU membership may not yet be sufficient to gauge fully the extent to which Sweden may affect EU environmental policy and, importantly, vice versa.

However, it is worth pointing out that although domestic restrictions on chemicals were, on balance, more stringent than existing EU rules, Sweden's standards were actually raised during the review process in a few cases (interview with a Swedish official in July 1999).

The environmental provisions of the Amsterdam Treaty

Sweden's core environmental objectives during the IGC (which negotiated the Amsterdam Treaty) were to achieve the strengthening of the 'environmental guarantee', to get the concept of sustainable development enshrined as one of the EU's core objectives and to make more explicit the need for better integration of environmental requirements. All of these Swedish objectives have been taken up in the Amsterdam Treaty which came into force in May 1999. However, there is considerable dispute over whether the Amsterdam Treaty has indeed strengthened the 'environmental guarantee' of Article 100A (reclassified as Article 95 under the Amsterdam Treaty). Stefani Bär and Andreas Kraemer have concluded that 'any doubt about the possibility for member states to introduce stricter national measures has been removed [in the revised Article 100A]. But at the same time, new interpretation problems and ambiguities have been produced' (Bär and Kraemer 1998: 320). The new Article 100A explicitly states for the first time that member states may be allowed (under certain circumstances) to adopt more stringent environmental national laws for issues already covered by EU legislation. However, the national measures must be vetted by the Commission within a six month period.

Sweden was opposed to an extension of qualified majority voting (QMV) for the environmental provisions for fear of being outvoted on nationally sensitive issues. QMV has been the rule in the environmental field since the Maastricht Treaty came into force in 1996 (although unanimity still applies for tax measures, town and country planning, water management and the choice of energy sources). The Swedish government (after introducing similar domestic measures) strongly supported the adoption of an EU-wide carbon dioxide/energy tax (Liefferink and Andersen 1998a) but this was vetoed, initially by the British and more recently by the Spanish. Because of its fears regarding QMV, Sweden did not support an alternative Danish proposal which would have allowed for the adoption by QMV of environmental taxes to tackle transboundary environmental problems such as climate change (see Molin 1999).

The Swedish government published its EU environmental policy priorities and strategy in March 1995; it has since updated it several times (Government Communication 1994/95; Government Report 1997a – Ds 1997: 68). As for domestic environmental policy, the concept of sustainable development plays a central role in the Swedish government's strategy which aims to make an environmental forerunner out of the EU in the international arena. Since joining the EU, Sweden has acted both as a forerunner which sets a good example as well as a pusher state which aims to raise environmental standards on a EU-wide level (Andersen and Liefferink 1997; Liefferink and Andersen 1998a). However, before these issues are assessed in more detail, it is worth focusing on the reasons why Sweden has exhibited a somewhat ambiguous climate change strategy.

Sweden's climate change strategy

Since joining the EU, the Swedish government has not taken on a leadership role with regard to combating climate change. This illustrates that even environmental leader states occasionally fail to live up to their reputation. On the one hand, Sweden has long made considerable efforts to cut its 'greenhouse gases' of which carbon dioxide is the most important (see, for example, Ministry of the Environment 1997). On the other hand, the Swedish government almost unravelled the EU's climate change strategy in early 1999 (*EWWE*, 21 May 1999: 8–11). Sweden (and the Netherlands) initially threatened to block efforts to put a ceiling on the use of the so-called 'flexible mechanism'. The 'flexible mechanism' was enshrined into the climate change convention at the insistence of the USA and allows for the substitution of domestic emission abatement measures with emission trading, that is, the buying up of certain quotas from other states. Most EU member state governments sought the ceiling as it was felt that at least 50 per cent of the national target should be achieved through domestic efforts (such as energy saving). However, the Swedish decision in the 1980s to phase out nuclear energy was not supported by a complementary strategy aimed at introducing alternative energy sources which would not bring about increased carbon dioxide emissions. Sweden's opposition to the ceiling should be seen in this context.

It is also the case that Sweden had already made considerable efforts in the 1970s and 1980s to reduce domestic energy consumption and, more recently, adopted tax measures to reduce energy consumption further. The Swedish government therefore wanted its early domestic measures to be taken into account during the negotiations about national ceilings with regard to the 'flexible mechanism'. The deep split which runs through the ruling SAP and, indeed, Swedish society at large on the nuclear power issue has left officials in a precarious negotiating position. It even triggered one of the rare occasions when Sweden was blamed by (domestic) environmental groups for slowing down progress on a very important EU environmental dossier. However, Sweden does not usually drag its feet with regard to the adoption of more stringent EU environmental measures.

Sweden's leading role in combating acidification

Since it joined the EU, Sweden has been the most important driving force behind a common strategy to combat acid rain. Acid rain has been a long-standing pollution problem which causes serious environmental pollution in Sweden (European Economic Agency 1999a; 1999b). Sweden has acquired considerable scientific expertise on acid rain and pioneered the so-called 'critical loads' principle, which became enshrined into the Sulphur Protocol of the LRTAP convention in 1994. The 'critical loads' principle constitutes a departure from the traditional approach to assign uniform emission reduction limits to a particular country; it instead aims to lower harmful (sulphur and nitrogen oxide) emissions to less than the critical (and environmentally damaging) threshold level on a regional or even local basis.

Reviving the EU's acidification strategy

Immediately after joining the EU, Sweden launched an initiative within the Environmental Council for a coherent EU strategy to combat acid rain. The Council subsequently asked the Commission to come up with a report which was published in 1995 (SEC(95) 2057). The Directorate General (DG) XI, which is a relatively small DG, is responsible for environmental issues within the Commission. It strongly welcomed the secondment of a Swedish expert who, in cooperation with a seconded British official, drafted most of the Commission's report. Unusually, the seconded Swedish expert was not a government official but had previously worked for the Swedish NGO Secretariat on Acid Rain, which is an NGO closely involved in negotiations of the LRTAP convention. The Swedish government was aware that its acidification strategy was likely to meet with stern resistance from the Southern member states (and Spain in particular). Swedish officials therefore sought close informal contacts with the most reluctant member state governments prior to Environmental Council negotiations in order to discover possible compromise solutions (Molin 1999).

The Commission's report was presented to the Environmental Council in December 1995. It concluded that the application of the BAT principle would leave many regions within the EU well above the 'critical loads' threshold (SEC(95) 2057: 19). However, mainly for cost reasons, several member state governments were not prepared to accept the relatively ambitious reduction targets put forward in the Commission's report. The Council conclusions finally accepted a Dutch compromise proposal (which drew heavily on advice from the Swedish expert) but also asked the Commission to come up with a less costly modified strategy. Subsequently, DGXI accepted support from two other Swedish experts, who were seconded to its offices in Brussels in 1996–98. Sweden has, therefore, made extensive use of trying to influence the Commission from 'within' (see also Liefferink and Andersen 1998a).

The Commission's modified acidification strategy, which reflected a number of Swedish priorities, was finally published in March 1997 (COM(97) 88). It proposed the adoption of a 50 per cent gap-closure target (namely that the 'critical loads' threshold level should not be exceeded in more than 50 per cent of the designated area) by 2010 compared to the 1990 base line. The most important measures proposed to achieve this aim included: the adoption of stringent national emission ceilings for sulphur dioxide, nitrogen oxides, and ammonia in a new directive; the revision of the large combustion directive; the adoption of a directive limiting the sulphur content of liquid fuels; the revision of the 1988 large combustion directive; the ratification of the 1994 LRTAP sulphur protocol; and the adoption of restrictions on emissions from ships. Sweden therefore not only succeeded in placing acidification onto the EU's agenda but also helped to frame the EU's pollution abatement strategy to counter acid rain.

Sweden has taken unilateral action with regard to limiting (sulphur and nitrogen oxide) emissions from ships. The measures adopted should have led to a 75 per cent reduction by 2000. They consist mainly of lower shipping dues for vessels which use low sulphur fuels and are equipped with advanced emission abatement technologies. This is another example of where the Swedish government has tried to set an example for others to follow and used policy instruments like taxes, which are commonly used within Swedish environmental policy.

The auto-oil programme

The transport sector constitutes the biggest single source of nitrogen oxide emissions in Sweden. This is the main reason stringent car emission regulations have long been a Swedish priority. Sweden adopted a modified version of the US car emission standards, which made necessary the adoption of the three-way catalytic converter by 1989. It also adopted cold start test procedures (to ensure that car emission abatement technology would also function within cold climate conditions) and stipulated durability requirements for the three-way catalytic converter. When Sweden joined the EU, it therefore had in place car emission legislation which was more stringent than existing EU legislation. Sweden was allowed to keep its national standards for the time being, mainly because the Commission had already embarked on a revision of the EU's car emission limits and fuel standards. However, the EU did not give any legal guarantees that the higher Swedish standards would ultimately be adopted within the EU.

At the time that Sweden joined the EU, the Commission's controversial Auto-Oil I Programme was already at an advanced stage (for a critical review see Friedrich *et al.* 1998). The Programme put forward car emission limits and fuel standards for 2000 (and 2005) that were derived from environmental quality objectives (EQOs) in a cost-effective manner. However, the member states were unable to influence this Programme because it was formulated jointly by the Commission and the automobile and oil industries; member state governments and Non-Governmental Organizations (NGOs) remained excluded from this stage of the complex EU policy formulation process. It was therefore initially of little relevance that Swedish officials had already gained access to the so-called Motor Vehicles Emission Group (MVEG) in 1994. The influence of the MVEG, which is a Commission ad hoc advisory group made up of Commission and member state officials as well as industry and NGO representatives, has declined since the mid-1990s.

The Commission's Auto-Oil Programme stipulated durability requirements but failed to put forward a cold start test, which was a Swedish priority (Molin 1999). The Swedish government therefore contacted some of the sceptical Southern member states but also Britain prior to the Environmental Council meetings to persuade them of the merits of such a test. Following elections in France which brought a more environmentally minded government to power, the French government later submitted a compromise proposal which was adopted by the Council. It seems that Sweden's strategy of taking for granted the support of the other 'Green' Northern member states and focusing lobbying efforts on the reluctant member states and France in particular appears to have paid off on this occasion. Sweden and Finland made identical demands during Environmental Council meetings which discussed the need for a cold start test. However, in the end, the Swedish government had to rely on the progressive views of the European Parliament (EP) which took up all of the Swedish demands (as well as those from other environmental leader states) during the co-decision procedure which grants the EP co-legislative powers together with the Council. The EP decisively tightened the Commission's original proposal and also forced the Council to accept more stringent standards. The car emission limits and fuel standards which were jointly adopted by the EP and Council in June 1998 therefore came very close to the original Swedish demands.

Conclusion

Sweden has taken on a very active role in EU environmental policy-making. As the brief case studies have already shown, Swedish policy-makers have opted for different strategies ranging from providing a model for others to follow to the concerted lobbying of reluctant member state governments. Overall, the Swedish approach to environmental policy fits recent trends on the EU level which emphasize cost-effective measures derived from environmental quality objectives. However, it should not be overlooked that 'Europeanization' of Swedish environmental policy and policy actors (see 'point' one of the 'Membership Diamond') has taken place unevenly and varies from issue to issue as well as from actor to actor. The government administration and most large corporate actors have adapted quickly to the new challenges while environmental NGOs often lack the necessary resources to exert similar influence on EU policy-makers and to form transnational alliances. The general public still perceives the EU mainly as a threat to ambitious national environmental policy measures. However, the profile of EU environmental policy is likely to be raised by the new Swedish Commissioner, Margot Wallström, who took over the environmental portfolio in September 1999.

The Swedish government has already moved beyond traditional two-level diplomacy, as was shown in the case studies. However, for Sweden to become a 'complete' EU member state it will be necessary for societal actors to become more strongly involved in the multi-level EU decision-making processes and to lobby actors such as the EP more effectively. Sweden's long tradition of a progressive domestic environmental policy and relatively consensual (despite the nuclear issue) and transparent policy-making procedures presents both opportunities and obstacles for its further integration into the EU. Sweden has much experience and expertise in the environmental policy field which it can offer to the EU. However, it must also be prepared to accept compromise solutions which important domestic actors may not always find palatable. In its first few years as an EU member,

Sweden has overall played a very successful role in EU environmental policy-making.

Note

1. Rüdiger Wurzel would like to thank the Nuffield Foundation for funding a related research project on which some of the findings put forward in this chapter are based.

CHAPTER 11

Swedish Agriculture

Ewa Rabinowicz

Introduction

Agriculture and primary processing were excluded from earlier forms of cooperation between Sweden and the European Union (namely, the FTA and the EEA). Hence, the impact of Sweden's EU accession on those two sectors is potentially more significant than on the rest of the economy. The aim of this chapter is to analyse the consequences of full EU membership for Swedish agriculture (including primary processing). What complicates the analysis, however, is the fact that Sweden's agricultural policy was the subject of extensive reform, and the government's decision to reform the country's agricultural policy was taken only one year prior to the application for EU membership being made. For this reason, the reform was sometimes perceived as being in preparation for eventual EU membership. The opposite is, however, the case. By moving Swedish agriculture in a more liberal direction than the existing CAP, the Swedish reforms actually made EU accession more complicated since the country's agricultural sector needed to be re-regulated again. In addition, the Swedish agricultural reform creates an ambiguity about what constitutes a proper point of reference in any evaluation of the Swedish farming sector and the implications of EU membership. Should the impact of full membership be evaluated from a historical perspective, and against the situation prior to EU accession or rather in terms of a hypothetical 'post-reform' scenario? Both comparisons are incorporated in this chapter, although greater emphasis is placed on the former, using comparisons with historical events and figures.

Swedish agriculture prior to accession: natural conditions and policy reforms

Natural conditions

From the fertile plains of southern Sweden to those areas with poorer soil and climatic conditions in the north, the natural conditions affecting agriculture vary considerably according to the region in question. The length of the growing season, for example, varies from between 220 and 170 days. Southern regions experience conditions similar to those in Denmark, northern Germany and Ireland whilst the country's northern regions have more in common with those in Finland and Norway.

Agricultural production in Sweden is based mainly on livestock. Such livestock production accounted for more than 75 per cent of the value of production, with milk production alone making up nearly 40 per cent in the late 1980s and early 1990s (*Yearbook of Agricultural Statistics* 1991; 1997). In addition, there were 90,000 farm holdings (of over 2.0 hectares each) in Sweden in 1994. Total arable land covers about 2.8 million hectares, whilst the total agricultural area is in the region of 3.4 million hectares (or some eight per cent of the total land area of Sweden). The average size of a Swedish farm was around 30 hectares, which is greater than the EU average farm size.

Employment in agriculture accounts for about three per cent of Sweden's total employment. However, the contribution of agriculture to the country's GDP has fallen from 1.8 per cent in 1985 to one per cent in 1994 (*Agricultural Yearbook* 1998). Indeed, a vast majority of farms in Sweden are family farms that derive most of their incomes from sources other than primary agriculture. The share of agriculture in relation to the total income of farm households has declined from 31 per cent in 1989 to 17 per cent in 1995 (*Yearbook of Agricultural Statistics* 1998). Food processing in Sweden is dominated by farmers' producer cooperatives, with, for example, farmers' cooperatives holding 99 per cent of the market in milk-processing. Their market share in the slaughter business is also around 75 per cent.

Swedish agricultural policy before the reforms

In the late 1980s, Swedish agricultural policy was fairly similar to the CAP. Border protection based on variable import levies and domestic market regulation resembling the EU's intervention system were the cornerstones of Swedish agricultural policy at this time. Sweden also applied supply control measures for sugar and milk, with quotas introduced at, more or less, the same time as in the Union. Set-aside schemes were in force for grain. However, Swedish agricultural policy was considerably more homogeneous than the CAP. Fairly similar types of regulations were applied to a wide range of commodities. For instance, beef and pork were regulated in the same way, with similar arrangements for poultry and eggs. The CAP, on the other hand, consists of commodity regimes based on very divergent principles. As a result, there were fewer variations in levels of support across individual agricultural commodities in Sweden than was the case for the EU. In 1990, the total level of support in Sweden (measured as Producer Subsidy Equivalent (PSE), the most commonly used measure of assistance to agriculture), was 57 per cent as compared to 46 per cent for the EU. In 1994 the difference narrowed to 51 per cent for Sweden and 49 per cent for the EU OECD (1996).[1]

A detailed explanation as to why Swedish agricultural policy was reformed largely falls outside the scope and remit of this chapter, although it is correct to state that such reform was not in preparation for Sweden's future membership of the Union. Nevertheless, the major features of the reform (including removal of milk quotas) are summarized below.

- The existing milk quota system was abolished already in 1989.

- Internal market regulations (the intervention system) were to be eliminated.

- Export subsidies were to be abolished.

- Semi-annual price reviews were terminated.

- The level of border protection remained unchanged in view of an expected and endorsed lowering of tariffs as a result of the GATT negotiations.

- Farmers were offered temporary compensations for an expected decline of prices due to reform on a per acreage basis. As an alternative, the whole compensation amount could be collected as one payment provided that the land has been 'restructured'. In other words, removed from food production for at least five years.

No other OECD country (excluding New Zealand as an important exemption) had attempted such a radical deregulation of agricultural policy. The Swedish reform was, in particular, much more fundamental than the 1992 CAP reforms that were to follow. In both cases, farmers were offered compensations for price reductions. Compensations that were paid in Sweden, however, were only temporary and rather modest when compared to the EU level. Market interventions and export subsidies were eliminated in Sweden, but retained in the EU.

Key actors involved in agricultural policy formation and implementation

The process of decision-making relating to agriculture, including, *inter alia*, parliamentary committees on agriculture and the deliberations between key interest groups (compare below), illustrates clearly two of the elements of the Miles 'Membership Diamond' – namely, the importance of consensual policy-making where policies are the outcome of lengthy and open deliberations ('point' one) and second, the significance of interest groups/corporatism in the shaping of domestic (and EU-related) policies ('point' two).

Certainly, the Social Democratic Party (SAP) has been the main actor in government in Sweden during the post war period and since the SAP does not compete directly for 'farm votes', it has emphasized consumer interests within agricultural policy formation. It was, for instance, a SAP government that created Consumer Delegation (CD) in 1963 (see below) and it was the Social Democrats that have initiated all radical changes of Swedish agricultural policy (most notably, key reforms in 1967 and 1990). In particular, these reforms took place at times when the SAP, for one reason or another, was not dependent on parliamentary support from the Centre Party to maintain the stability of the respective government.

In contrast, the Centre Party (which was known as the Peasant Federation until the 1960s) represents middle-sized farmers. Large farmers and land-owners tend, to some extent, to vote for the Moderates (Conservatives). Indeed, the declining number of farmers forced the Centre Party to empha-size other issues, such as the protection of the natural environment, to maintain electoral support. Yet, the protection of farming interests has remained a key priority. Due to its centrist position, the Centre Party has been an attractive cooperation partner for both political blocs. Moreover, until the 1980s, the Centre Party (or its predecessor) was the only right-of-centre party that the SAP could consider seriously as a coalition partner. Nonetheless, the SAP cooperated on several important issues (such as tax reform) with the Liberal Party during the 1980s. This political reorientation was probably an important precondition for the agricultural reform of 1990.

The primary organization representing the country's farmers is the Fed-eration of Swedish Farmers (LRF). This Federation was created in 1971 by an amalgamation of the Federation of Swedish Farmers' Association and the National Swedish Farmers' Union, which created a strong organization uniting both the cooperative movement and the farmers' trade union organization.

The unique feature of the Swedish system was the existence of consumer representation (CD) in agricultural policy matters.[2] Together with the LRF, the CD participated in parliamentary committees on agricultural policy, in semi-annual price reviews intended as discussion forums for deliberations between the LRF and the CD and, finally, in the implementation of agricultural policy. In effect, the CD was an artificial organization repre-senting consumers' interests and appointed by the Swedish government.

Implementation of Swedish reforms

The implementation of the (reformed) agricultural policy was to begin on 1 July 1991. One day after, the Swedish government submitted an application for full membership. Since the adjustments imposed on Swedish agriculture by the domestic reform process, when compared to those that were expec-ted to follow from joining the Union, were substantially different, Sweden's EU application placed the country's agricultural sector, as well as the politicians, in a troublesome position. However, there was also no simple solution to the problem. The domestic reform process could hardly be interrupted, nor could any substantial pre-accession adjustment be realized, since this would undermine the credibility of the government's commitment to abide by the result of any future referendum on EU accession. In short, the government could not be seen publicly as assuming that Sweden would join the EU automatically and before a referendum on EU membership had been held.

Hence, the implementation of the 1990 reform proceeded as if nothing had happened. Yet, the reform process became increasingly difficult to sustain as time passed, and the EU accession negotiations proceeded quite quickly. In particular, the Swedish farmers, quite reasonably, applied a 'wait and see' strategy and it soon became clear to everyone that no 'irreversible' decisions relating to Swedish agriculture would be taken until the EU membership issue was finally settled.

A detailed account of the implementation of the reform is largely beyond the remit of this chapter. Suffice to say that two aspects are relevant in relation to Sweden's EU accession. First, that internal market regulations (as well as the previous milk quota system) were removed or simplified in accordance with the original scheme of reform. Some arable land (about 380,000 hectares) was removed from agricultural production or 'restructured'. However, only 80,000 hectares were estimated to have been transferred permanently to different uses. Indeed, the eligibility of such 'restructured' land for acreage payments (following the 1992 CAP reform) later became an issue which featured in the accession negotiations.

Second, the fact that the Swedish government applied for EU membership so soon after the reform had been decided raised the question about whether the possibility of joining the EU in the near future was considered by the agricultural policy reformers. It is obvious from the design of the reform, not least from the fact that almost everything had to be reversed, that this was not the case. Moreover, the Centre Party and the LRF, which had only accepted the 1990 reforms reluctantly in the first place, conceivably could have used a reference to future EU membership as a way of blocking, or at least delaying, the domestic reform programme.

The 1990 reforms resulted in two major implications as regards Sweden's EU accession and future full membership. First, a large number of practical complications were created, since regulations and institutions that had been removed by the 1990 reform would have to be reintroduced to meet CAP obligations. When agricultural policy reform is considered in the light of the first research theme – the 'fit' of Swedish institutions into the process of European integration (see Chapter 1) – it is correct to say that the 1990 reform resulted in a decline in the degree of 'Europeanization' of Swedish institutions, and thereby, implied a greater need for adjustment after EU accession. The second implication was that Sweden joined the EU with a strong commitment to a liberal agricultural policy and an ambition to reform the CAP.

The impact of EU accession – a proper point of reference

The fact that Swedish agricultural policy was reformed shortly before the EU membership application creates some ambiguity as to a proper point of reference for any evaluation of the impact of full membership on Swedish agriculture. Should the comparisons be made largely from a historical perspective and with the situation before EU accession or rather with a hypothetical post-reform scenario? Yet, this issue is not a trivial one since the expected, but never fully realized, consequences of the 1990 reform were, by no means, insignificant. Swedish agriculture, which was producing considerable surpluses of some commodities, was intended to adjust in the face of domestic market pressures. According to estimates by Jonasson (1993), grain prices were expected to fall by 20 per cent, beef prices by 9 per cent, the price of pork by 5 per cent and the price of milk products by 3 per cent. The 1990 reform was, moreover, expected to cause a substantial reduction in producer surplus and to push land values close to zero (with the exception of the fertile plains of southern Sweden).

It could be argued that the latter alternative is the proper one. It could hardly be possible for Sweden as a non-EU member to go back to the pre-reform situation especially since several changes have been implemented already. Moreover, no official decision to abandon the 1990 reform was taken. A study commissioned by the EU Consequences Committee (Rabinowicz 1993), of the expected implications of full EU membership on Swedish farming, was based on the assumption that the 1990 reform would continue. The study concluded that EU accession would not imply great change to the aggregate value of production. Nevertheless, the composition of production would alter considerably. Livestock sectors would shrink somewhat, although grain production would expand strongly. Farmers, especially landowners, were also expected to gain considerably (compared with the situation if and when the domestic reform had been finalized). A modest gain was expected for consumers.

However, as time passes, it becomes more and more questionable to evaluate the impact of full membership based on a comparison with a domestic reform process that was never fully realized. Such comparisons with a 'semi-factual' (or even fictional) situation (which assumes the full implementation of the 1990 reform and, thus, can never be known in detail), are also increasingly difficult to make. Hence, the analysis incorporated in the remainder of this chapter is based on comparisons with historical data.

The negotiations

Following Putnam (1988), international negotiations are often analysed as 'two-level games'. Rabinowicz (1999) has attempted to use this framework to analyse the unfolding Eastern enlargement of the Union. A somewhat similar concept is a distinction between external and internal negotiations (Raiffa 1982) or 'double-edged diplomacy'. In the aforementioned studies, the European Commission acts as the chief negotiator with the respective applicants (Level I). However, the Commission must also receive negotiating directives from EU member states, which requires internal negotiations (Level II). In terms of the analysis included in this chapter, Level II comprises the negotiations by government with domestic interests. Indeed, such internal negotiations are sometimes more demanding than the external ones.

This was not, however, the case for agriculture because it was a non-socialist government (a four-party coalition elected in 1991) which was responsible for negotiating the terms of Swedish EU entry. From the agricultural perspective, the change of government in Sweden made a lot of difference, since Mr K-E Olsson from the Centre Party became Minister of Agriculture and this gave the LFR direct access to the accession negotiations. There is no doubt that the LFR considered this situation to be very advantageous.[3] Within the government, the issue of whether lower demands for Swedish agriculture could be 'traded' for more substantial requests in other issue areas in the negotiations (such as on the budget rebate and regional policy) was raised. Nevertheless, resistance from the Centre Party, as well as the perceived low chance of eventual success for such a strategy deterred the government from pursuing it.[4] The Level II negotiations did, however, not involve the SAP, which turned out to have significant consequences (see below).

Sweden negotiated with the EU alongside Finland, Norway and Austria and this fact probably influenced the accession negotiations as well as the outcome. The agricultural issues featuring in the negotiating process were quite similar for all applicants and centred on the following points (Schneider 1997):

1. The adjustment of national price levels to EU conditions.
2. National production quotas and the reference levels for direct payments and other subsidies.
3. The leeway allowed by the EU for special policies (dealing with environmental, regional and structural characteristics and, to a large degree, focusing on disadvantaged regions).

Until the 1995 accession round, the issue of bridging any price gaps was handled by introducing 'Accession Compensation Amounts' (ACAs), which were temporary payments added or subtracted at the border in order to avoid any disruption of trade that would follow from applying different prices for the same commodity in various member states. By phasing out these payments over an agreed time span, this mechanism guaranteed a smooth alignment of domestic price levels to the new environment. All the applicants except Sweden requested that ACAs should also be used this time. Nevertheless, the European Commission, having largely completed the Single Market by 1992, insisted that this mechanism was unfeasible in the new 'post-Maastricht' setting and refused to apply ACAs to this forthcoming enlargement. The Commission argued primarily that ACAs would be impractical border controls within the Single Market.

Understandably, the objectives of the Swedish government, with respect to production quotas and reference levels, was to safeguard pre-EU levels of agricultural production at the very least. In the case of production quotas, base acreage and the numbers of animals eligible for headage payments, the demands were in excess of present production and herd sizes (see Table 11.1).

The issue of support to agriculture in northern Sweden was very sensitive since 'Arctic agriculture' was not believed to be able to cope with the challenges arising from EU accession without some kind of a special treatment. It can be observed that the EU was, for the first time, confronted with a situation in which joining the EU would result in *worsening* conditions for agriculture within a new member country (or at least some of its regions). Indeed, 'Arctic agriculture' raised special questions for the EU since agriculture occupies only a tiny share of land in northern Sweden and is important for the preservation of bio-diversity. The region is also sparsely populated, with few employment opportunities in rural areas. Moreover, all Swedish political parties supported the preservation of agriculture in northern Sweden. Hence, in terms of the EU permitting some leeway for special policies, the Swedish government demanded that the 'means must be found to maintain and develop agriculture in Northern Sweden, which implies a maintained support system with adequate co-financing by EU' (Swedish Position Paper, Agriculture, position No. 39).

Sweden placed a strong emphasis on sanitary and phyto-sanitary issues – in particular, salmonella, other diseases in live animals (such as swine pest) and the use of antibiotics as feed additives. The Swedish government demanded guarantees that imported animals are free from salmonella, which could be achieved by testing imported animals. Similar demands were also made in relation to other diseases in live animals. Furthermore, certification by veterinary surgeon was required for the import of feed. The use of antibiotics as a feed additive was forbidden in Sweden, which also demanded EU authorization to continue with its ban. These demands reflected the preferences and fears of the Swedish population (and were duly intended to make Swedish EU membership more palatable for the general public). Yet, they were also in line with the position of the LRF which argued that assurances of high sanitary standards would act both as import protection and facilitate the promotion of Swedish exports.

The outcome of the negotiations: the accession agreement

Sweden (and the other countries) had to adopt the basic mechanisms of the CAP at the time of accession. Border controls were fully abolished in terms of intra-EU trade, which caused the different price levels to adjust immediately and without delay. The agricultural contents of the Accession Treaty can be divided into four parts dealing with: (i) production volumes and

Table 11.1   Production quotas and reference quantities

Quotas and reference quantities		Swedish position	Production or use of resources in 1994
Milk quotas (1000 tons)			**Milk production**
Deliveries	3.3		
Direct sales	3		
Reserves	175	3500	3400
Sugar quotas (1000 tons)			
A Quota	336.4	380.0	372
B Quota	33.6	60.0	
Beef and Sheep reference quantities			
Suckler cows	155,000	165,000	165,000
Male cattle	250,000	300,000	240,000
Ewes	180,000	230,000	187,000
Crop reference areas (1000 hectares)			
Grains	1737	2100	1600

Source: Swedish Board of Agriculture

factors, (ii) support areas and level of support, (iii) environmental policies and (iv) veterinary issues.

With respect to the quota levels, the Swedish government has, hardly surprisingly, received less than they demanded, but the outcome was close to the previous level of production and/or use of resources. Table 11.1 compares the actual quota allocation with the Swedish position and levels of production. It is worth noting that the crop reference area for grains included 'restructured' land and was not based on the lower land use apparent in the post-1990 reform period. Sweden was apparently successful when its demands could be substantiated by relevant figures and data. However, additional Swedish requests, for instance, for the adjustment of acreage payments upwards on the basis of the lower than normal yields experienced during the reference period, were not successful.

The 'Arctic problem' was solved by granting Sweden (and Finland) permission to pay so-called agricultural national support, which was available to those to the north of the 62° parallel and some adjacent areas. The details were not decided at the time of the entry negotiations, but left for the future. This national support is subject to certain restrictions, however, since it is tied to a specific geographical area and/or the number of animals, as well as to fixed production ceilings, which are determined on the basis of earlier production. The support may not, in effect, increase production or its intensity and is differentiated according to particular region. This national support is also paid on top of LFA support and environmental support (see below).

The main problem in the accession negotiations relating to the Less Favoured Areas (LFA) was actually that the existing policy in Sweden was not compatible with directive 75/268/EEC. According to calculations made by SBA (in 1993), only a tiny fraction of arable land would qualify for support if the existing EU rules were applied in Sweden (compared to 55 per cent amongst the incumbent members of the Union). By modifying definitions of eligibility at the EU level, 47 per cent of arable Sweden qualified to receive LFA payments.

Another important factor was the perceived ecological impact of EU accession on Sweden. Under existing EU regulations, every country is allowed to set up an individual agri-environmental programme based on Regulation EEC 2078/92, which guarantees sufficient flexibility to meet domestic requirements. Generous use of agri-environmental support, which is mainly allocated to the LFAs, was an important device aimed at preserving 'Arctic agriculture' in Sweden. According to the Accession Treaty the EU agreed to pay ECU 165 million to Sweden.

Concerning veterinary issues, the negotiations were particularly fraught. The opening bid from the Commission was substantially revised in order to accommodate Swedish demands for controls on the importing of live animals and food of animal origin in order to prevent the spread of salmonella. For other diseases (swine pest and PRRS) a transition period of three years applies. The same is the case for use of antibiotics in feed stuffs. The transition period has now expired but in the meantime the EU decided to ban the usage of some antibiotics as feed additives.

Swedish farmers and the LRF were generally pleased with the negotiated agreement, but this is hardly surprising given the role the LRF played in the accession process. Moreover, the alternative to the accession agreement – the continuation of the domestic reform process – was not very attractive to Swedish farmers. Therefore, Swedish farmers supported full EU membership in sharp contrast to their colleagues in other EFTA applicant countries. Thus, aspects of 'double-edged diplomacy' did work and were apparent between domestic farmers and the Swedish government (which also managed largely to protect the interests of Swedish farmers in the accession negotiations). The success was, however, only temporary as the internal negotiations excluded some key players. The SAP considered, for example, that the deal was 'too good' to farmers or at least was too costly in financial terms. Several leading Social Democrats, most notably Mrs Winberg, Minister of Agriculture after September 1994, declared during the 1994 EU membership campaign that domestic farmers should not count on receiving all the negotiated subsidies because Sweden could not afford them given the need for co-financing and the precarious financial position of the country.

Evaluating the accession negotiations from the point of view of the development of European integration, it could be claimed that the outcome constitutes a big leap towards a re-nationalization of the CAP (Rabinowicz and Bolin 1998). As a result of the EFTA enlargement, the Union now contains countries with permanent and considerably higher levels of support than previous members. This support is, to a large extent, paid from national budgets and involves measures that are specific to the respective countries in question.

Implementing the accession agreement

The change in government and the legacy of severe financial crisis affected the implementation of the accession agreement, especially with respect to measures that required co-financing on the part of the Swedish government. As a result, the funds which were negotiated and accepted by the EU have remained partly unused. Their utilization increased gradually as new environmental programmes were introduced, but even in 1999 only about 85 per cent of the funds were expected to be utilized[5]. This fact resulted in the reduction of funds allocated to Sweden for the period 2000–5 as the Commission argued that the country evidently does not need the money. It could be argued accordingly that the impact of EU accession has not fully materialized as yet.

The Swedish government has chosen ambitious implementation alternatives under the CAP, especially where the Swedish Environmental programme for Agriculture is concerned. Under an EU Regulation (EEC 2078/92), Sweden had 12 various support schemes (1995–99) and, furthermore, several different support regions (see Table 11.6). The overall impression is that the implementation of the CAP is administratively rather costly. According to official figures, major parts of the CAP's implementation accounts for about SEK 600 million per year (figures from the Swedish Board of Agriculture 1998).

The impact of EU membership

Agriculture and primary processing have been most affected by EU accession since those sectors were hitherto the most protected (and excluded from the Swedish–EEC Free Trade Agreement (FTA) and EEA agreement). This section compares the situation before and after EU membership with respect to prices, production, consumption, trade and incomes. It is implicitly assumed that most of the observed differences can be attributed to accession. However, given that Sweden has been an EU member for five years or so, this period may still be too short to evaluate fully the impact of accession, especially since the CAP has been implemented only gradually. Farming is, moreover, a business with long time horizons and, thus, adjustments to and in the agricultural sector may take a considerable time.

The development of prices

For the first time in the EU's history, the EFTA-3 enlargement, including Sweden, followed a 'big bang' approach, removing the impediments to trade from the first day of EU accession. In Finland, prices dropped by almost 40 per cent. In contrast, prices in Sweden declined modestly, as the 1990 agricultural reform produced larger effects on prices than that of EU accession. The development of producer prices is shown in Table 11.2.

Table 11.2 Development of producer prices in Sweden (indices)

1990	1991	1992	1993	1994	1995	1996
100	98.9	96.6	94.3	97.7	96.4	92.3

Source: Livsmedelsekonomiska samarbetsnämnden 1997

When the impact on consumer prices is analysed, it may be interesting to examine retail prices that include and exclude VAT (see Tables 11.3 and 11.4), although for an assessment of the impact of the membership only the latter is relevant. However, the perceptions of consumers about EU membership is more likely to be influenced by the prices they actually pay in the shops. VAT on food was reduced on 1 January 1996 from 21 per cent to 12 per cent.

Table 11.3 Development of consumer prices of food covered by Agricultural Regulations (KPI-J) inclusive of VAT in Sweden (indices)

1990	1991	1992	1993	1994	1995	1996
100	104.1	98.5	97.3	97.7	97.0	90.3

Source: Livsmedelsekonomiska samarbetsnämnden 1997

Table 11.4 Development of consumer prices of food covered by Agricultural Regulations (KPI-J) exclusive of VAT in Sweden (indices)

1990	1991	1992	1993	1994	1995	1996
100	103.4	103.7	99.8	100.2	99.6	101.1

Source: Livsmedelsekonomiska samarbetsnämnden 1997

As in the case of producer prices, the impact of full membership on consumer prices was not only modest, but also smaller than those effects accruing from the changes in domestic policies, agricultural policy reform and the reduction of VAT on food, that have occurred during the 1990s in Sweden. Somewhat bigger changes can be observed if different groups of commodities are examined. Compared to 1994, the prices of bread, flour and pasta declined by 0.2 per cent; the prices of meat and edible fats also declined by 3 per cent and 2.3 per cent respectively in 1995. Milk products rose by 4 per cent and fruit and vegetables by 0.9 per cent. The absence of a significant and positive impact on food prices led to some discontent amongst consumers. In spite of being completely irrelevant,[6] comparisons with the favourable development of consumer prices in Finland were often made in the media, thereby contributing to the population's discontent. Indeed, the lack of a positive impact probably contributed to public's general unhappiness with the EU and/or did not help to improve the image of the Union in the eyes of the average Swede.

Development of production and farm incomes

On aggregate, the production decisions of Swedish farmers have not been influenced significantly by EU accession. First, prices have not changed markedly. Second, agricultural production is governed by a number of production control parameters (such as quotas, base acreage and the number of animals eligible for support) and Sweden managed to achieve an equivalent level for those parameters that were close to Sweden's historical patterns of agricultural production and land usage (see Table 11.1). Moreover, it should be kept in mind that Swedish agricultural production was affected during the first years of accession by the turmoil created by the reintroduction of some regulations, which had been removed previously. Production trends are illustrated in Table 11.5.

The favourable development of aggregate farm income between 1990 and 1991 – the year the implementation of the reform started – depended upon temporary adjustment support paid to farmers at the beginning of the 1990 reform period.

Taking into account the importance of the issue of 'Arctic agriculture' in the negotiations, it may be interesting to analyse the development of farm incomes at the regional level. According to calculations made by the SBA (1998), the profitability of Swedish agriculture (calculated as Gross Value Added including direct payments (GVA) per Annual Work Unit (AWU), which is the most commonly used indicator assessing farm incomes in the EU), increased considerably (see Table 11.6 in accordance with the official delimitation of support regions). Region 1 is the northernmost and most

Table 11.5 Development of production values 1990–97 in fixed prices (1991) and corrected for variation in weather, total costs, subsidies and net farm income at the sector level (indices)

	1990	*1991*	*1992*	*1993*	*1994*	*1995*	*1996*	*1997*
Crops	100	88	84	85	83	81	81	84
Livestock	100	92	94	101	103	103	104	104
Subsidies*	100	122	74	66	56	103	111	115
Total costs	100	85	87	90	93	88	89	90
Net income	100	104	89	92	89	102	105	110

*Subsidies refer to direct payments and include temporary compensations

Source: Own calculations based on Livsmedelsekonomiska samarbetsnämnden 1997

Table 11.6 GVA per AWU (including Regional Support) in different support areas in 1994 and 1995 (millions of SEK, rounded values)

	1994	*1995*	*% change*
Region 1	161,700	160,660	−0.7
Region 2a	200,700	207,300	3.3
Region 2b	187,300	198,100	5.7
Region 3	156,400	181,600	16.1
Region 4	161,200	187,900	16.6
Region 5a	142,900	172,400	20.6
Region 5b	174,400	199,100	14.1
Region 5c	180,500	209,300	15.9
Normal areas	273,500	292,100	6.8
Regions covered only by environmental support	252,700	278,900	9.9
Whole country	220,700	241,600	9.5

Source: SBA, *Rapport* 1998:2

highly supported, followed by regions 2a–b. The largest increase in incomes can be observed in the new Less Favoured Areas (regions 4 and 5a–c), which were not supported previously. For agriculture in the north, the change was negligible.

A good indication of the level of profitability in agricultural production is the development of land prices and rent levels for agricultural land. Yearly investigations in land rent prices indicate an upward trend for the later years. Using 1994 as the reference year (index = 100), the average land rent prices have index values of 102, 107 and 112 for the years 1995, 1996 and 1997 respectively (*Yearbook of Agricultural Statistics* 1998). This trend is similar for the whole of Sweden, except for the northern parts.

Consumption

In Sweden, changes in consumption were relatively small; even for beef where prices dropped most. The biggest change can be observed for poultry, where Swedish markets are still protected by veterinary rules and, accordingly, not much was affected by EU accession.

The food industry

Prior reform of Swedish agricultural policy, which may have, on the one hand, complicated the incorporation of Sweden's agriculture into the Union's CAP, was, nonetheless, beneficial for the processing industry since the deregulation of the sector before EU accession largely prepared the industry for the more competitive situation once Sweden became a full EU member. In contrast to farmers, the industry could start preparing in advance, although these circumstances make it more difficult to analyse the impact of EU accession. The analysis below focuses on the changes that can be attributed to joining the EU regardless of when they actually occurred.

According to economic theory, high protection rates and small domestic markets experiencing low competitive pressures are likely to result in limited efficiency. Primary processing could be expected to exhibit both technical inefficiency (not producing on the production frontier) and poor economies of scale. In a protected industry, which is also dominated by producer cooperatives, and includes not only opposition from hired labour but also from the owners themselves, structural change is often inhibited. Small-scale producers, cum owners, tended especially to oppose such change, preferring to maintain smaller plants in close proximity to their farms rather than have larger plants at a longer distance (Kola *et al.* 1999). Empirical analyses of the competitiveness of Swedish food processing industry that were made prior to EU accession confirm this theoretical prediction (see Bolin and Swedenborg 1992 for a summary). In particular, the meat processing industry was identified as facing great difficulties (Hanf and Böckenhoff 1993).

Sweden's processing industries especially feared competition from Denmark. Geographic and cultural proximity was expected to make expansion in the Nordic market easy for Danish firms. Swedish insistence on not using ACAs was, to some extent, a product of self-confidence but also a response to pressures from domestic processing industries who hoped to expand into Finnish (and Norwegian) markets if Danish competition became too severe.

Direct investment in EU countries and other applicant countries also constituted an important form of adjustment. Swedish Cerealia, for instance, invested in Denmark (Kola *et al.* 1999). Swedish firms have also formed alliances with other companies in the EU. For example, Arla, the largest milk cooperative in Sweden, formed an alliance with French Sodiaal. The major reaction on the part of Swedish companies to the increased competition was, otherwise, an intensification of merger activities involving plant closures and employment reductions. Concentrating on the meat processing industry, or rather on the cooperative part of the industry (as private meat processors have been coping reasonable well with the challenges arising from the Single Market), dramatic changes can be observed. On 1 January 1999, all meat processing cooperatives (except a small cooperative in Kalmar) merged into one, called 'Swedish Meat'. Such a large merger would never taken place unless no other options were available. Since the new cooperative faces overcapacity, a reduction in the number of plants and employment seems inevitable and was specifically mentioned in the relevant documentation inviting members to join the new organization. The number of employees in the merging cooperatives has already been reduced by 39 per cent (between 1991 and 97) and the number of slaughterhouses dropped by 26 per cent (between 1991 and 95).

Table 11.7   Export of food products from Sweden, according to country (millions of SEK, rounded values)

	1990	1991	1992	1993	1994	1995	1996
EU15	3475	3434	3217	3626	4454	8230	8678
CEEC	149	177	413	458	955	746	858
OECD	2355	2127	2081	2696	3603	3588	3785
Other	1359	1246	752	893	1410	977	1190
Total	7339	6984	6464	7673	10,422	13,541	14,511

Source: Livsmedelsekonomiska samarbetsnämnden 1997

Table 11.8   Import of food products to Sweden, according to country (millions of SEK, rounded values)

	1990	1991	1992	1993	1994	1995	1996
EU15	10,286	11,287	11,941	14,472	16,932	20,018	21,879
CEEC	679	738	758	791	1049	652	732
OECD	4434	4623	4934	5561	6651	5195	5116
Other	4400	4298	3880	4611	6555	4946	4541
Total	19,799	20,946	21,513	25,435	31,187	30,811	32,267

Source: Livsmedelsekonomiska samarbetsnämnden 1997

The impact on trade

A custom union affects international trade in two ways. On one hand, the lowering of trade barriers amongst participating members leads to trade creation. The raising of a common trade barrier against non-members can, on the other hand, divert trade, replacing previous partners by members of the customs union. Both phenomena can be observed in the case of Swedish agricultural trade.

Looking at Swedish exports, it can be observed that total exports rose as a result of EU membership (see Table 11.7). The increased exports have mainly been directed to other member countries. In the case of imports, trade seems to be diverted from all other groups of countries to imports from the EU (see Table 11.8).

The Swedish position *vis-à-vis* the CAP after EU accession

Sweden joined the Union with a very negative perception of the CAP. During the accession campaign preceding the 1994 referendum, opponents of Swedish EU membership pointed to the CAP as an example of a wasteful policy that could be avoided by staying outside the Union. Proponents of full membership argued that Sweden should join in spite of the CAP. These negative perceptions of the CAP amongst both EU opponents and proponents and a commitment to further reform of the CAP were reconfirmed by the work of a public committee examining the CAP (KomiCAP). The final report of the committee (SOU (1997d): 1997: 102) stated that the CAP needs to be reformed in a more marked-oriented direction, which places greater emphasis on the natural environment, animal welfare and rural development issues simultaneously. The Swedish Riksdag took a decision (Swedish Government (1997/98) Prop. 97/98: 142) in accordance with those recommendations.

Indeed, the most visible manifestation of this critical attitude was Swedish participation in the 'London club' – a group of four countries committed to a more radical reform of the milk regime than the Agenda 2000 proposal formulated by the Commission envisaged. The countries in question (Sweden, the UK, Denmark and Italy) demanded a reduction of intervention prices by 30 per cent (compared to the 15 per cent advocated in the Agenda 2000 proposals) and an increase of milk quotas by four per cent. Since Sweden was not utilizing its milk quota fully, the main incentive for participating in this initiative was not a desire to increase milk production (as seems to be the case for the other participants in the 'club'), but rather a rejection of the milk quota system as such. Moreover, Sweden's previous system had been abolished as early as 1989.

With respect to Agenda 2000, the Swedish government considers that the CAP reforms that have been agreed so far are insufficient to cope with the challenges of further EU enlargement and the next WTO round. In terms of other issues, such as adherence to budgetary discipline and the reform of the EU sugar regime, Sweden has placed the principle of securing broader CAP reform before the politics of narrow national interest. Such an unusual attitude often creates confusion both in the Commission and in other member states which are more familiar with the practice of EU members pushing their own national interests as the primary objective.

The commitment to CAP reform has been criticized repeatedly by the LRF who would prefer the government to look after the interests of Swedish farmers instead. Farmers' newspapers have been echoing this criticism. Under the heading 'Agriculture will pay a high price for the mistakes of the government', ATL, a professional newspaper dedicated to farming, wrote in an editorial comment on the Agenda 2000 agreement that: '... Swedish demands concentrated on deregulation and lower costs. The interest of Swedish agriculture has been second priority. This is very worrisome'. (ATL, No. 9, March 1999.) The general public has also remained critical of the CAP and public concerns have been fuelled by the fact that Sweden is a considerable net contributor to the EU budget and farming is one of few sectors benefiting from (high) subsidies.

Indeed, one of the themes of this book relates to the degree of Europeanization experienced by Sweden (see Chapter 1). Joining the Union has required institutional adjustments that were essential to the implementation of the CAP in Sweden. It can be argued that this adjustment represents a kind of 'compulsory Europeanization'. In a deeper sense though, the process of Swedish policy formulation on agricultural questions has not altered much. When defining the Swedish position on the future of the CAP, KomiCAP has followed similar procedures (in terms of the organization, composition and topics addressed and analytical approach) as previous parliamentary committees on (domestic) agriculture. KomiCAP identified a preferable long-term development of the CAP from the standpoints of 'equity' and 'efficiency' – rather than concentrating on desirable and achievable changes of the CAP in the shorter perspective – which takes into account the interests of other member states and/or potential strategies to achieve such short-term reforms.

When recent Swedish initiatives towards the CAP are considered, Swedish politicians have been focusing largely on efficiency-improving CAP reforms instead of looking exclusively after the interests of Swedish farmers. If similarity with other member states is taken as a measure of 'Europeanization', Sweden has hardly been 'Europeanized'. Moreover, Sweden has often adopted much more radical positions than those of other member states. In the consensus-oriented culture of EU decision-making, such behaviour is generally not successful. A question needs to be asked about whether this conduct on the part of Sweden can be attributed to the fact that the country can still be considered as a comparatively new EU member (the third research theme identified in Chapter 1). This tendency to adopt more radical positions has declined over time, supporting the view that Swedish behaviour can be, at least partly, explained by Sweden being a new member.

Summary and conclusions

It is not easy to assess the implications of EU accession for Sweden's agricultural and food processing sectors. The fact that the country's agricultural policy was reformed prior to EU accession and that Sweden has continued with its liberal attitude towards agricultural policy reform even when an EU member indicates that Swedish agricultural policy would, most probably, be much more liberal than the CAP is today if policy discretion over this field had remained at the national level. However, it is not possible to construct a reliable and detailed picture of Sweden's agricultural policy with the country as a non-EU member. There is no doubt, however, that Swedish farmers have gained from EU accession and the continuing strong support of the LRF for full EU membership suggests that this remains the case.

When the effects of full membership are evaluated using historical comparisons of level of production and farm incomes, the impact is modest but, using this methodology, farmers also seem to gain. In spite of all the fear at the outset that less favoured areas would not be able to cope with the CAP, no negative effects can be detected. Thus, it could be argued that perhaps the most interesting observation is not what happened, but what has *not* happened. The most probable explanation for this modest impact is that the provisions of the Accession Agreement largely ensured that the level of support remained unchanged. Two major devices were relied upon as part of the process of reaching a lasting compromise with the EU as regards the level of support to 'Arctic agriculture': the generous use of environmental support and the national support.

The debate on agriculture and food in the pre-accession period concentrated on, amongst others, issues relating to 'Arctic agriculture' and farm incomes, rather than on food processing. The impact of the accession seems, however, to be much more dramatic on this latter sector than on primary agricultural production. This is especially the case for the cooperatives in meat processing who had previously enjoyed an easy life in the shelter of domestic regulations.

Turning to one of the other key themes of this book – namely, to what extent Swedish institutions and policies 'fit' into the general process of European integration (see Chapter 1), it can be observed that the 1990 agricultural reform meant that Swedish institutions were less able to 'fit' directly and easily into the EU's common framework governing agricultural policy. Whereas Sweden liberalized, the EU kept on regulating agriculture. This, in turn, ensured that a fast readjustment – a speedy 'Europeanization' – would be essential. Yet, this 'Europeanization' is primarily an administrative process. In a deeper sense, Sweden has not been 'Europeanized' so far.

Notes

1. The PSE is an indicator of the value of the monetary transfers to agriculture resulting from agricultural policies in a given year. Percentage PSE is the total value of transfers as a percentage of total value of production valued at domestic prices.
2. Consumer Delegation ceased to exist in 1990.
3. Cooperation between the Centre Party and other participants in the government coalition was not free from tensions, mainly over environmental issues such as construction of a bridge between Sweden and Denmark which was strongly opposed by the Centre Party. At one point, the vice-chairman of the Party, Mrs Nilsson, suggested that the Party should leave the government coalition rather than compromise on the environment. Her suggestion provoked a strong reaction, almost an outrage, from B. Dockered, the leader of LRF, who argued that such a move would deprive the Party of access to the negotiations.
4. This analysis is based on a discussion with Professor C. B. Hamilton, Under-Secretary of State in the Ministry of Finance for the Liberal Party during the period.
5. It should be remembered that the utilization depends also on the interest of farmers to apply for support schemes.
6. CSE (Consumer Subsidy Equivalent), a measure of taxation of consumers by agricultural policy, calculated by the OECD (1996), amounted in 1994 to 65 per cent for Finland and 41 per cent for Sweden.

PART IV

Social Issues

CHAPTER 12

Swedish Social Policy and the EU Social Dimension

Arthur Gould[1]

Introduction

It is the first three 'points' of the 'Swedish and Membership Diamonds' (see Chapter 1; also Miles 1997a) which seem of most relevance to the analysis of social policy. The welfare state, prior to EU membership, formed part of Sweden's 'Integrative and Consensual Democracy' ('point' one of the original 'Swedish Diamond' – see Miles 1997a). Concern about it – in material collated for this chapter – was often expressed in terms of national sovereignty. It was, and is, a source of national pride – something the Swedes felt they were better at doing than other countries. Most political parties are committed to it. It was a way of ensuring that all Swedish citizens belonged. Everyone contributed, everyone benefited. High benefits and good quality services ensured that Swedes were not at the mercy of the market. People were not commodities – they were de-commodified (Esping-Andersen 1990). The degree to which this picture represented a genuine reality or a mythical golden age is open to debate, but this is how it is remembered.

The welfare state was also part of the 'Swedish Corporate Model' ('point' two of the original 'Swedish Diamond'). Pay negotiations between SAF and LO could influence and be affected by state welfare provision. The national boards for welfare, employment and education were all administered on a tripartite basis. Supporters of the welfare state also claimed that it helped Sweden adapt to the consequences of 'Economic Interdependence' (the 'Swedish Diamond's' third 'point') since individual employees and their families were provided with security and opportunities to help them cope with whatever economic restructuring was deemed necessary for Sweden's economic survival.

For many decades after the Second World War, Swedish governments had sufficient national autonomy to be able to preserve and advance the concept of a 'People's Home' (*Folkhemmet*) to a point where public expenditure reached over 60 per cent of GDP, social expenditure over 30 per cent of GDP and public sector employment constituted one third of the total working population (Gould 1993). The income replacement value of social insurance benefits was 90 per cent, elderly people retired on pensions often equivalent to 60 to 70 per cent of their previous income and the unemployment rate, even in the 1980s, was usually well below four per cent. It is not surprising therefore that, for many Swedes, entry into the EU raised anxieties about the possible threat to the Swedish welfare state. In the run up to the referendum in November 1994, concern was expressed about a number of social policy issues: the possible dilution of Swedish welfare by the process of harmonization and the impact this might have on the status of women, the lack of priority given to unemployment and the liberalizing threat to public health policies on alcohol and illegal drugs.

To discover the extent to which these fears were justified, visits were made in 1998 to interview Swedish Members of the European Parliament in Strasbourg, to interview a range of policy actors in Stockholm and to conduct a literature search in various academic and public agency libraries.[2] Interviewees were asked to comment upon whether they thought that membership of the EU had influenced the major social programmes of the welfare state and whether Sweden did have an impact on EU social policy.

The Swedish welfare state

There is no doubt that social expenditure in Sweden has been reduced in recent years – from a high of almost 39 per cent of GNP in 1993 to 35 per cent in 1996 (Socialdepartementet 1998). Public expenditure has also come down from a peak of 70 per cent of GDP in 1993 to 64 per cent in 1997, with a further predicted fall to 58 per cent by the year 2000 (Ministry of Finance 1997: 13). There have been cuts to benefits and eligibility rules have been tightened. Hospitals have had to declare staff redundancies and some services for the elderly have been privatized. Unemployment has risen from less than two per cent in 1990 to over eight per cent in the middle of the decade with a further 5 per cent on labour market measures, such as job creation and training schemes. Inequalities have widened and poverty has risen. The costs of social assistance to local municipalities has increased at the same time as their income has fallen. The emphasis in the public sector for some years now has been on budgetary discipline and effectiveness. Whatever the domestic pressures, the OECD and EU have, for some years, been encouraging the Swedish government to cut taxes and expenditure even further.

But to what extent these changes are due to EU membership is a matter of conjecture. Most sources – published and personal – recognized that the EU had no mandate to regulate *directly* the nature of member states' systems of state welfare. There had been some changes to social insurance regulations to facilitate the free movement of labour. Swedish workers whose companies transfer them to other parts of the EU continue to enjoy rights to Swedish benefits. Other EU nationals who take up jobs in Sweden under certain circumstances have rights to benefits in Sweden (SoS-rapport

1996: 16; Direktiv 1997: 84). Similarly, negotiations have taken place con-cerning the mutual acceptability of health care qualifications to enable Swedish doctors, nurses, dentists and midwives to work in other EU countries and medical personnel from elsewhere in the EU to work in Sweden with the minimum of administrative fuss. In the case of dentists and midwives, it was found to the surprise of the Swedish authorities that their own training needed to be improved. When it came to minimum standards for health and safety at work, employment rights and most recently the directive on parental leave, it was found in most cases that Swedish provi-sion was already of a higher standard. These adjustments can hardly be said to have a significant impact on the Swedish welfare state. They are more a matter of what one of those interviewed called 'social regulation' than social policy.

There have, however, been a number of debates about the *indirect* impact of full membership upon Swedish welfare. First, there is the issue of whether Swedish welfare has suffered because of the impact of tying the krona to the ERM prior to membership and subsequently of trying to meet the con-vergence criteria of EMU (see Chapter 9). Second, there is a concern that there should be a stronger social dimension to the EU. Third, there is the impact on women to consider. Fourth, there is a claim that mutual influence has occurred through informal meetings and exchanges between member states.

EU economic policy and EMU

Prior to the 1994 referendum, there were those clearly in favour of EU membership, those against and a large body of 'don't knows'. In collecting post-referendum material for this chapter there seemed to be those one could classify as pro- and anti- the EU but also a large group who one can only describe as 'reluctant Europeans'. The last consists of those who have come to accept membership as necessary but still regard the whole enter-prise with caution, apprehension and some reservation. It has to be remembered that in Sweden it is those on the Right who tend to be in favour of the EU. They endorse its pro-market ethos but remain unhappy about its corporatist tendencies. It is those on the Left who tend to be sceptical, expressing concern about national sovereignty, institutions and traditions (see Chapters 5 and 7).

The Moderate Party (Conservatives) and employer organizations obvi-ously felt that being part of the more market-oriented EU would result in a slimmer public sector and a reduced role for state welfare. Amongst some Social Democrats, there were those who claimed that Sweden would have been in a worse position for maintaining its welfare standards had it not gone into the EU (Wetterburg 1995). The EU meant that the Swedish model would survive. Welfare depended upon the ability to afford it. Membership would mean higher economic growth and healthier public finances. The promise of economic growth seemed to be the main attraction of the EU; the threat of competition from East Asia the principal threat (Wetterburg 1995). Other Social Democrats took the line that the economic policies which the EU promoted made it unlikely that social policy would be unaffected (Johansson 1997). A generous welfare state depended upon the maintenance of full employment, which in turn depended upon a willingness to stimulate the economy even at the risk of increasing inflation – something EU economic policy[3] was, in 1998, unwilling to contemplate.

Although Sweden, like the UK, has decided not to become part of EMU in the first wave, the Social Democratic governments of the 1990s tried to meet the convergence criteria. Under the Centre–Right coalition, the public sector deficit and national debt rose to 14 per cent and 90 per cent of GDP respectively. Through a mixture of measures – cuts in public expenditure, higher taxes and the sale of public assets (*Riksdag och Departement* 1995a) – the public sector deficit was brought down to nil by 1997, well under the three per cent limit set for EMU. The national debt, however, remained at 81 per cent, well above the 60 per cent limit (National Institute for Economic Research November 1997).

These trends were welcomed by the business community. *Industriförbundet* (The Industry Association) felt that EMU would encourage the growth of small and medium-sized companies (still a relatively underdeveloped part of the Swedish economy) sufficiently to solve the problem of mass unemployment (Industriförbundet 1997). A Moderate Party (Conservative) MEP and SAF representatives felt that the convergence criteria had forced Sweden to be more strict about its public finances. It would have to happen anyway because of international pressure but, in their view, EMU had forced the pace. You could only have security if you had a healthy economy.

Anita Gradin, Sweden's European Commissioner and a former government minister, has claimed that the EMU will protect the Swedish welfare system:

> Stability is what EMU is about. Stable prices and sound public finance so that budget policy can concentrate on important questions such as jobs instead of interest payments on the national debt. (Gradin 1997)

Her view was not shared by the Minister for Social Affairs or a senior LO official who at a conference in 1997 expressed serious doubts that the welfare state could be defended were Sweden to join EMU (*Dagens Nyheter* 1997a). Anti-EU MEPs who were interviewed blamed EMU for the cuts in public and social expenditure. Others took a different line and said either that EMU had hastened the need for public sector restraint or that it had helped the government achieve what it needed to do anyway. Most of those interviewed in Stockholm 'blamed' international economic influences generally for the need to cut back rather than EMU in particular.

Other Eurosceptic MEPs – the Social Democrat Sören Wibe, the Environment Party's Per Gahrton (not among those interviewed) and the leader of the Left Party, Gudrun Schyman, have all attacked EMU. Wibe criticized the whole concept of a single currency because the EU lacked appropriate balancing policies to deal with the consequent regional unemployment (Fredén 1996). He clearly favoured a more flexible policy which would stimulate demand. The consequences of inflation rates of 3 to 4 per cent 'ought not to be a problem', he claimed (Schuck 1997). Gahrton insisted that when Sweden decided to apply to join the EU in 1990 unemployment stood at 2 per cent. As a result of tying the krona to the ECU, unemployment rose drastically. 'We managed to tear down in less than ten years a welfare state that took several generations to build up,' he said in a vitriolic attack on the EU for being undemocratic and the European Central Bank for its lack of accountability (Gahrton 1997: 70). Schyman clearly saw EMU as responsible for the cuts in the public sector which meant, 'In practice, an adaptation to the lower levels of public services, women's opportunities for paid employment and the present system of social security which exists in other EU countries' (Schyman 1995).

A less extreme view was expressed by LO's chief economist, who, while recognizing that EMU took too little account of the effects on employment, felt that LO and socialists generally should seek to make the EU 'a project of the Left' (Edin 1995). A single currency was desirable but only if a balance between economic and employment objectives could be sustained. Like his colleague Gudmund Larsson, he shared the optimistic aim of a 'Red Europe'. Larsson took the view that Europe was the cradle of socialism and the welfare state and that the EU project needed to be rescued from the Right (Randqvist 1995).

There was little mention of the welfare state in the Commission of Enquiry – the Calmfors Report (SOU 1996b – 1996: 158) – into the 'pros' and 'cons' of EMU but amongst the responses to it there were a number of concerns expressed about employment and welfare (Government Report 1997b – Ds 1997: 22). The Labour Market Board was not convinced that unemployment would not increase in the long term. The Association of County Councils feared for public sector jobs while the Association of Municipalities was more worried about local autonomy as national finance policy pursued more stringent goals. The Health and Social Affairs Board clearly felt that the social costs had already been too high and pleaded for more research before an irrevocable decision was made.

Amongst the trade union federations, SACO felt that Sweden would be more vulnerable outside EMU than within. LO was, like the government, unwilling to enter in the first round, preferring what it called the core countries to initiate the experiment. It was, however, concerned that the degree of labour mobility required to avoid more unemployment would be unattainable. It was TCO – the majority of whose members are women – which was most hostile to EMU. It was concerned about being trapped within a system overly concerned with inflation, and more likely to lead to social inequality and lower social expenditure. It recognized the possible advantages of higher growth and lower interest rates but feared the likely growth in unemployment. Amongst those organizations concerned about the social impact of EMU, the fear for the loss of national autonomy was strongly linked with a lack of national control over measures to tackle unemployment and the level of public expenditure. This view was neatly encapsulated in an interview with Sten Johansson (former Director of SCB – Central Bureau of Statistics – and now of FIEF – the Trade Union Research Institute) when he said that EU economic policy:

> 'was not attuned to the different circumstances of various countries. They're all doing the same thing and getting unemployment as a result. Swedish social policy was designed for full employment. When you have mass unemployment, you have to make room for the increased costs, by making public expenditure cuts.'

For analytical and political reasons some respondents sought to play down the EU's direct responsibility for the erosion of the Swedish welfare state. They either claimed that the government could have acted to preserve it (the autonomy argument) or that it was the wider international environment which was to blame (the dependence argument). Semantics aside, it is difficult to resist the compelling role played by the convergence criteria. The institutional characteristics of the Swedish welfare system may persist but its scale is likely to converge with that of its EU partners.

The EU social dimension

One criticism of the EU in general and of the EMU project in particular was the inadequacy of the social dimension. It was said that there was too great a concern with flexibility, competition and efficiency and not enough with the social consequences of a pro-market philosophy. However, there were clearly difficulties in getting member states (including Sweden) to agree upon what kind of social provision they wanted. An article in *Dagens Nyheter* put it nicely when it said that there was an acceptance of the 'subsidiarity principle' which meant a large degree of autonomy for member states when it came to social policy (*Dagens Nyheter* 1993). This, in turn, implied that EU social policy should only guarantee a minimum level of provision. But this still meant that countries with a high level of social provision perceived other lower spending ones as being guilty of social dumping. This was a charge levelled at the UK by Sture Nordh, the former leader of SKTF – the union for public sector 'white-collar' workers – for its initial refusal to accept the Social Chapter (Lapins 1995). Ideally, many Swedes would like to see other EU countries come up to Nordic standards. Safety at work, for example, is still an area where Sweden excels. Parental leave might exist in other countries but not to the extent that it does in Sweden. In the absence of such a movement, both the social dumping implied by subsidiarity and the harmonization implied by EMU remain a threat to high welfare-spending countries.

The view of *Svenska Dagbladet*'s EU correspondent was that social policy harmonization was proceeding slowly but incrementally and only in certain limited areas. She mentioned the failure of the French to get social policy on the agenda in 1995 and cited the varied and complex welfare systems as a contributory cause for the lack of progress. She thought that what social policy measures were agreed often came about because of a concern with related issues such as citizenship and rights, the implications of which were not initially thought through. Social policy crept in 'not from social policy causes or social policy reasoning' (Nilsson 1995a). A year later she argued that the Italians had been more successful but only in relation to the prevention of 'benefit tourism'. 'Further than this, in regard to the harmonization of social policy, no EU country is prepared to go' (Nilsson 1996).

The impact on women

It is generally accepted that women in particular have benefited from the expansion of the Swedish welfare state. It provided them with jobs in the public sector (Sweden is one of the most segregated labour markets amongst industrialized countries), a related access to social insurance benefits, rights to parental leave and extensive child care provision. It is not surprising then that in the 1994 referendum when the population as a whole voted 52 per cent to 47 per cent in favour of membership, women voted against in the same proportions – the younger the woman the more likely she was to vote 'no' (*Riksdag och Departement* 1994). Since membership, the relative position of women and men has widened. Of women, 57 per cent were against EU membership in May 1996 compared with only 48 per cent of men (Olsson 1997). When the government sought public responses to the EU in 1996, it was mostly women who replied, and then negatively (*Dagens Nyheter* 1996).

The Commission of Enquiry which examined the implications of membership for welfare and for women was criticized by two of its female members for underestimating the impact on social expenditure and on jobs for women. They said that women in Catholic countries were still expected to bear the unpaid burden of caring for children and the elderly; women were 'pressed out to the margins of the labour market' (SOU 1993b – 1993: 117: p. 239). These views continue to be expressed. In a socialist journal it was said that the EU only considered gender equality in relation to jobs and education, not in relation to the home and family relationships (*Folket i Bild* 1996). Women were not credited in social insurance terms for their work as carers. The leader of the Left Party wrote that the strength of women's position in Sweden was dependent upon full employment and a developed public sector – 'Poverty in EU countries' she claimed, 'hits women the most' (Schymann 1995). Women were more likely to be directed to part-time work with little social protection. 'Women in Sweden are also losers and the situation will be worse with the EMU convergence programme.'

One of the interviewees, a female academic, argued that women, particularly working-class women, were losing out because of the more market-oriented approach to welfare. In her view, only a state run welfare system committed to equality could ensure good quality schools and care for all. Highly educated women could thrive in the private sector, but their working-class counterparts needed good nurseries for their children, not unregulated child-minding. Moreover, women who worked for privately owned care companies were being offered inferior hours and pay compared with what they had enjoyed when employed by local authorities. While this situation, in her view, was more to do with internationalization than the EU, the Union was clearly part of the whole process.

Mutual influences

The only other way in which interviewees felt that Swedish welfare had been influenced through membership of the EU was through mutual interaction and the exchange of ideas. At times it was difficult to tell whether such influences had much substance. When specific examples were mentioned Swedish influences tended to be positive and EU influences negative or vague. For example, it would be said that the Spanish or the Portuguese had shown considerable interest in the Swedish system of elderly care or that Sweden led the world in clean food production and was influencing other countries. What Sweden had to learn from other countries was how to cut public finances, how to manage tenders for care contracts, how to deal with the unfamiliar problem of poverty. Only the Moderate Party (Conservative) MEP and the representatives of the employers saw privatization and competition in a positive light. Others regarded them as necessary evils to which Sweden had little choice but to adapt.

EU social policy

The Amsterdam Treaty

EU social policy still seems to consist of little more than attempts to promote the free movement of labour through the setting of minimum standards in matters of health and safety at work, training opportunities for the unemployed, social security for migrant workers and gender equality. Even the 1994 White Paper does little to move towards a genuine social concern for citizens as a whole or the marginalized and excluded (European Commission 1994). In the view of Georg Vobruba, 'social policy projects are pared away to almost nothing in the complex negotiation processes at European level' (Vobruba 1995). Although there are a number of directives in the field of employment, the general picture that emerges both from the literature and the interviews is that by and large, Swedish provisions were already superior prior to membership. There were occasional exceptions, such as the directive on working time and/or the protection of Swedish workers when their companies were taken over by another. Once it had been accepted by the EU that collective agreements between the labour market partners (unions and employers) in the field of employment rights had a similar binding status in Sweden as legislation had in other countries, there was little legislative change necessary.

The Swedes seemed well organized to take advantage of the different programmes under the Social Fund. The EU programme office provided considerable help and support for applicants to the 'Objective 3' programme for the long-term unemployed, young people, women and people with disabilities. The literature provided by the office seems to contain many examples of groups who have benefited. A survey of Swedish small and medium-sized companies found that 6000 jobs had been created by the Mål 4 programme. In British terms, the equivalent would be about 40,000 jobs (TEMO 1997). Not a large amount perhaps but important in a country whose economy has hitherto been dominated by large companies. One interviewee pointed out, however, that the resources provided by the Social Fund were dwarfed by those devoted to labour market schemes by the Swedish government itself.

So far we have been discussing the impact on Swedish social policy of EU membership, but Swedish politicians had their own priorities when the country became part of the EU. The Social Democrats intended, for example, to encourage other member states to adopt a more proactive line on unemployment, other employment issues and gender equality (*Riksdag och Departement* 1995b; Regeringens skrivelse 1996/97: 80). The meeting of Ministers in June 1997 was an initial success but disappointingly vague for Göran Persson. The Swedes were not keen on proposals concerning workforce flexibility and the harmonization of labour market policy. In contrast, the *Dagens Nyheter* correspondent thought that the new British Prime Minister sounded like a management consultant in his advocacy of workforce flexibility (*Dagens Nyheter* 1997b).

The subsequent meeting at Amsterdam concluded with an agreement on an \$18 billion package to create 12 million new jobs (*Dagens Nyheter* 1997c). The Treaty itself included a chapter on employment in which the EU laid down objectives of promoting: a high level of employment and social protection, a coordinated strategy for employment, a skilled, trained and adaptable workforce, and labour markets responsive to economic change with the added requirement that the European Council would consider a joint annual report on progress from member states (Duff 1997: 59–60). In a commentary on the Treaty, Duff claimed that the origin of the chapter lay with a Swedish proposal in 1995. However, he also claimed that the commitment to 'adaptable' workforces and 'responsive' labour markets represented a 'substantial drift to liberal opinion' (ibid.: 65).

While there was considerable agreement that the combined influence of the Swedish government and Allan Larsson (a former Swedish Finance Minister and Director-General of the Labour Market Board) within DGV had been considerable, there were disagreements about the interpretation of the significance of the Treaty – even within the Swedish cabinet. The Finance Minister seemed to think that concrete goals had been set for reducing unemployment whereas the Minister for Employment thought that the figures quoted had merely been illustrative (*Dagens Nyheter* 1997d). Amongst those interviewed there were divided views. The MEPs from the Centre Party and Environmental Party thought Amsterdam marked an important Swedish achievement but Social Democrat and Left Party MEPs were dubious about whether the final outcome would be worthwhile. A Moderate Party (Conservative) MEP accepted that the Swedish active labour market policy had been influential but its reputation was undeserved. She wanted to see less state intervention in employment in both Sweden and the EU. In his book, attacking the federalist tendencies of the EU, the Environmental Party MEP, Per Gahrton, pointed out that whereas the Treaty *required* a degree of budgetary discipline which was to be enforced by sanctions, the employment chapter consisted only of non-binding resolutions (Gahrton 1997: 80–1).

Civil servants and administrators in Stockholm thought Amsterdam was significant. One interviewee even thought that the EU might be moving in a Swedish direction. Spokespersons for the employers federation (SAF) agreed with the Conservative (Moderate Party) view cited above and felt that labour market measures by themselves could achieve nothing without a commitment to lower taxation and employers' social security contributions. An academic thought the significance of Amsterdam was demonstrated by Germany's Chancellor Kohl who after the agreement was said to have laughed at it. Others felt that in the absence of a commitment to stimulate demand labour market measures would achieve very little. In its remiss response to the Amsterdam Treaty, even the Labour Market Board felt that the employment proposals were weak (*Dagens Nyheter* 1998).

A more worrying aspect of the Amsterdam agreement was the inclusion of a requirement that member states reduce their levels of taxation and employer contributions as a way of creating more jobs. Persson's response at the Luxembourg meeting to approve the proposals was to say that he did not accept that reducing taxes had any 'particularly dynamic effect on the labour market' (*Dagens Nyheter* 1997e). Social Democrats had been aware of pressure to harmonize taxes for some time and earlier in 1997 EU Finance Ministers had urged Sweden to reduce taxes and cut public expenditure. The tax minister had made it clear that the Swedish desire for a 'strong welfare society' demanded a higher level of taxation than in other countries.

> All are included in our system. Everyone pays for welfare and everyone benefits from it. . . . If we were to abolish property taxes we would break the country. (*Dagens Nyheter* 1997f: 3)

Were the EU to make strong moves towards the harmonization of taxation, he implied, the impact on Swedish welfare would be considerable.[4]

The EU and gender equality

The possible impact on women of EU membership has already been considered but gender equality is another of those areas where Sweden would like the EU to make greater progress. The Swedes see themselves as the most gender equal country in the world with, for instance, the 1994–98 cabinet comprising 50 per cent women and a parliament of 40 per cent. Given the electoral importance of women and their hostility to the EU, it has been important for government to show that it is concerned about the relative lack of gender equality in the rest of Europe. In neither the European Parliament nor the decision-making bodies of the EU was it thought that women were well represented.

In a number of reports on the EU the government expressed its intention to press for a gender perspective in all areas of EU activity, for more equal representation for women in EU decision-making, for positive discrimination where women are underrepresented in a particular form of employment and to make the burden of proof in cases of sex discrimination less stringent (Statsrådsberedningens skiftserie 1995; Regeringens skrivelse 1996/97: 80; 1997/98: 80).

Hobson compared equal opportunity policies in Sweden and the EU and saw deficiencies in both. However, she concluded that under much EU legislation there lay male breadwinner assumptions. Gender issues within the EU were discussed only in relation to the labour market and employment. Although Sweden was known for its 'soft' law on sex discrimination, by placing gender equality within the framework of family policy Sweden had achieved a greater degree of integration of women into the labour force and given women a greater status than elsewhere in the EU (Hobson 1997).

Alcohol and drug policies

Sweden has long had a strong temperance tradition which expresses itself today in what are called *restrictive* policies. In relation to alcohol this meant keeping prices high and limiting availability. In terms of illegal drugs, the aim is to achieve a *drug-free society* (Gould 1994). Both are seen primarily as public health issues. There was a fear that entry into the more liberal EU would result in alcohol and drugs flooding into the country. There is a certain amount of evidence for both.

The travel allowances for alcohol have had to rise and it was generally felt that by the year 2003 they might have to rise still further. Moreover, Sweden's policy of high prices was under threat from increases in illegal smuggling. Even more directly, the EU demanded the abolition of four of the state's five monopolies leaving only the state-run liquor store company – *Systembolaget* – to continue a threatened existence (Ugland 1997).[5] Eurosceptics felt this abandonment of an important aspect of public health to be a betrayal of government promises made prior to entry (Surell 1997). But as on many other issues concerning the EU both the Moderates (Conservatives) and SAF felt that it was time for liberalization for economic and social reasons.[6]

Sweden then has almost given up the right to maintain its own public health policy on alcohol but in the area of illegal drugs there is a remarkable national consensus. Neither on the Right nor the Left were the remotest of liberalizing tendencies evident. Other countries in Europe, such as the Netherlands, with its coffee shops, and Britain, with its harm reduction programmes, were seen as having capitulated to the drug problem. However, while some felt the loss of border controls were catastrophic, others argued that alternative ways had been found to reduce illegal imports.

Within the EU, the Swedes have tried to promote their *restrictive line* (Nilsson 1995b). The resignation of Emma Bonino has been called for because of her views on legalization (Cederschiöld 1996). Within the European Parliament, a great deal of effort went into opposing the D'Ancona report.[7] The report has, amongst other things, called for a harmonization of member states' drug policies around the principles of harm reduction and the decriminalization of drug *use* (European Parliament 1997). Most of the wrecking amendments were tabled by Swedish MEPs (European Parliament 1998a). The final version of the report shows that harm reduction is hardly mentioned, decriminalization has been removed and the aim of a drug-free society inserted (European Parliament 1998b).[8] Clearly this was not achieved by Swedes alone, but their evangelical consensus was very influential.

Conclusion

Support for the welfare state is no longer a source of national consensus to the extent that it was. The Moderates (Conservatives) embraced the EU partly in the hope that it would weaken the extent and strength of the public sector. They would like to see a process of harmonization precisely because it would entail lower taxes and employer contributions. It is the latter on which they tend to focus rather than directly argue against social provision which still attracts significant public support. However, the other bourgeois parties – and possible coalition partners in any future government – are by no means as hostile to the welfare state. A 'Fragmenting of Democracy' (consistent with 'point' one of the Miles 'Membership Diamond') has occurred but not enough to create a strong anti-welfare consensus (see Chapter 1). Public hostility to the EU is likely to be bound up with fears about the perceived threat to the 'People's Home'. The erosion of the

Swedish welfare may not be entirely due to the EU, but it has played its part in the international neo-liberal economic hegemony.

'Declining Corporatism' (the 'Membership Diamond's' second 'point') is certainly evidenced by the reluctance of SAF to continue with tripartite arrangements. It too has supported the emerging European consensus that high labour costs weaken competitiveness. But the bond between LO and the Social Democratic government, though strained, remains strong. Both fear the possible adverse consequences for welfare and employment were Sweden to join the EMU. Both are happy to leave the decision to join to a later date. Swedish corporatism may even be strengthened by its EU equivalent if, as the Green Paper suggests, employers and employees are an important part of the democratic process particularly in relation to EU social policy (European Commission 1993; Vobruba 1995: 311).

There is no doubt, however, that there have been 'New Challenges of Economic Interdependence' as identified by Miles as part of the third 'point' of his 'Membership Diamond'. While Eurosceptics 'blame' the EMU convergence criteria for what has happened to Swedish welfare, others accept that the 'realities' of international trade and competition leave Sweden little alternative but to change. Neither large annual deficits, a growing national debt nor the use of devaluation are seen as attractive devices for preserving the welfare state and the public sector. It is said that the Swedish model cannot survive alone. 'Reluctant Europeans' refuse to surrender, however. They still see merit in the Swedish way of doing things and would like other European countries to adopt Swedish practices – such as the Active Labour Market Policy – rather than Sweden adopt a minimal approach to welfare. They would also prefer to raise minimum standards within the EU rather than accept their dilution as a consequence of EU harmonization. A crucial element in the whole EU debate is gender. Swedish women perceive themselves as beneficiaries of the public sector and the welfare state and have no desire to find themselves reduced to the inferior status of their European counterparts.

The economic imperative has also weakened Sweden's restrictive policy on alcohol. While many Swedes might be pleased to see a liberalizing of the country's approach to alcohol, there remains a fear of the possible public health consequences. But there would seem to be little likelihood of an acceptance of a more liberal approach to drug policy. If other member states attempt any such harmonization they will meet a strong and united opposition. The slogan of a *drug-free society* has come to represent what is different about Swedish culture. And if – as seems likely in a society plagued with high unemployment – substance misuse problems grow, it will strengthen the already strong anti-EU sentiments which the Swedish people express.

Many Swedes accepted the EU for material reasons, hoping that the Union would provide them with the economic growth which would enable them to maintain their welfare state and own 'unique' way of life. It is this which makes them – like the British – reluctant Europeans. It is also this aspect which makes it difficult, if not impossible, for the Swedish government to take the European project forward in a positive way.

Notes

1. The author wishes to thank the Nuffield Foundation for funding his research visits to Strasbourg and Stockholm. Without its support the kind of work I do would have been impossible. I am also grateful for the many Swedes who agreed to be interviewed and for the insights and information they gave me.
2. While those selected for interview on this occasion could not be said to be representative of the wider policy community in any statistical sense, they did come from a variety of private and public organizations and can be said to illustrate a range of political perspectives:
    (a) Members of the European Parliament interviewed in Strasbourg:
       Two representatives from the Social Democratic Party and one each from the Conservative, Centre, Environment and Liberal parties;
    (b) Policy actors interviewed in Stockholm:
       Drawn from the Swedish National Union of Local Government Officers; Trade Union Institute for Economic Research; Institute for Social Research, Stockholm University; EU correspondent for a national newspaper; Parliamentary Committee on EU affairs (EU nämnd); Swedish Employers' Federation; Ministry for Health and Social Affairs and the Ministry for Employment; EU Programme Office; National Administrative Board for Health and Social Affairs; Central Council for Information on Alcohol and other Drugs; National Public Health Institute.
3. While there is no single 'EU economic policy' as such, the pursuit of a single market and economic and monetary union and the need for coordination of national economic policies has led to a fairly coherent economic strategy. Certainly, those interviewed perceived the EU as having a set of economic priorities which they either endorsed or rejected.
4. In 1996, taxes and contributions as a percentage of GDP came to 54.5 per cent (*Eurostat Yearbook* 1998: 235). Denmark's figure was also above 50 per cent but the next nearest countries were Finland with 48.7 per cent and Belgium with 45.9 per cent. Harmonization would clearly mean further substantial cuts to public and social expenditure.
5. Harry Franzén, a grocer in the south of Sweden, appealed to the European Court of Justice against the refusal of the authorities to allow him to sell alcohol in his shop. The Court rejected his appeal in October 1997.
6. Public opinion has also become more liberal in Sweden. The experience of travel in other countries has led to the adoption of more social and more moderate drinking habits.
7. The report took its name from the Chair of the Committee on Civil Liberties and Internal Affairs, Hedy D'Ancona, a Dutch MEP.
8. This was not the end of the story. When the final version went to the vote in October 1998, a majority of MEPs replaced 'the aim of a drug-free society' with 'the goal of treatment should be a drug-free life'.

CHAPTER 13

Sweden: a Mainstream Member State and a Part of Norden[1]

Hans E. Andersson

Introduction

This chapter examines Swedish perspectives in relation to institutional questions affecting the policy areas of asylum, immigration and policing and argues that, in these areas, Sweden does not deserve its general reputation as a troublesome member state. Despite the population's quite negative attitudes towards the European Union, Sweden has, nevertheless, approved of the inclusion of asylum and immigration issues within the EU's supranational arrangements. However, the chapter will also explore, in some depth, Sweden's additional role as a member of Norden – the region consisting of the five Nordic countries (Denmark, Finland, Iceland, Norway and Sweden) and three autonomous territories (the Faeroe Islands, Greenland and Åland). The region's long history of informal cooperation, it is argued, is of importance in shaping Swedish policy positions in the areas of asylum, immigration and policing. As part of this discussion, the chapter will also address aspects of the Miles 'Membership Diamond' and, to a lesser degree, comment upon the four research themes as outlined in Chapter 1.

Collaboration in police and criminal matters

It is well known that the member states have experienced difficulties in advancing cooperation when it comes to the area of policing. However, since the 1970s, limited cooperation between the member states has begun to develop and with the signing of the 1992 Treaty on European Union (TEU) a framework for initiatives in the policing sphere came into being. In this section, Swedish perspectives concerning the Europol Convention and the 1997 Treaty of Amsterdam will be highlighted.

The aim of the European Police Office (Europol) is to improve police cooperation between the member states. Given that the basis for such cooperation is an international convention, it would be logical to assume that Europol cooperation ought to be purely intergovernmental. However, where there are disputes between member states, the vast majority (with the exception of the UK) have declared that they will bring related actions to the European Court of Justice for judgement. The Swedish government could accept rather easily that the Court should have the authority to adjudicate in such disputes.

However, the government has been much less inclined to accept the possibility of allowing the Court to submit preliminary rulings to the national courts. The reason for this was that the issue is seen as a sensitive one and concerns core areas of nation-state competence. The Minister of Justice, Laila Freivalds, argued that it was not a question of great ideological character and that the Swedish government did not want to tie itself to any specific position.[2] At the end of the day, Sweden did accept that the Court should be allowed to submit preliminary rulings. Thus, with this book's first research theme in mind (how Sweden 'fits' into the general process of European integration), one can say that Sweden took a pragmatic stance in this particular instance – and in spite of its objections to the involvement of the supranational European Court of Justice. Swedish pragmatism is also evident in that it has been declared that the government will decide from convention to convention if the Court should have this right.[3]

On 29 October 1997, the Riksdag approved Sweden's participation in Europol by 258 votes for to 38 against (1 abstention and 52 absent). Thus, there was little resistance and, on all the key questions, it was just the Left Party (19) and the Green Party (16) that voted against approving the Europol Convention. Thus, in line with both parties' resistance to Swedish EU membership, they are continuing their opposition. In the case of the Europol Convention, the two parties argued, amongst other things, that the Convention does not guarantee respect for the integrity of citizens and that there is an almost total lack of parliamentarian control on how the Convention is implemented.[4] One should also note that one MP from the Social Democratic Party and two from the Centre Party also did not approve of the Europol Convention. However, the overall impression is that an overwhelming majority supported advancing police cooperation between the member states.

The Riksdag ratified the Europol Convention, but also assigned to the government the task of trying to initiate an overview of the system within the Union with respect to privileges and immunity. What is of particular interest is the key arguments put forward by the Riksdag's Committee on Justice. It argued in its report that an essentially domestic-orientated perspective must be taken when it comes to the Union and this perspective makes the system of immunity and privileges look old-fashioned (1997/98: JuU2). These arguments suggest that Swedish parliamentarians are striving to become accustomed to the fact that the Union is not purely a question of international relations. However, the Persson government shortly thereafter (2 December 1997) asked the Riksdag to approve a protocol on privileges and immunity relating to Europol and its officials, which was accepted by 270 votes for to 35 against (nil abstentions and 44 absent).

On 30 November 1995, the Social Democratic government reported to the Riksdag on its basic position in relation to the 1996–97 IGC (that culminated in the 1997 Treaty of Amsterdam (Skr. 1995/96: 30)). The government concluded that cooperation in the area of Justice and Home Affairs (JHA) was not working well. It stated that Sweden should strive to keep related cooperation on an intergovernmental basis, but also suggested a limited strengthening of the EU's institutions. The government proposed that the Commission should be given the task of surveying the progress of member states in fulfilling the obligations of previous EU agreements in the JHA area. It also urged that there should be consideration given at the IGC as to whether the European Commission should be given the right to initiate on all aspects of JHA. Furthermore, the government also argued that there should be some discussion on how the European Parliament's role in the decision-making process could be broadened. It suggested that the Parliament should participate, to a larger degree, in the formulation of binding decisions on the member states. Evidently, this was an exercise to ensure that the European Parliament should have the opportunity to express its views.

Not too surprisingly the Green Party (Mot. 1995/96: U29) and the Left Party (Mot. 1995/96: U22) made it quite clear in their bills to the Riksdag that they wanted to see JHA remain as a strictly intergovernmental affair. The Left Party stated that the work within the UN, the Council of Europe and Interpol, rather than EU cooperation, was more important in the fight against international drugs (Mot. 1995/96: U22). The Centre Party's position is somewhat difficult to differentiate from that of the Social Democratic government. The Party does also explicitly say that it places great value on the Riksdag remaining united on Swedish viewpoints (Mot. 1995/96: U25). However, the other parties wanted to go further than the government. The Christian Democratic Party argued that Europol should, under the lead of national police forces, have the authority to take greater direct action (Mot. 1995/96: U21). In addition, the Moderate Party proposed that some measures against drug abuse ought to be transferred from the third to the first 'pillar' (Mot. 1995/96: U23) and the Liberal Party was happy to see Europol cooperation develop in a supranational way (Mot. 1995/96: U19). It was not surprising then that the Riksdag (29 April 1998) ratified the Treaty of Amsterdam by a considerable majority – 229 votes for to 40 against (4 abstentions and 76 absent). A clause concerning new forms of decision-making within the third 'pillar' was adopted by 229 votes for to 34 against (10 abstentions and 76 absent).

Even given its interest in furthering European police cooperation, there are limits that the Swedish government is not ready to go beyond. During the 1996–97 IGC, it was proposed that Europol should be able to 'call on' the police forces of member states, but Sweden, along with others, resisted this, ensuring that the proposal failed.[5] The Swedish government also objected to the transfer of some civil law issues from the third 'pillar' to the first. However, Sweden's position was similar to those of France, the UK, Ireland, Denmark, Austria and Portugal.[6] Thus, Sweden's reluctance to sanction the development of these policy areas under the auspices of the EU supranational institutions was in no way unique.

What it evident is that the Green Party and the Left Party are continuing their resistance against Swedish EU membership, including even opposition to limited forms of intergovernmental cooperation, such as the Europol Convention. However, the governing Social Democratic Party seems to be able to rely on the support of other parties – holding 290 of the Riksdag's 349 seats altogether. Thus, when the first 'point' of the Miles 'Membership Diamond' (a fragmenting 'Europeanized' democracy) is considered in this context, there seems to be few problems for the government in achieving an overarching elite consensus in favour of its policy on EU collaboration in police and criminal matters.

It is also apparent that Sweden is now trying to utilize EU membership and thus handling aspects relating to the Diamond's third 'point' (the new challenges of economic interdependence) by trying to ensure that EU cooperation becomes more efficient. There was widespread agreement that cooperation within the third 'pillar' was not working effectively and that something had to be done. Miles's Diamond suggests that as a result of the relationship between the Diamond's third and fourth (the attachment to non-alignment) 'points', the governing Social Democrats are cautious as regards CFSP development, but favour more ambitious supranational integration on other selected issues. However, when it comes to the issue of police cooperation, Sweden seems to be a rather mainstream member state. During the 1996–97 IGC negotiations, the country did not adopt a stance similar to either of the (relatively) extreme positions of Germany or the UK. The German government wanted to see the transfer of as many policy fields as possible, including Europol, to the first 'pillar', whilst the British government resisted the transfer of any policy areas and/or radical reform of the EU institutions. At present, there seems to be little reason to expect that the Swedish position will change in the foreseeable future.

Collaboration in asylum and immigration matters

Asylum and immigration are examples of other policy areas where the member states have experienced difficulties in developing ambitious European cooperation, although important steps were taken with the signing of the 1990 Dublin Convention[7] and later the 1997 Treaty of Amsterdam.

On 28 May 1997, the Riksdag approved Sweden's participation in the Dublin Convention by 272 votes for to 34 against (with nil abstentions and 43 absent). The vote was in accordance with the referendum of Autumn 1994. All of the present members of the Green Party (17) and the Left Party (17) voted against accepting the Convention. As a rule, the two parties often criticize the Government's policy on asylum and immigration for being too restrictive. Their main criticism of the Dublin Convention was that it could result in negative consequences for refugees (Committee report 1996/97:

SfU16, reservation). General criticism of government policy on asylum and immigration can also be found in the Liberal Party, although the Liberals do accept the principle of cooperation in these areas at the European level.

In the 1995 report to the Riksdag before the IGC, one of the government's points of departure was that the EU would continue as an association of independent states in which member states might, in some cases, transfer decision-making authority to the Union. The Social Democratic government also commented that small member states are relatively stronger in terms of influence within the EU's first 'pillar', compared to those areas covered by more traditional intergovernmental relations. Given these considerations, it is not surprising that the government (when it came to JHA questions) stated that the transfer of 'appropriate parts' of asylum and immigration was acceptable. The government argued that such a transfer would create conditions facilitating the realization of the free movement of persons. A transfer of power from the third to the first 'pillar' also ought to contribute to a fairer sharing of responsibility between the member states.

What is interesting is that the Swedish Social Democratic government entered the IGC negotiations with an explicit acceptance in principle of the transfer of policy areas from the intergovernmental third 'pillar' to the first 'pillar' with its supranational elements. Yet, an aspect that did not feature in the government's 1995 report was that concerning these issues it also considered it appropriate that voting by unanimity in the EU Council of Ministers should be maintained. Nevertheless, across the range of opinion articulated by the various member states, including several that opposed (quite categorically) any major transfer of powers from the third to the first 'pillar', the Swedish position was, more or less, in the centre.[8]

In bills written by the Christian Democratic Party (Mot. 1995/96: U21), the Moderate Party (Mot. 1995/96: U23) and the Liberal Party (Mot. 1995/96: U19), there was a clear support for the transfer of asylum and migration policies from the EU's third to first 'pillar'. The bill from the Centre Party was slightly more cautious, but even this party argued that if intergovernmental relations could not ensure a fair sharing of the responsibility for giving refugees a safe haven, there would be legitimate grounds to consider whether the EU should not develop a common asylum and immigration policy in the longer term (Mot. 1995/96: U25). In contrast, the Green Party (Mot. 1995/96: U29) and the Left Party (Mot 1995/96: U22) were mostly negative to the idea of transferring powers from the third 'pillar' to the first in their bills.

The result of the IGC negotiations was that the issues of immigration and asylum should be transferred from the third to the first 'pillar'. On 29 April 1998, the Riksdag ratified the 1997 Treaty of Amsterdam by 229 votes for to 40 against (4 abstentions and 76 absent). At the time, all the parliamentarians from the Green Party (17) and the Left Party (17) voted against ratification, but they were also accompanied by MPs from the Social Democratic Party (2), the Centre Party (3) and the Liberal Party (1). Thus, there still were small pockets of resistance within the parties. However, in spite of these divisions within these latter parties dating back from the time of the 1994 membership referendum, the overall impression is that EU opposition (at least to full membership) has, for the most part, gone. Certainly, there is evidence to suggest that in terms of the book's second research theme (as outlined in Chapter 1), the Riksdag at least has been further 'Europeanized' and that the divisions within the parliamentary parties have become smaller.

A vote about a particular clause of the Amsterdam Treaty illustrates the point that the Riksdag has been further 'Europeanized' and that Sweden, *vis-à-vis* other member states, is not the most 'troublesome' member state. During the negotiations, Denmark, Ireland and the UK succeeded in gaining exceptions concerning those issues that were moved from the third to the first 'pillar', since they disapproved of the supranational arrangements. In the Riksdag, the 'EU dissidents' argued that Sweden ought to follow these examples and ensure that JHA-related issues operate on a strictly intergovernmental basis. They also demanded a vote on this particular issue. During this vote, the MPs from the Green Party (17) and the Left Party (17) voted alone and the clause was agreed by 231 votes for to 34 against (8 abstentions and 76 absent).

It is fair to say that Sweden was not 'foot-dragging' on institutional questions associated with the areas of asylum and immigration policy. Yet, how can one, for example, reconcile the notion that Sweden – a country that is widely regarded as being not that enthusiastic about furthering EU integration – accepts the EU's supranational development in the areas of asylum and immigration? An initial and natural response would be to state that the former (rather general) impression often cracks when the picture is scrutinized closely. However, given the Swedish government's cautious policy on EMU (see Chapter 9) and the domestic population's quite negative attitude towards both EU membership and the 'Euro', there are also good reasons to view Sweden as a hesitant member state.

Yet, when it comes to questions of asylum and immigration policy, it can be argued, quite convincingly, that there are two issue-specific motives behind Swedish interest in furthering cooperation in these particular policy areas on a European level. First, the Swedish government's objective is to secure a more equitable burden-sharing of the costs of receiving refugees between member states. Sweden was, for instance, one of the countries that – counted in terms of per capita – accepted the most asylum seekers during the war in former Yugoslavia in the early 1990s. Second, there are the more humane motives of wishing to help those in plight and the realization that Sweden alone cannot handle large waves of refugees. Consequently, this matter must be resolved on a common European basis. Nevertheless, asylum and immigration policy is an area where nation-states are, in general, rather cautious, especially when it comes to the possibility of decreasing their sovereignty and powers.

Hence, in order to understand Swedish support for the transfer of asylum and immigration questions from the EU's third to the first 'pillar', it is equally important to appreciate the significance of the code-word 'minimum standards'. In the Treaty of Amsterdam, the code-word 'minimum standards' allows an individual member state to take a more generous stance with respect to, for instance, the qualification of nationals of third countries as 'refugees'. It was due to the inclusion of this code-word that Sweden during the IGC negotiations could accept qualified majority voting.[9] The implication, for example, is that if the policy towards refugees on a European level became restrictive, it would still (at least theoretically) be possible for Sweden to maintain a more generous policy. In terms of this book's first research theme, there is clear evidence to show that Swedish policies (concerning these specific issues) 'fit' rather nicely into the general process of European integration. Nevertheless, it is regrettable that in spite of the coinciding crisis in Kosovo, the question of cooperation in these areas (as well as in police matters) received little attention in the party campaigns for the June 1999 direct elections to the European Parliament (see Chapter 5).

As was the case with collaboration on police matters, it can be concluded that the Social Democratic government has easily secured an overarching elite consensus behind its policy. In the area of asylum and immigration, the parties continue to be divided along the lines adopted for the 1994 referendum. However, these divisions are mainly between the parties and not so much within them. In line with the assumptions of the first 'point' of the 'Membership Diamond' (a fragmenting, 'Europeanized' democracy), there is reason to believe that this has had an impact on the Persson government's policy in these areas.

Indeed, when the 'Membership Diamond' is considered in detail, it is easy to see how Swedish policy towards EU cooperation on asylum and immigration fits nicely within the Diamond's third 'point' (new challenges of economic interdependence) and also the relationship between 'points' three and four. If, as the Diamond suggests, it is crucial that EU membership is viewed by policy-makers as a question of securing the fullest utilization of benefits for Sweden, then the Swedish stance on these questions is self-explanatory. Sweden can benefit economically if asylum and immigration policy is transferred from the third to the first 'pillar' since EU supranational cooperation should lead to greater 'burden-sharing' amongst member states when handling flows of refugees.

In terms of the relationship between the Diamond's 'points' of economic interdependence (three) and Swedish security policy (four), the Diamond quite accurately predicts the Social Democratic government's position on institutional issues relating to EU collaboration on asylum and immigration. Miles argues that tension between these two 'points' has shaped Sweden's EU policy at the governmental level. The Persson government has, on the one hand, taken a cautious attitude towards the future development of the

CFSP and, on the other, displayed selective acceptance of supranational integration, depending on the policy area in question. Clearly, Swedish policy on asylum and immigration is an example of the latter.

With the Diamond in mind, it should also be noted that in the areas of asylum and immigration, there has been quite an overarching consensus behind government policy. This pattern was also evident in Swedish discussions on policy in relation to the 1996–97 IGC. Four of Sweden's political parties in their party bills – written in response to the government's 1995 IGC report – agreed, more or less, with the Social Democratic government that asylum and immigration issues ought to be transferred from the EU's third to the first 'pillar'.

The Nordic Passport Union

Although Sweden has been interested in furthering EU cooperation in the areas of asylum, immigration and policing, attention also needs to be paid to the fact that the country is a part of Norden. The benefits for Sweden of further cooperation between the member states in these specific areas has to be balanced against any risk of damaging the existing Nordic Passport Union. This was especially apparent during the mid-1990s, when Schengen cooperation was to come into force.

The EU member states have been successful in establishing the free movement of goods, services and capital in the EU, although when it comes to the 'fourth freedom' – the free movement for persons – EU cooperation has not been that successful so far. This is primarily because the member states found it difficult to agree on so-called 'compensatory measures' (measures that compensate member states for some of the problems arising from the abolition of border controls), which include, amongst others, closer cooperation in the areas of asylum, immigration and policing. The compensatory measures include the setting of a common standard when it comes to the external border controls since the removal of internal border controls by member states is perceived as needing to be balanced by the establishment of an effective external border control against third countries. During the mid-1990s, this seemed to threaten the future of the Nordic Passport Union.

In 1985, France, Germany and the Benelux countries signed the Schengen Agreement, with the aim of gradually phasing out customs and border controls between the participating states – although significant difficulties meant that it took another five years before the Schengen Implementation Convention was also signed in 1990. Although Schengen cooperation hastened the realization of the free movement of persons between participating member states, it remained a separate intergovernmental affair taking place without the involvement of the EU's institutions. It was always intended, however, that Schengen cooperation would be replaced by arrangements within the European Union. This is achieved through the 1997 Treaty of Amsterdam.

In contrast, Nordic cooperation can, in general, be characterized as low-level collaboration with few formal agreements and definitely no supranational ones (see for instance, Andrén 1967; Sundelius 1982; Thomas 1996). With some simplification, Nordic cooperation has traditionally been based on a community of common languages and perceptions of a shared cultural and historical background. One of the most celebrated results of Nordic cooperation is, of course, the Nordic Passport Union, which has enabled citizens to not have to carry their passports when visiting other Nordic countries since the mid-1950s. During 1994–99, the Nordic Passport Union seemed to be at great risk of being dismantled.

The Schengen Implementation Convention began to be applied from 26 March 1995, but even during the preparatory stage Germany stated in 1994 that it was prepared to strengthen its border controls on the German-Danish frontier. This was not only due to the fact that Schengen was going to take effect, but also that German policy was influenced by the fact that the country was receiving many illegal immigrants. Even though few of these immigrants used Denmark as a 'transfer country', the German government was sensitive to the problem. Hence, in order to avoid stricter controls on its southern border, Denmark applied for observer status in May 1994, with the aim of becoming a full member of Schengen. In its application, the Danish government declared that it would be essential that the free movement of persons between the Nordic countries was maintained and respected. During Autumn 1994, there were regular contacts between the Nordic countries and later, in February 1995, the five countries' Prime Ministers issued a common statement asserting that the Nordic countries should take a positive position *vis-à-vis* their participation in Schengen.[10] It should be noted that at this stage it was not clear at all whether Iceland and Norway, as non-EU states, would be accepted into Schengen. Moreover, it was also unclear whether the Norwegian population, which had previously rejected full EU membership in 1994, would not object strongly to participation in cooperation that was so closely connected with the Union.

As a central part of the author's forthcoming doctoral thesis, the relationship between the Nordic countries and the Schengen states is explored[11] and the focus of this research is to discover whether the Nordic 'identity' has influenced the respective countries' perspectives on European integration, using Schengen as a case-study. In addition to extensive use of official documents, the author has interviewed ministers, parliamentarians and senior officials in Denmark, Norway and Sweden.

In this research, a distinction needs to be drawn between the 'motives' and 'motivations' of policy-makers. The former is the actual reason why a person acts in a particular way whereas the latter is the justification. For example, politicians rarely rationalize their actions with reference to the motivation that they want to be re-elected, but rather refer in public to more 'acceptable' motives. There is, almost needless to say, nothing preventing an actor in having different motives for acting in a specific way.

Having made this distinction between 'motives' and 'motivations', the next sections do not deal explicitly with it. Suffice to say that the arguments suggesting that the future of the Nordic Passport Union was at stake were central to Swedish debates concerning Schengen. Certainly in this context, it can be argued that what is important is not whether the involved actors really had the motives they are referring to (something that there is little reason to doubt), but rather whether the Nordic Passport Union was of such importance that it had the potential to influence Sweden's position *vis-à-vis* the Union.

The Swedish government's application in June 1995 was said by its opponents to have been made as a consequence of full EU membership. Yet, this is not denied by the 'pro-Schengen' people in Sweden. As the former Prime Minister, Ingvar Carlsson, argued in the author's interview with him in May 1998, 'Since the nation-state neither in that area was good enough, it was important to take part in the fight against criminality. Moreover, Denmark had decided to become a member, but that was just another reason. For me, it was natural to follow on from [EU] membership.' The proponents of Schengen were obviously interested in *both* the maintenance of the Nordic Passport Union and the development of Sweden's EU membership.

In the Swedish case, it is possible to discern two major reasons for joining Schengen. One reason was the interest in participating in general EU integration: more specifically, the EU's efforts at promoting the free movement of persons and increasing cooperation in the areas such as immigration, asylum and policing. The other reason was Sweden's commitment to maintain the Nordic Passport Union. It is to these aspects that this chapter will now turn.

In March 1995, the first substantial debate about Schengen took place in the Riksdag (Prot. 1994/95: 74). In the introduction by the Minister of Justice, Laila Freivalds, she argued that Denmark had previously adopted a reserved attitude towards taking part in Schengen cooperation, but has now applied for observer status with the eventual aim of becoming a member. Thus: 'In order to make it possible to maintain the currently 40-year-old unrestricted movement of people between the Nordic countries, even with the Danish participation in the Schengen cooperation, the question has been raised regarding the other Nordic countries' relation to this cooperation.'

It has been suggested that Swedish interest in taking part in Schengen was purely a result of being an EU member. The Swedish government, in order to further Swedish interests and present itself in general terms as being very 'pro-EU', wanted to be involved in as many parts of European cooperation as possible. Thus, using the arguments about the Nordic Passport Union could just be an excuse to join Schengen. However, the Minister of Justice also stated that the question of Swedish participation in Schengen cooperation had arisen because of Sweden's desire to maintain the free movement of persons between the Nordic countries. Can this statement be corroborated?

During interviews with three officials at the Departments of Justice and Foreign Affairs they all responded to an open question by stating that it was the Danish application which brought the 'Schengen question' to the fore.[12] One of them also stated that the general impression was that the work carried out under the auspices of Schengen was probably unnecessary, since it could be done within the Union's framework.[13] There are also other indications strengthening the argument that it was not immediately obvious that Sweden would join Schengen. One is that there was over a month between the time when the Finnish government in May 1995 declared its intention to apply to join Schengen as an observer (with the eventual aim of becoming a member) and the time that the Swedish government followed suit. If the Social Democratic government had been eager, then it is reasonable to assume that the Swedish announcement would have come sooner.

Given that Swedish interest in Schengen cooperation was 'awakened' by the Danish application and that the government sought, even then, to maintain the Nordic Passport Union, it would seem that the Passport Union was important to Sweden. An examination of the views of parliamentarians working against Swedish membership of Schengen should indicate, albeit to a limited extent, the level of importance. First of all, did the parliamentarians involved from the Left Party and the Green Party – the parties that were, after all, against Swedish membership of Schengen – perceive that the Nordic Passport Union was at stake? If they did not, this would suggest that the Swedish government was merely making excuses.

However, Bengt Hurtig, a Left Party MP, concerned with the risk that Norway would not participate in Schengen cooperation, commented that, 'In consideration of Denmark's conditions, there will be a discussion regarding, to what extent, Schengen's external border will be between Denmark and Sweden or between Denmark and Germany'.[14] Peter Eriksson, an MP from the Green Party, also stated, 'Shall we have this strict border between Denmark and Sweden or should it be towards Norway? This debate is not so easy to hold.'[15] During an interview in June 1998 with Peter Eriksson, attention was drawn to his prior statement and he maintained that in the short-run and after Denmark's application, there really was a risk that Sweden may have to choose between initiating border controls against either Denmark or Norway. However, he also added that, 'Yes, in the short perspective that was the case. When Denmark applied that was the case. If the Swedish government had so decided, it could have found a solution. The Nordic countries could have introduced such a solution and, thus, could have obtained an imposition of minimal border controls from the Schengen countries.'

Obviously the Left Party and the Green Party did perceive that the Nordic Passport Union was at stake and given that they disapproved of the governmental solution (joining Schengen) it is interesting to consider any recommended policy alternatives. In February 1995, Gudrun Schyman, leader of the Left Party, argued that, 'Of course it must be possible to discuss partial solutions with the countries that are taking part in Schengen. Solutions which could make it possible to keep the passport freedoms without having to cooperate in the areas of policing, asylum and so on.'[16] Given that a prominent party leader argued that there must be other partial solutions to the problem, it is also reasonable to assume that other policy alternatives would feature in the political debate. However, in a debate in early April 1995, the Minister of Justice, Laila Freivalds, asked for examples of the potential alternatives that her Department was ignoring (Prot. 1994/95: 84). Schyman's answer is illustrative: 'I am expected to present alternatives, but I do not have any alternatives. I just ask the simple question: Is it possible to solve this in another way rather than have to accept the whole package?'

Amongst other things, the opponents of Schengen usually highlight the organization's lack of democratic controls and the risk of establishing less generous practices towards asylum seekers. What is interesting is that in the debates on Schengen cooperation, the Swedish opponents (with one exception and that was not in a debate specifically on Schengen) never articulated an option that was raised in Norway. Hence, in spite of the things that Swedish opponents criticized Schengen cooperation for, they never argued that these things were of such an importance that they outweighed the benefits of the Nordic Passport Union. In the Swedish debate, such an argument was simply not put forward with any force. Thus, it was never suggested that in order to avoid the 'evils' of Schengen, Sweden ought to abolish the Nordic Passport Union.

This discussion on the (lack of) alternatives to Sweden joining Schengen illustrates the importance that domestic actors placed on the Nordic Passport Union, even though it does not provide us with a definitive answer to the question about which alternative (Schengen cooperation or the Nordic Passport Union), the government preferred. During the interviews, a hypothetical question was asked on the likelihood of whether Sweden would have applied for membership of Schengen if Denmark had not done the same. Of course, it is in the 'pro-Schengen' people's interest to answer, as Laila Freivalds did in June 1998, 'Not at that time'. Or as the former Prime Minister, Ingvar Carlsson, commented (May 1998), 'Schengen is good, but we were not prepared to give up something so important as the Passport Union'. However, it is more interesting when a prominent figure against Swedish membership of Schengen also agrees. As Peter Eriksson, an MP of the Green Party, answered (June 1998), 'No, I don't think so. That would not have been possible. ... It was a prerequisite.'

On 16 April 1998, the Parliament voted on Swedish participation in

Schengen cooperation. In line with their respective parties' official stances, the present 34 MPs from the Left Party and the Green Party voted against. They were accompanied by two MPs from the Social Democratic Party, two from the Centre Party and one from the Liberal Party, with a further four MPs from the Social Democratic Party abstaining from voting. Thus, even within the pro-Schengen parties, there were small pockets of resistance. In general they, as well as the Left Party and the Green Party, objected to any increase in supranationality, but in spite of these concerns, the over-whelming majority of the MPs – 231 for to 39 against (5 abstentions 74 absent) – were in favour of Schengen cooperation.

Even though the Nordic states, together with the Schengen countries, found a solution during 1995–96 that made it possible to retain the Nordic Passport Union and avoid the imposition of stricter border controls from the Schengen countries, the problems were, nevertheless, not over. As part of the 1997 Amsterdam Agreement, Schengen cooperation became part of the European Union. Elements of Schengen's intergovernmental coopera-tion (asylum and immigration) will eventually become part of the EU's first 'pillar'. Thus, the question of Icelandic and Norwegian status was of immediate interest and the future of the Nordic Passport Union was again at stake.

However, the Treaty of Amsterdam was amended with a protocol on the integration of Schengen. In the protocol, the member states agreed to take into account the need to maintain a special relationship with Iceland and Norway. The issue is somewhat controversial within the EU since some members disapproved of the idea of letting countries that not are full member states cooperate so closely with the existing European Union. However, given the importance that the Nordic countries attached to the maintenance of the Nordic Passport Union, it is not that surprising that the negotiations in 1999 resulted in the continuation of the free movement of persons between the Nordic countries.

Conclusion

It can be concluded that Sweden, when it comes to the institutional ques-tions relating to the areas of asylum, immigration and policing, behaves rather like a 'mainstream' member state, contradicting the usual picture of Sweden as a hesitant member state. In terms of the 'Membership Diamond', it seems that Sweden is now trying to utilize the benefits of EU membership and furthers its national interests in different ways. This is also the case even if it requires a transfer of EU competencies from the intergovernmental third to supranational first 'pillar', such as with asylum and immigration issues. However, like most of the other member states, Sweden does not show any interest in a similar transfer as regards policing aspects. The use of force continues to be a highly sensitive and thus a policy arena in which member states want to keep their monopoly and sovereignty.

However, even though there is Swedish interest in these specific policy areas, Swedish policy can be heavily influenced by the fact that the country is a part of Norden. It is obvious that the decision-makers have attached great importance to the maintenance of the Nordic Passport Union. Irrespective of the fact that a distinction can be drawn between 'motives' and 'motivations' (the former being the reasons why a person behaves in a particular way and the latter the justification for these actions), there is little to suggest that Swedish decision-makers would not be interested in the maintenance of the Nordic Passport Union. Using the terminology of Putnam's 'two-level games', it can be concluded that Swedish decision-makers have quite a small Level II 'win-set' in relation to these specific policy areas. That is, Swedish political leaders would experience difficulties in their national environment with any international agreement that envisaged the ending of the free movement of persons between the Nordic countries. Indeed, it is highly unlikely that any Swedish politician would sanction such an international agreement and risk inflaming the electorate's anger.

Putnam's 'two-level game' analogy is also useful in explaining the 'not so reluctant' Swedish stance towards EU collaboration in the areas of asylum, immigration and policing. The Swedish electorate's general dissatisfaction with the Union stems from, amongst other things, its perception of the Union as an expensive, bureaucratic giant which pays too much attention to the size of Swedish strawberries. However, when it comes to cooperation against international crime and ensuring that other European countries 'take their share of the responsibility' for refugees, it seems reasonable to assume that Swedish politicians enjoy having quite a large 'win-set' at the national level.

Miles argues that it is likely that it will take until well into the new century for the transitional stages affecting the Diamond's first and second 'points' to be completed (see Chapter 1 and Miles 1998b). His Diamond framework suggests that Swedish governments may find it difficult to convince public opinion of the benefits of the country being a member state. However, as regards the policy areas covered in this chapter, Sweden has, for the most part, left these transitional stages. Indeed, if the first research theme (see Chapter 1) is considered then, certainly as regards asylum, immigration and policing issues, Swedish priorities 'fit' rather well into the general process of European integration, even if in the last area (policing), Swedish governments are, at present, rather reluctant to accept supranational arrangements. Yet, there is nothing extraordinary in this. The vast majority of member states also raise objections to the extension of such arrangements to cover policing.

It is perhaps more difficult to assess to what degree Sweden has been 'Europeanized' and has adjusted fully to being an EU member state. Yet, given that Sweden is starting to initiate policies, such as crime prevention, on the European level, there is some evidence to suggest that this is the case.

A more clear-cut answer can be given to the fourth research theme. There are real difficulties in foreseeing any changes in Swedish EU policy (concerning these three sensitive policy areas) that will be anything but 'elite-led'. Indeed, the EU's arrangements governing the third 'pillar' are so complex that it takes quite an effort to understand these institutional arrangements. Nevertheless, it can, for the most part, be assumed that Swedish citizens want EU member states to cooperate as regards these specific policy areas, although the question of the Nordic Passport Union also indicates the limitations that Swedish governments have to work within.

Notes

1. Given the large numbers of Riksdag documents referred to in this chapter, the editor has decided not to list them all in full in the Bibliography as they are cited in the correct fashion as would appear in Sweden. As a rule of thumb for the 'non-Swede', those documents prefixed with 'Mot.' are usually motions put forward in the Riksdag by the parliamentary parties (and/or their members) outlining their respective positions. All other references (mostly prefixed by date only, Skr. or Prot.) usually refer to the reports and/or proceedings of the Riksdag's parliamentary committees and/or plenary debates.
2. Stenographic transcripts from the Swedish Parliament's Advisory Committee on EU Affairs (16 June 1995).
3. Under-Secretary of State Kristina Rennerstedt. Stenographic transcripts from the Swedish Parliament's Advisory Committee on EU Affairs (31 May 1996).
4. Committee report 1997/98: JuU2, reservation no. 1.
5. The Swedish chief negotiator Gunnar Lund. Stenographic transcripts from the Swedish Parliament's Advisory Committee on EU Affairs (4 April 1997). The paragraphs are often classified when they concern other countries. In this case the Swedish chief negotiator maintained that some other member states agreed with the Swedish viewpoint.
6. The Swedish chief negotiator Gunnar Lund mentioned the four small countries at the meeting on 11 April 1997 and France and the UK at the meeting on 25 April. Stenographic transcripts from the Swedish Parliament's Advisory Committee on EU Affairs (11 and 25 April 1997).
7. The Dublin Convention was signed by the (then) 12 member states in June 1990 but was first applied during 1997. The aim of the Convention is to regulate in which country an application from an asylum-seeking person should be considered. It should be noted that the Dublin Convention is a traditional Convention between independent states and thus has no supranational elements.
8. The Swedish chief negotiator Gunnar Lund. Stenographic transcripts from the Swedish Parliament's Advisory Committee on EU Affairs (15 November 1996). At a meeting with the committee on 28 February 1997, the Swedish chief negotiator Gunnar Lund maintained that, like Sweden, most member states were willing in due time to accept the use of a qualified vote, but few were advancing that it should be done immediately.
9. The Swedish chief negotiator Gunnar Lund. Stenographic transcripts from the Swedish Parliament's Advisory Committee on EU Affairs (4 and 11 April 1997).
10. Protocol from the Nordic Council's 46th session (February 1995), appendix 1.
11. The dissertation is intended to appear by the end of 2000 or early 2001. Andersson, Hans E., Department of Political Science, Göteborg University.

12. Department of Justice: Hans Frennered and Peter Strömberg. Department of Foreign Affairs: Anders Olander.
13. Department of Justice, Peter Strömberg.
14. Stenographic transcripts from the Swedish Parliament's Advisory Committee on EU Affairs (20 December 1996).
15. Stenographic transcripts from the Swedish Parliament's Advisory Committee on EU Affairs (20 December 1996).
16. Protocol from the Nordic Council's 46th session (February 1995), p. 67.

CHAPTER 14

Conclusion: Polishing the 'Membership Diamond'

Lee Miles

Revisiting the book's four research themes

This book and its component chapters should provide the reader with a relatively extensive assessment of Sweden's experiences of the first years of full European Union (EU) membership. This conclusion returns to the four research questions/themes (introduced in Chapter 1) and their application to Sweden, then assesses the implications for the 'Membership Diamond' and finally proposes a number of scenarios outlining Sweden's relationship with the Union.

> *Theme 1: Swedish priorities regarding European integration and the extent to which existing Swedish institutions and policies 'fit' into the general process of European integration*

A survey of the various chapter analyses suggests that Swedish governments do not, by and large, have a specific vision of how European integration and the 'New Europe' is to evolve. Like the good 'functionalists' they are, the Swedes have tended to take a rather pragmatic view on how the European Union should develop. To some degree, this reflects the legacy that successive Swedish governments face since the outcome of the 1994 referendum on Swedish EU accession, and that the Carlsson and later Persson administrations were and are constrained by the lukewarm enthusiasm for the European Union of most Swedes (see Chapter 7). It is accurate to say that most Swedes only accepted membership of the European Union on the basis that it would be good for the country's economy and not because they are enthusiastic about any future vision of a supranational integrated 'Political Europe'. Swedish policy on European issues has tended to be at times rather defensive – directed at protecting existing domestic legislation and policy priorities. In short, and at least in the Swedish case, it is more appropriate to talk of Swedish priorities towards Europe, instead of 'visions' of European integration.

Yet, this does not imply that the old term coined by Toivo Miljan of Sweden (along with the rest of the Nordic countries) as a 'reluctant European' is entirely correct either (Miljan 1977). Indeed, as Part III of this book especially highlights, Sweden has developed specific policy priorities on

European integration or, at least, emphasized a number of key policy areas, where the Swedish government believes it can make a contribution to the European Union. Broadly, these policy priorities fall into three broad (if not exclusive) categories:

1. *'Championed policy priorities'*. Swedish governments are driven by the 'priority' of making a 'positive' impact on the EU's future development. In practice, various Swedish governments have selected various issues as being of primary importance and have duly 'championed' these within the EU's policy-making process. Most of them are related to: (i) Swedish desires to improve the democratic credentials of the Union, such as greater EU openness and transparency; (ii) those policy areas where the Swedes are usually perceived to be 'market leaders', such as in the environmental and social policy spheres (see Chapters 10 and 12); (iii) those aspects of the EU's external relations portfolio which Sweden believes (if developed) will reinforce its existing foreign policy priorities, such as in the Baltic Sea and/or European crisis management. In terms of policy priorities, it could be argued that these are largely 'defensive', aimed at bringing the Union up to Swedish standards or at least are recognized by Swedish governments as 'policy opportunities' where the Union can be 'shaped' along Swedish lines. Nevertheless, in these areas, the Swedes are very proactive and usually support the development of EU supranational policies and arrangements in these specific areas.

2. *'Normative policy priorities'*. The major priority here is that Sweden is viewed by others to be a 'mainstream' member state and a 'good European'. In reality, these are policy areas which Swedish governments do not overtly 'champion', but in which they prefer to remain engaged because they perceive that there will be political and/or economic advantages from such participation. Swedish governments welcome, or at least have no major objections to, involvement in these respective policy areas as a 'normal' member state. In these policy portfolios, such as in Research and Technological Development (RTD) (see Chapter 8) and Schengen cooperation (Chapter 13), Swedish activity is more 'neutral'. However, these are also areas where the Swedes have usually come to favour further supranational cooperation, or, more accurately, now have fewer reservations about the Union developing policies in these areas. Examples are the evolution of the CFSP (Chapter 2) and also Schengen cooperation (Chapter 13). It is, perhaps, in these areas where Swedish attitudes have changed to the largest degree and where Sweden has adjusted the most as a 'new' member state.

3. *'Policy dilemmas'*. The priority of Swedish government in these policy areas is to 'defend' overtly and usually 'protect' national interests, even if this requires Sweden to be placed on the periphery of EU develop-

ment. Nevertheless, the Swedes also want to input into such EU developments so that their views do not become largely ignored by other member states in other spheres. In practice, Swedish governments remain cautious about the viability of EU integration in these contexts and are wary of the negative impacts on Swedish domestic policies and debates. In short, they usually favour intergovernmental solutions or at least resist the extension of the EU supranational arrangements. This may be because Sweden is concerned about the undue impact of the Union on the country because it is a 'small state', such as on some EU institutional reform questions, but it is also usually based on the fact that there is lack of Swedish party, interest group and public support for EU development in these areas. A good policy example would be, for instance, the protection of Swedish alcohol monopolies, and, to a lesser extent, Swedish attitudes towards EU monetary integration. Nevertheless, the usual outcome is that the Swedish political elite are unconvinced of the benefits of European integration in these areas and, more specifically, have difficulties in pushing forward domestic debates in these areas as they strike at the heart of 'Swedish domestic concerns'.

There will, of course, always be tensions between the national and EU levels as regards the evolution of EU supranational policies. However, the net outcome has been that Swedish government continues to follow a 'mixed' approach to European integration. Sweden, as a small, mature industrial democracy, is keen to ensure its leadership in certain policy fields by 'pushing forward' the parameters of EU policy. Where this is unlikely to be achieved – perhaps due to, amongst other things, the opposition of other member states – Swedish governments seek to 'defend' Sweden's domestic procedures and standards, especially in those areas deemed as politically sensitive and affecting public opinion on the EU.

Nevertheless, even in the latter policy areas, there are signs that Swedish policy priorities increasingly 'fit' into the more general scheme of European integration. The Persson government, for example, has softened its tone on developing the EU's military capabilities in 1999 and the Prime Minister has also, more or less, accepted that the country will join the single currency one day (see *Financial Times* 1999c). To some extent, this is due to the fact that Sweden is increasingly influenced by the momentum of the European Union of which it voluntarily decided to join. As Ulrika Mörth highlights (Chapter 8), the European Union consequently begins to shape Sweden's own domestic agenda. Yet, it is also a reflection that as aspects of the Swedish government's agenda are incorporated within the European Union's legislative framework (such as in the 1997 Amsterdam Treaty), the EU starts to become more 'acceptable' to the mainstream of Swedish political society. Both these dynamics are integral parts of the inevitable learning process associated with EU membership.

Theme 2: To what degree has Sweden been 'Europeanized'?

This perhaps leads us nicely into a discussion on to what extent Sweden has been 'Europeanized'. The Swedish political elite have, for most purposes, been 'Europeanized' as these actors have been drawn even further into the EU's policy-process. Even the mainstream political parties (Chapter 5) and interest groups (Chapter 6) have largely accepted, sometimes grudgingly, the economic logic associated with European integration and that the country's interests are better served by being 'inside' the Union. This is reflected, albeit to a limited degree, within Sweden's EU policy priorities and in some areas, like RTD, Sweden has been actively involved (see Chapter 8). Nonetheless, although there may be some evidence of the 'Europeanization' of Swedish political institutions, it is exceedingly difficult, as Olof Ruin (Chapter 4) argues, to differentiate these from the other trends operating in the Swedish polity and/or their specific degree of impact.

Yet, as Ekengren and Sundelius (1998) suggest, the degree of 'Europeanization' may be roughly gauged in terms of its impact on the 'Swedish state' and on 'Swedish society'. Swedish policy-makers are susceptible to, and aware of, the pressures emanating upon them from 'Europe'. The 'Swedish state', or, more accurately, the country's political machinery and administration is now geared to conducting its affairs in relation to the Union especially since the EU's policy portfolio has affected both foreign and domestic policy arenas, further enhancing the existing 'grey' area between the international and national dimensions of foreign policy management. Nevertheless, the 'Europeanization' of Swedish society (in this context translated to meaning 'EU-ization') has been much slower. The 'grass roots' members of Swedish political parties (Chapter 5), interest groups (Chapter 6) and, for the most part, the general public do (Chapter 7), at this stage, perceive themselves to be hardly affected by the Union. Consequently, they are also largely unconvinced of the perceived or real consequences emanating from European Union and/or that the Union plays any relevant role in their everyday lives.

At face value, it would seem that even though 'Europeanization' continues, political scientists are still somewhat uncomfortable with estimating accurately how it operates. The size of the overall impact of Europeanization and its implications for specific sectors of Swedish polity and society remain significant, if largely unanswered, questions – other than the conclusion that it remains important and that its impact has, to date, been rather uneven across a nation-state like Sweden. This is an area crying out for further research to be undertaken. Thus, it is difficult to analyse the pace of 'Europeanization' and if, indeed, when or where, it will stop.

Theme 3: Has Sweden adjusted fully to life as an EU member state and can Sweden still be regarded as a 'new' member of the European Union?

This theme/question focuses on the 'time' and/or 'spatial' dimension of EU membership. In a technical sense, Sweden will cease to be a 'new' member state when the EU enlarges once again (as others will be the 'new' ones). Yet, as British and, to a lesser extent, Danish experiences of full EU Membership indicate, 26 years, let alone the few years of Swedish membership covered by this book, may still not be enough to allow member states to 'adjust fully' to the obligations of EU membership. At least in part, the nature and time-scale of adjustment depends on the 'psychological state of mind' of the member state at the time of joining. Unlike the British case, and more similar to the Danish one, Sweden has at least conducted an extensive debate as part of the 1994 accession referendum on the merits of joining the Union.

Hence, in 1999, as this conclusion is being written, it is fair to say that the major battles between and within Sweden's mainstream political parties and interest groups on EU membership have, to all intents and purposes, been won by the 'pro-EU camp'. The European policies of Swedish governments will remain committed to, and be conducted within, the context of EU membership for the foreseeable future. Those groups within the Swedish political elite advocating the country's withdrawal from the Union have been, for the most part, marginalized within the mainstream political parties by their existing leaderships, ensuring that the main skirmishes between the 'pro-' and anti-EU membership camps now take place at the periphery of the political spectrum. EU withdrawal is championed by smaller parties like the Left Party and the Greens, and by certain key interest groups but, for the most part, features only in very general public debates in the country. From this perspective, Sweden has adjusted to life as a full EU member since the debates surrounding EU accession and withdrawal have slowly become less influential.

Yet, 'full adjustment' must be construed in other ways for these aspects do constrain the freedom of manoeuvre of Swedish governments when following EU-related policies. 'Full adjustment' can be roughly translated into two elements. First, that Sweden plays an active role in the future policy evolution of the Union and second, that not just the 'Swedish state', but also 'Swedish society' becomes 'comfortable' with Sweden playing such a role in further European integration (separate from the EU membership question).

Certainly, as regards the first point then, successive Swedish governments have seen the Union as an 'opportunity' to play a larger role in certain policy areas, such as on improving the EU's role in crisis management and Baltic Sea questions, which will be popular back home in Sweden (see Chapters 2 and 3). The concept of 'two-level games' is also illustrated here. The Persson government remains concerned with 'selling the European Union' to the domestic population and utilizing the shaping of the EU's agenda during international negotiations to further this task. This appears to have been a successful strategy on 'secondary' issues relating to the EU's first 'pillar' (for example, on EU employment and environmental policies) and, particularly, in shaping policy associated with the second (CFSP) and third (criminal and police matters) 'pillars' of the Union, where the EU's ambitions are perhaps more muted. It is also the case that in these areas, the policy interests of the larger EU member states have also been sympathetic to and in accordance with that of Sweden.

However, Sweden's EU policy has been less influential in terms of its impact on 'first rate' big questions, such as EMU, associated with the EU's development. In these areas, the interests of larger EU countries have been brought to bear and the level of division with the Union has been more notable. To some degree, this is due to Sweden being one of the smaller EU member states and thus, has only a marginal impact on the EU's primary agenda, but it is also a reflection of the fact that these 'bigger' questions of European integration have much deeper political implications and thereby have been highly divisive in terms of domestic political debates.

The success of Swedish governments in influencing the EU's agenda is also affected by the high degree of 'Euro-scepticism' prevalent in Swedish society. This largely explains, for example, the tentative 'wait and see' policy of the Persson government towards Swedish membership of the 'Euro' between 1995 and 99 (see Chapter 9) and why issues like the degree of transparency and openness of EU decision-making are highlighted by the Swedish government. As long as the slow pace of adjustment continues at the societal level and Swedes remain 'uncomfortable' with their country's participation in deeper European integration, then Sweden's political adjustment will also, to some degree, remain incomplete. Swedish policy-makers will continue to close some policy options at the EU level that they might otherwise prefer to pursue – limiting the degree of impact that Sweden may have on the Union's agenda.

Theme 4: The potential scenarios for future institutional and policy change in relation to the European Union and whether changes in Swedish EU policy and priorities are 'elite-led' or 'societal-influenced'

During the majority of the time period discussed in this book, Swedish governmental policy has tended, on balance, to be 'societal-influenced', although there are clear indications that Swedish policy priorities are becoming 'elite-led'. It should be made clear, however, that the two terms are not exclusive and there is a high degree of interaction between them. Hence, what is being discussed is the 'emphasis' within and placed on the selection of governmental EU policy priorities.

Certainly, the EU policies of the Carlsson and Persson governments were largely concerned during the early days of membership with securing the EU's acceptance of those policy issues raised by Sweden but not subsequently accepted by the Union during the 1993–94 accession negotiations. In other words, Sweden's EU policy agenda had been mainly preset by the legacy of the accession negotiations and the 1994 membership referendum debates, which cast a 'long shadow' on the priorities of respective Swedish governments during the early years of membership.

To all intents and purposes, if the Swedish political elite 'led' then it was mostly in those areas left over from the EU accession experience, which were heavily 'societal-influenced'. The EU policies of the Carlsson and later Persson administrations were directed at ensuring that issues, like greater transparency in EU decision-making, an EU employment chapter, more stringent environmental provisions and a stronger EU role in crisis management were incorporated at the first appropriate opportunity after membership had been secured. This was the prerequisite if the political elite were to go on to 'lead' society on some of the more controversial issues placed on the EU's agenda by the 1992 Maastricht Treaty. In fact, the Swedish political elite were successful in laying down many of these aspects within the EU's treaty framework through the 1997 Amsterdam Treaty. Hence, the 'long shadow' has now, for the most part, disappeared as the Amsterdam Treaty represents 'a beacon of achievement' for Swedish EU policy.

At the time of writing, Swedish EU policy may be entering a new era. The country's political elite, now increasingly free of the shackles imposed by the early EU membership debates, are now clearly trying to take Sweden forward and to at least start to initiate a more focused debate on Sweden's role and participation in some of the thornier areas of EU policy. Moreover, this more confident role on the part of the government must be placed in the context of Sweden preparing itself for its first tenure as President of the European Council in 2001.

Prime Minister Persson, for example, softened his tone in 1999 on the evolution of an EU military capability (provided it was to be used alongside an enhanced EU role in European crisis management) and stressed that a greater EU military persona is compatible with Sweden's continuing 'non-alignment' and EU membership. Successive Swedish governments continue to take ever more flexible interpretations of the country's 'non-alignment'. In addition, the Social Democratic government has pushed forward the debate on the country joining the 'Euro'. Persson, for instance, insisted, in November 1999, that the government's 'wait and see' strategy cannot continue indefinitely. In an interview with the *Financial Times*, he argued, 'It's impossible for us to say No [to the Euro]. We have only two options. Yes, we want to enter now or Yes, we want to enter later' (*Financial Times* 1999c: 8). This more assertive stance on questions of further EU integration on the part of the Persson administration can also be seen within EU external relations (see Chapters 2 and 3).

In summary, it implies that, at last, Swedish governments are pushing forward domestic debates on the central questions affecting European integration. Although not without risk, this is central to further legitimization of governmental EU policy back home and to Sweden playing a more active role in the Union. It may be the case that Swedish governments are now moving from a 'defensive' to an 'offensive' strategy aimed at mobilizing public support for European integration. However, this is also partly due to the fact that external pressures emanating from the EU's own policy timetable may be becoming a stronger influence on the Persson government, rather than because the governing Social Democrats are confident that, in domestic terms, Sweden is ready for a more prominent role in European integration. But what does all this mean in terms of the Miles 'Membership Diamond'?

Polishing the 'Membership Diamond'

Each contributor was asked not only to consider (to varying degrees and where applicable) these four research themes/questions, but also given the task of beginning their initial analysis of their various subject areas from the perspective of the Miles 'Membership Diamond'. Of course, authors were free to move away and use other frameworks if they deemed this appropriate, but it is accurate to state that the 'Membership Diamond' concept was intended to (and largely has) provided the book with a reasonably coherent conceptual framework on which cross-chapter evaluations can be conducted. Although the application of the Diamond varies (quite correctly) according to the chapter and subject area concerned, the continuing relevance of the 'Membership Diamond' framework has been, to some extent, vindicated by the fact that the vast majority have found aspects of the 'Membership Diamond' to be relevant to their respective analyses. Indeed, there are several general conclusions as regards the 'Membership Diamond' that can be drawn.

Point 1: A 'more divided' and 'Europeanized' democracy

Many of the chapters, and especially those in, not surprisingly, Part II of the book, highlight the continuing relevance of domestic factors in constraining Swedish governmental policy on Europe. In particular, the constituent chapters emphasize most aspects of the first element of 'point' one. The EU's impact on elite searches for consensual policy-making, the nature of democratic questions associated with the EU, the division these aspects create within the Swedish political elite and especially political parties, and finally the continuing scepticism of the country's populace towards the European Union are still inhibiting dynamics. The chapters suggest that all these dynamics will usually pressure Swedish governments to follow a limited number of policy options (and a narrow 'win-set').

Governments have tended to be cautious in contentious areas of EU policy and focused on ensuring that those areas of the EU's development which are most contentious with the domestic population are redressed as quickly as possible. In short, the Swedish political elite may be now largely happy with and in favour of Sweden's participation in the European Union, but they have as yet been less successful in winning the 'rhetorical battle' with the electorate and convinced it of the benefits of European integration *per se*. This is, of course, a very slow process. Indeed, there is now evidence through Eurobarometer surveys to indicate that the sizeable level of Swedish opposition to EU membership is softening, but given that public opinion remains volatile it seems equally likely that political parties will be very careful when handling EU-related issues. The country will still be regarded by many as one of the least enthusiastic members of the Union.

What perhaps needs to be emphasized, however, is that EU questions may have reinforced domestic political divisions, but the process of 'fragmentation' has not been anywhere like as damaging as that associated with what happened say in Denmark or Norway in the 1970s and it is doubtful whether this will be a permanent feature within the Swedish party system in the longer term. Yet, it must also be made equally clear that this was *never* foreseen or argued by Miles in the first place. Rather it is more the case that in the late 1990s the level of division associated with EU questions may have stabilized within the Swedish political and party system, or at least the political elite within the mainstream political parties have become more adept at managing these sources of possible tension and dispute.

The Liberals and Moderates are the most happy with further European integration. Yet, the EU remains a source of internal friction within the Social Democratic, Centre and Christian Democratic parties, with the Left Party and Greens being the most hostile (see Chapter 5). In addition, the big questions to be considered within the context of 'point' one are now no longer associated with EU membership for the most part. The centre ground of Swedish politics has largely reconciled itself that EU membership is now a permanent feature of the Swedish polity. Rather it is on questions of Swedish participation in future 'deepened' European integration that remains the source of tension and division within and between most political parties.

Thus, even after the 1998 general election, which led to a minority Social Democratic government under Göran Persson assuming office (with the parliamentary support of the anti-EU membership Greens and Left Party), this has not so far had any dire consequences for Persson's EU policy or resulted in any notable changes of emphasis within that policy area. In particular, the areas of EU and foreign policy have been 'ring-fenced' out of the agreement with the Left Party and the Greens and in these areas Persson will seek the support of the non-socialist parties for parliamentary support on questions relating to EU policy.

The labelling of the first 'point' as a 'fragmented' democracy may be slightly too strong a word to describe the actual process now going on in the late 1990s. After all, the Swedish political (and party) system is nowhere near collapse, least of all because of EU-related questions. However, once again, this was *never* argued by Miles since the original coining of the term 'fragmenting' was used to indicate *a degree of emphasis on 'change'* within the Swedish polity in the early-mid 1990s and *not* to intimate that the author foresaw the collapse of the Swedish political system. Nevertheless, it is probably the case that the name of the first 'point' should be altered slightly to a 'more divided, Europeanized democracy'.

Given the slow acceptance of the population of EU membership and that the political parties have become more efficient in dealing with the domestic friction emanating from EU questions, then is this more effective management due to the fact that the country's political institutions are 'Europeanized'? According to Ruin, the jury remains out on this one, but perhaps what can be concluded at this point is that the country's existing political processes have adjusted in order to facilitate consensus policy-making on EU questions, even if they are not fully 'Europeanized' on all matters. In other words, apart from fairly minor institutional reforms to governmental machinery after accession, and the Riksdag establishing supervisory mechanisms such as the Advisory Committee on European Affairs, then, for the most part, the country's political machine has operated quite successfully in dealing with EU questions using existing apparatus. As Miles (1998b) has argued, for example, the Swedes had relatively few major problems when formulating policy proposals for the 1997 Amsterdam IGC and/or in securing wider domestic support for them from other political groups. It looks as if this will also be the case when Sweden assumes the Presidency of the European Council in 2001.

The 'litmus test' of the strength of the Diamond's first 'point' in the next few years will probably be how Sweden handles the question of full participation in the 'Euro'. Certainly, any future public referendum on Swedish EMU participation will be the last chance for those arguing for Swedish EU withdrawal to present their case with any real force. It will also indicate the degree of division within and between the major political parties and disposition of the Swedish population. The first 'point' of the Diamond continues then to be the major constraint on governmental EU policy and its specific development. Nevertheless, the revised first 'point' suggested in this conclusion includes first, a stronger focus on further integration questions (rather than EU membership) as the basis for any division and second, that it is perhaps more correct to talk of 'more division' rather than 'fragmentation' within the first aspects of 'point' one (see Figure 14.1).

Point 2: 'Changing corporatism'

Any political commentator studying Swedish political discourse in the 1990s would, most probably, highlight the growing internationalization of Swedish

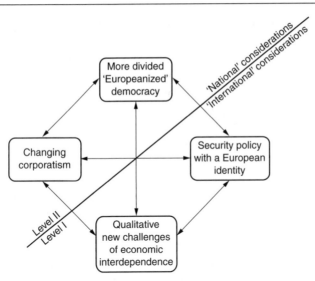

Figure 14.1 The polished 'Membership Diamond'

business in the 1990s. Political issues, such as the fragile competitiveness of Swedish firms and the economy in general, as well as the worryingly large number of foreign acquisitions of 'flagship' Swedish 'national champions' such as Volvo cars in 1999, are constant features of domestic political debates in the late 1990s. After the dark years of economic recession in the early 1990s, Sweden's economy is still in sizeable transition. Such internationalization of business has, according to the Diamond's second 'point', gone hand in hand with interest groups' views on European integration and more general debates linking 'de-corporatization' and 'neo-corporatism' with EU accession. This continues to be the case.

Indeed, as Karlsson argues, the Diamond 'does give a clearer picture of the role of interest groups in the making of Swedish policy' (Chapter 6). Yet, in line with the more stable elements appearing within the Diamond's 'point' one and that the process of 'de-corporatization' (begun in the early 1990s) is still fresh in the minds of the political elite, Sweden remains an essentially corporatist country at heart. Those corporatist elements that remain in the Sweden of the late 1990s are likely to be characteristic features of the country for the foreseeable future. In short, although the internationalization of interest groups continues to be perceived as going hand in hand with EU membership and European integration, it also seems that the process of 'de-corporatization' may be slowing in Sweden (even if it will probably continue). Indeed, as Karlsson also argues (see Chapter 6), Sweden's most prominent interest groups may be declining in terms of general influence, but they have also undergone substantial changes to maximize their influence on governmental EU policy and at the supranational EU level. There are even some minor areas where EU membership has actually increased corporatism by institutionalizing the role of corporate actors within EU policy-making.

If this is the case and although the general trend is towards a slower kind of 'de-corporatization', it may be pertinent today to talk no longer about the second 'point' as 'declining corporatism' but rather to re-label it as a more settled version of 'changing corporatism' (see Figure 14.1). Certainly the corporatism now practised in Sweden is slightly different from that of a decade ago and these changes have been facilitated, albeit to some degree, by Sweden's EU membership, but what perhaps is less clear is whether corporatism is in terminal, rather than just relative, decline.

Whatever the scenario, Sweden's corporate actors are now more familiar with dealing with EU questions as the latter have become more everyday parts of the Swedish political agenda and as EU policies infringe upon those policy ambits where interest groups are more interested. Nevertheless, although the country's corporate actors may be ready and able to cope with EU membership from an institutional perspective, this does not mean that the Union is not a controversial area for most interest groups to deal with. Just as with the major political parties, contemporary EU questions, such as Swedish participation in the 'Euro', have led to and in some cases compounded divisions within, for example, the Swedish labour movement. The differences of opinion between certain leaders of the Swedish trade unions and their 'grass roots' members, between component trade unions within the same trade union congress and, indeed, between the trade union congresses on EU policy questions, have further weakened the ability of Sweden's corporate leaders to 'lead' their members and to maximize their influence upon aspects of Swedish EU policy. Not only this, but there are also sources of division between the labour movement and their Social Democratic colleagues in government over the nature and pace of Sweden's role in European integration.

Given these latter points, it may be the case that Swedish corporatism is 'changing corporatism' and that these 'changes' are far from complete. Yet, the various chapter analyses also vindicate the Diamond's main assertions of the second 'point' that: (1) the changes to Sweden's corporate structure are perceived as being linked (rightly or wrongly) with EU membership and (2) the more stable, but still, to some extent, incoherent role of Swedish interest groups on EU questions affects governmental policy. They remain accurate. However, the subtle changes within the second 'point' may actually mean that its overall importance in shaping Swedish EU policy is perhaps less. Thus, 'point' two is now much less influential than 'point' one in restricting governmental enthusiasm for European integration. Indeed, as Sweden's interest groups continue to be more firmly rooted with EU decision-making and Swedish business continues to internationalize, the changes in the 1990s will mean that the second 'point' will slowly alter from a constraint to a facilitator of Swedish governmental action towards the EU.

The evaluations contained in this book suggest that this process has already begun.

Point 3: The new 'qualitative' challenges of economic interdependence

Above all, the various chapters confirm the central role of 'point' three in shaping Swedish governmental policy towards European integration and that this 'point' remains the dominant aspect pushing forward Swedish participation in key EU policy areas. It is worth remembering that the third 'point' was informally divided into two elements: 'internal' EU-related aspects (policies directed at and affecting Sweden as a member of the Union – FDI and EMU) and 'external relations' aspects (Swedish influence on the formulation of the Union's policies regarding third states and especially the Baltic Sea and EU enlargement).

As regards the former 'internal policies' then a number of conclusions can be drawn from the study. First, that although the specific question of Foreign Direct Investment (FDI) is perhaps no longer a constant feature of domestic debate on European integration, the related question of maintaining and protecting Sweden's economic competitiveness through participation in the European Union is. The Swedes still perceive the European Union primarily (if not exclusively) as an economic organization based around the Single European Market (SEM) concept (see Chapters 6, 8 and 9, for instance). From this perspective, this allows Swedish governments to 'sell' the European Union to its domestic population as a positive 'wealth-creator' for Sweden. Indeed, the domestic population's acceptance of EU membership and Swedish participation in EU projects is largely conditional on this being the case. In rather oversimplistic terms, if the Swedes have accepted the EU for essentially economic reasons, then their country's participation in new EU policies is dependent on the Union providing some kind of economic 'benefit' to Sweden. This is the 'performance related criteria' on which the Swedish population continues, at least for the present, to judge the EU and is also one of the major reasons for their large-scale disillusionment with it.

Second, it is now EMU that is the primary feature within Swedish political debates relating to the third 'point'. Indeed, the fact that the EU has now started to implement the 'third stage' of the EMU timetable has placed a highly visible external pressure on the Swedish government and on the domestic political agenda. This policy area has reinforced the perception in Sweden that the country cannot remain divorced from the Union (and has thereby limited the impact of the EU membership critics) and that, in some way, the country must maintain its influence on the EU's monetary agenda. In other words, whether the Swedish populace like it or not, the 'Euro' has arrived, and the Persson government has on the basis of this, 'raised its game'.

Third, European economic integration has, in many ways, also bridged a 'qualitative' threshold in which the implications of its policy developments are now substantial both for EU and non-EU states (see Figure 14.1). Sweden is required in the next few years to decide on whether it wants to be involved (and to what degree) in the main policy underpinning the EU's economic interdependence – EMU. Yet, this policy is also different in a 'qualitative' sense, since it requires participating member states to accept a larger degree of political management from Brussels in the formulation of domestic economic policy. The 'Euro' increasingly raises new 'qualitative' challenges of economic interdependence since the debate in Sweden now has to focus not only on whether Sweden can afford for economic and/or political reasons to remain outside, but also if the country does participate then the implications arising from EMU are also highly political, mostly irrevocable and fairly long term. Whatever the choice, the implications of European economic integration are controversial for Sweden in domestic terms.

Furthermore, the centrality of the EMU question in shaping the nature of the first element of the third 'point' as a facilitator of Swedish perspectives on European integration has been complemented by the rising profile of Sweden's role in the EU's external relations (the 'external' element of 'point' three). In other words, although EMU will remain the main 'economic' reason for drawing Sweden closer into the Union, this process is reinforced by the attractiveness that the Union offers in furthering Sweden's economic and political interests in the surrounding region. Not only will EU enlargement be a semi-permanent feature on the EU's agenda well into the new millennium, but Sweden's role as a supporter of particularly Baltic enlargement has been further reinforced as the Union has developed new external policies in which Sweden plays a central role (such as the EU's Northern Dimension – see Chapter 3). These 'external relations' elements highlight the advantages that the EU offers to Sweden and are concrete areas where the Persson government can claim to have been successful. The 'internal' and 'external' elements of the third 'point' are moving Sweden forward in the same direction towards a 'deeper' relationship with the Union and are of such magnitude that they have become the most important features of Swedish EU policy in 1999.

Point 4: Security policy with a European identity

Chapters 2 and 3 assess the sizeable changes influencing Swedish foreign and security policy. Indeed, it is accurate to state that over the last few years both the Swedish policy of 'non-alignment' and the EU's CFSP and crisis-management functions have altered considerably. In broad terms, Sweden's 'non-alignment' is now interpreted so flexibly that its compatibility with the EU's CFSP has become progressively less controversial.

Moreover, since the signing of the Amsterdam Treaty and with the continuing expansion of both the EU's remit and power in European crisis management since then (which has largely been accepted by the Swedish government), the late 1990s may finally represent the time when the fourth 'point' is no longer a major restricting factor on Swedish government policy at all. Indeed, the Persson government has gradually come to regard the Union's external relations portfolio as an opportunity for European cooperation. In particular, the EU's peacekeeping functions are being expanded under the auspices of the 'Petersberg Tasks' and fit nicely alongside the Union's attempts at establishing an EU Northern Dimension and a common strategy with Russia.

As long as the CFSP is cloaked within the language of 'soft security', 'confidence-building measures', 'conflict resolution' and 'crisis management', then the fourth 'point' is now more of an international facilitator of a more open Swedish EU policy which is more sympathetic towards cooperation in European foreign and security policy matters. It is only the question of the EU developing a military role with a 'hard security', collective defence dimension that remains controversial (even if the eventual likelihood of this being the case seems at this point fairly remote). In short, then, the fourth 'point' is now less restrictive and has moved more towards facilitating a more open Swedish EU policy. The Persson government's 'win-set' is therefore larger than before.

Following on from this, the relationship between the third and fourth 'points' is now more complementary and less taut than before. The changes to the fourth 'point' so that Swedish objections to a strengthened CFSP are progressively diminishing and that the EU crisis-management role is increasingly attractive to the Swedes have tended to reinforce those trends apparent within the third 'point' (which remains as the dominant 'driver' behind a closer Swedish relationship with the Union). The net outcome is that Sweden has become more comfortable with supranational solutions in both the monetary and CFSP portfolios. After all, the EU's initiatives at closer monetary and foreign policy cooperation are, for the most part, here to stay.

From the perspective of Putnam's 'two-level games' (1988), it can be argued that, on the one hand, the domestic constraints (Level II) on Swedish EU policy, although present, are lessening given that the first 'point' (a more divided, Europeanized democracy) is now more stable, and the second 'point' (changing corporatism) is now more settled and perhaps less influential on Swedish policy than before. In addition, the combined international pressures (Level I) emanating from a more ardent third 'point' (the new 'qualitative' challenges of economic interdependence) and a changing fourth 'point' (security policy with a European identity) suggest that Swedish EU policy has, and will, become gradually more open to European integration initiatives (see Figure 14.1). In other words, the size of the overall Swedish 'win-set' is 'widening' over time. Certainly, the elite are largely content with EU membership. The biggest challenge remains within 'point' one and convincing the Swedish population of that fact.

Conclusion: Sweden and the European Union: where next?

Given these conclusions, several future scenarios are possible. These scenarios are rather broad and by no means exclusive and, of course, nuances exist both within and between them.

Scenario 1: A pessimistic scenario: Swedish withdrawal from the Union and the dominance of 'Swedish society' over the 'Swedish state'

Under this scenario, aspects of 'Swedish society' become so disillusioned with the country's experiences of membership that public opinion moves firmly and categorically in favour of Swedish withdrawal from the Union. In other words, both EU membership and the country's role in further European integration remain highly controversial. Certainly, questions like Swedish participation in the 'Euro' and in future EU collective defence arrangements are too progressive for the Swedish population to accept.

This could provoke a substantial improvement in the electoral fortunes of the anti-EU membership Left Party and Greens and/or a wholesale decline in the performances of the pro-membership parties, including the Social Democrats, forcing the last group to change their existing policies. It may take place at a forthcoming general election leading (perhaps if rather unlikely) to the formation of a Left Party/Green government (elected on an anti-EU mandate) or require a future government of another or more varied political persuasion (more likely) to hold another public referendum on whether the country should leave the Union. In the latter case, the population would then vote to leave the Union at the subsequent referendum.

In other words, aspects of the 'Membership Diamond's' (Level II) first 'point' would ultimately constrain Swedish policy and, in one sense, would reverse the pressures emanating from the Diamond's third and fourth 'points'. In Putnam's terminology, (Level II) domestic considerations have a decisive influence on Sweden's (Level I) international orientation. This scenario would require the adjustment of 'Swedish society' not to take place and indeed, for existing Europeanization trends to be reversed, placing pressure on the 'Swedish state' to alter its existing governmental policies. This is probably the least realistic or likely scenario to take place, although it cannot be completely discounted. None of the chapters suggest that this scenario will prevail.

Scenario 2: A 'balanced' scenario: continuing tension between 'Swedish society' and the 'Swedish state'

This scenario envisages the more or less continuation of existing trends, whereby the Swedish political elite and governmental apparatus continue to be drawn into the everyday workings of the Union and become, to varying degrees, protectors of Swedish EU membership. At the same time, the Europeanization of 'Swedish society' is slower. The scepticism of the population to European integration remains. In simple terms, the long-term future of Swedish EU membership is resolved in favour of continued membership. It is only the country's participation in future integration that attracts controversy.

Swedish governments will therefore continue to remain tentative and the differences of opinion on the benefits of the EU are sustained between the Swedish political elite and the wider public. This will ensure that Sweden (or at least the 'Swedish state') will continue with, at best, its selective enthusiasm for a supranational Europe and follow a 'mixed' approach to European integration (as long as the population continues to have substantial reservations towards the Union). From the perspective of the 'Membership Diamond', the tension between the first 'point' on the one side and the second, third and fourth 'points' on the other will continue in some form. On a positive note, this will enable the Swedish government to champion some areas of the EU's policy portfolio and on others to be more cautious. Moreover, it may also entail that were there to be slight negative changes within Swedish public opinion on EU questions, then the government may, perhaps, advocate 'multi-speed' approaches to European integration and/or even 'multi-tier' solutions in certain policy areas, such as Danish-style 'opt-outs' from specific provisions of future EU treaties. This is mainly the strategy adopted by the Persson government today, or at least during the early years of EU membership. It is also the scenario implied as being the most accurate by most of the chapters in this book.

Scenario 3: An optimistic scenario: the complete Europeanization of the 'Swedish state' and 'Swedish society'

This final scenario predicts that the changes in Swedish governmental policies (more evident from 1999 onwards) become even more concrete. In short, the question of Swedish EU membership is permanently resolved and, in addition, the country's participation in some of the Union's 'flagship' supranational policies is accepted by both the political elite and increasingly (if rather reluctantly) by the electorate. This therefore enables successive Swedish governments to participate fully in European integration, perhaps even to the point of being regarded by others as being part of the Union's 'political core'.

From the perspective of the 'Membership Diamond', the pressures emanating from its third and fourth 'points' become overwhelming. The Persson and/or successive governments can, therefore, join the 'Euro' and probably abandon 'non-alignment' in favour of a strong EU/WEU military capability (and perhaps even allow the country to join NATO?). In short, the 'Swedish state' (now fully Europeanized) will have been successful in shaping 'Swedish society' and convincing it, for the most part, of the benefits of European integration. To some extent, this process may have begun if Swedish public opinion polls are to be believed (see Chapter 7). What is probably far less certain is the extent to which this process will be completed.

The editor's tentative conclusion is probably that Sweden at the start of the new millennium will lie somewhere between scenarios 2 and 3 (if closer to the former than the latter). The majority of evidence in 1999 and in these chapter evaluations suggests that scenario 2 is the most accurate description of the position today, although there are clear indications that the movement on the road towards scenario 3 is on the cards and had begun by 1999. Good luck Sweden!

References

Aarebrot, F., Berglund, S. and Weninger, T. (1995) 'The View from EFTA', in O. Niedermayer and R. Sinnott (eds), *Public Opinion and Internationalized Governance*, pp. 344–67, Oxford: Oxford University Press.

Andersen, M. S. and Liefferink, D. (1997) 'Introduction: The Impact of Pioneers on EU Environmental Policy', in M. S. Andersen and D. Liefferink (eds), *European Environmental Policy: The Pioneers*, pp. 1–39, Manchester: Manchester University Press.

Andrén, N. (1967) 'Nordic Integration', *Cooperation and Conflict*, 2(1), 1–25.

Andrén, N. (1997) *Säkerhetspolitik: Analyser och tillämpningar*, Stockholm: Norstedts Juridik.

Archer, C. (1998) *Norden and the Security of the Baltic States*, Det sikkerhetspolitiske bibliotek nr. 4, Oslo: Den Norske Atlanterhavskomite.

Archer, C. (1999) 'Nordic Swans and Baltic Cygnets', *Cooperation and Conflict*, 34(1), 47–71.

Archer, C. and Jones, C. (1999) 'The Security Policies and Concepts of the Baltic States – Learning from their Nordic Neighbours', in O. F. Knudsen (ed.), *Stability and Security in the Baltic Sea Region*, pp. 167–82, London: Frank Cass.

Arter, D. (1999a) 'Sweden: A Mild Case of "Electoral Instability Syndrome?" ', in D. Broughton and M. Donovan (eds), *Changing Party Systems in Western Europe*, pp. 143–62, London and New York: Pinter.

Arter, D. (1999b) *Scandinavian Politics Today*, Manchester: Manchester University Press.

ATL (1999) No. 9, March 1999, Malmö: LRF Media HB.

Aylott, N. (1997) 'Between Europe and Unity: The Case of the Swedish Social Democrats', *West European Politics*, 20(2), 119–36.

Bär, S. and Kraemer, R. A. (1998) 'European Environmental Policy After Amsterdam', *Journal of Environmental Law*, 10(2), 315–30.

Barnes, P. (1996) 'The Nordic Countries and European Union Environmental Policy', in L. Miles (ed.), *The European Union and the Nordic Countries*, pp. 203–21, London: Routledge.

Beckman, B. and Johansson, K. M. (1999) 'EU och statsförvaltningen', in K. M. Johansson (ed.), *Sverige i EU*, pp. 113–28, Stockholm: SNS Förlag.

Bennulf, M. and Holmberg, S. (1990) 'The Green Breakthrough in Sweden', *Scandinavian Political Studies*, 13, 165–84.

Bergquist, M. (1970) *Sweden and the EEC*, Stockholm: Nordstedt and Söner.

Bieler, A. (1999) 'Globalization, Swedish Trade Unions and European Integration: From Europhobia to Conditional Support', *Cooperation and Conflict*, 34(1), March, 21–46.

Bolin, O. and Swedenborg, B. (1992) (eds) *Mat till EG-pris*, Stockholm: SNS Förlag.

Brundtland Report (1987) *Our Common Future* (World Commission on Development and Environment), Oxford: Oxford University Press.

Brunsson, N. (1989) *The Organization of Hypocrisy – Talk Decisions and Actions in Organizations*, Chichester: John Wiley.

Buzan, B. (1991) *Peoples, States and Fear: An Agenda for International Security Studies in the Post-Cold War Era*, 2nd edn, Hemel Hempstead: Harvester Wheatsheaf.

Calmfors, L., Flam, H., Gottfries, N., Lindahl, R., Matlary, J. H., Jerneck, M., Berntsson, C. N., Rabinowicz, E. and Vredin, A. (1997) *EMU – A Swedish Perspective*, Dordrecht: Kluwer Academic.

Cederschiöld, C. (1996) Press Release, Stockholm City Hall, 8 December.

Centre Party (1999) *'Förnya samarbetet i Europa'. Program inför valet till europaparlamentet den 13 juni 1999*, Stockholm: Centre Party.

Childs, M. (1980) *Sweden – The Middle Way on Trial*, New Haven: Yale University Press.

Cini, M. and McGowan, L. (1998) *Competition Policy in the European Union*, London: Macmillan.

Cirkulär 1-8, *EU-sekretariatet*, Stockholm: Regeringskansliet.

Dagens Nyheter (1993) 'Reformer i snigelfart mot växande misär', 30 April.

Dagens Nyheter (1996) 'Folket skriver mot EU', 11 August.

Dagens Nyheter (1997a) 'EMU kan hota välfärd', 15 May.

Dagens Nyheter (1997b) 'Jobben splittrar unionen', 16 June.

Dagens Nyheter (1997c) 'EU satsar på jobben', 2 October.

Dagens Nyheter (1997d) 'Spricka om EU-mål inom regeringen', 2 November.

Dagens Nyheter (1997e) 'Persson halvnöjd med EU-konferensen', 22 November.

Dagens Nyheter (1997f) 'Svårt slå vakt om hög skatt', 15 June.

Dagens Nyheter (1998) 'Ny EU grundlag döms ut', 31 January.

Dahl, A.-S. (1999) 'Sweden and the Baltic Sea Region – Activism on a New Arena or the End of Free-Riding?', in Knudsen, O. F. (ed.), *Stability and Security in the Baltic Sea Region*, pp. 140–54, London: Frank Cass.

Defence Bill (1991/92) 'Totalförsvarets utveckling till och med budgetåret 1996/97 samt anslag för budgetåret 1992/93' (1991/92: 102).

Defence Bill (1995/96) 'Totalförsvar i förnyelse' (1995/96: 12).

Defence Bill (1998/99) 'Förändrad omvärld – omdanat försvar' (1998/99: 74).

de Vestel, P. (1998) 'The Future of Armament Cooperation in NATO and the WEU', in K. Eliasson (ed.), *Foreign and Security Policy in the European Union*, pp. 197–221, London: Sage.

Direktiv (1997), *Genomförande av EGs direktiv om utstationering av arbetstagare* (1997: 84), Stockholm: Arbetsmarknadsdepartementet.

Dohlman, E. (1989) *National Welfare and Economic Interdependence. The Case of Sweden's Foreign Trade Policy*, Oxford: Clarendon Press.

Dryzek, J. S. (1997) *The Politics of the Earth. Environmental Discourses*, Oxford: Oxford University Press.

Duff, A. (1997) *The Treaty of Amsterdam*, London: Sweet and Maxwell.

Edin, P.-O. (1995) 'EMU måste bli ett vänsterprojekt', *LO-Tidningen*, No. 33.

Ekengren, M. (1996) 'The Europeanization of State Administration: Adding the Time Dimension', *Cooperation and Conflict*, 31(4), 387–416.

Ekengren, M. and Sundelius, B. (1998) 'Sweden: The State Joins the European

Union', in K. Hanf and B. Soetendorp (eds), *Adapting to European Integration: Small States and the European Union*, pp. 131–48, London: Longman.

Elder, N., Thomas, A. H. and Arter, D. (1988) (second revised edition) *The Consensual Democracies?: The Government and Politics of the Scandinavian States*, Oxford: Blackwells.

Eliassen, K. (1998) (ed.) *Foreign and Security Policy in the European Union*, London: Sage.

Elvander, N. and Seim Elvander, A. (1995) *Gränslös samverkan. Fackets svar på företagens internationalisering*, Stockholm: SNS Förlag.

ENDS Daily (various years) Daily e-mail service, London: Environmental Data Services, 40 Bowling Green Lane, London EC1R 0NE.

Esaiasson, P. (1996) 'Kampanj på sparlåga', in M. Gilljam and S. Holmberg (eds), *Ett knappt ja till EU. Väljarna och folkomröstningen 1994*, pp. 35–42, Stockholm: Norstedts Juridik.

Esping-Andersen, G. (1990) *The Three Worlds of Welfare Capitalism*, Cambridge: Polity Press.

EU Consequences Committee (1994) *Sweden and Europe Committee of Enquiry: Consequences of the EU for Sweden – The Economy: Summary and Conclusions* (SOU 6), Stockholm: EU Consequences Committee.

Eurobarometer (various years) *Public Opinion in the European Union*, Brussels: European Commission.

Eurobarometer (1995) *Europeans and the Environment*. Survey Conducted in the Context of the Eurobarometer 43.1 bis., Brussels: Directorate General Environment, Nuclear Safety and Civil Protection.

European Commission (1993) *Green Paper – European Social Policy: Options for the Union*, Brussels: European Commission.

European Commission (1994) *White Paper – European Social Policy: A Way Forward for the Union* (COM (94) 333), Brussels: European Commission.

European Commission (1996) *The Challenges Facing the European Defence-related Industry: A Contribution for Action at European Level* (COM (96) 10 Final), Brussels: European Commission.

European Commission (1997a) *Concerning the 5th Framework Programme of the European Community for Research, Technological Development and Demonstration Activities* (COM (97) 142 Final), Brussels: European Commission.

European Commission (1997b) *Implementing European Union Strategy on Defence-related Industries* (COM (97) 583 Final), Brussels: European Commission.

European Commission (1998) *Communication from the Commission: A Northern Dimension for the Policies of the Union* (COM (98) 589 Final), 25.11.1998, Brussels: European Commission.

European Environment Agency (1999a) *Environment in the European Union at the Turn of the Century*. Environment Assessment Report, No. 2, Copenhagen: European Environment Agency.

European Environment Agency (1999b) *Environment in the European Union at the Turn of the Century*. Appendix to the Summary. Facts and Findings per Environmental Issue, Copenhagen: European Environment Agency.

European Parliament (1997) *Report Containing a Proposal on the Harmonisation of the Member States' Laws on Drugs* (A4-0359/97), Strasbourg: European Parliament.

European Parliament (1998a) *Amendments to the D'Ancona Report*, Strasbourg: European Parliament.

European Parliament (1998b) *Second Report Containing a Proposal on the Harmonisation of the Member States' Laws on Drugs* (A4-0211/98), Strasbourg: European Parliament.

Eurostat Yearbook 1997 (1998), Luxembourg: European Statistical Office.

Evans, P., Jacobson, H. and Putnam, R. (1993) (eds) *Double-Edged Diplomacy: International Bargaining and Domestic Politics*, Berkeley: University of California Press.

EWWE (various years) Environmental Watch: Western Europe, Arlington: Cutter Information Corporation.

Fagerberg, J. and Lundberg, L. (1993) (eds) *European Economic Integration: A Nordic Perspective*, Aldershot: Avebury.

Financial Times (1999a) *Baltic Sea Region Survey*, 11 June 1999.

Financial Times (1999b) 'The Northern Dimension Fails to Come Up to Scratch', 13 November 1999: 6.

Financial Times (1999c) 'Sweden will Join Euro, says Premier', 15 November 1999.

Finnish Ministry of Foreign Affairs (1999) *Foreign Ministers' Conference on the Northern Dimension 11–12 November 1999*, HELD 421-73, Helsinki: Finnish Ministry of Foreign Affairs.

Folket i Bild (1996) Kvinnor, jämställdhet och socialförsäkring i EU, No. 8.

Fredén, C. (1996) 'Två vänsterperspektiv på EMU', *Tiden*, No. 8.

Friedrich, A., Tappe, M. and Wurzel, R. K. W. (1998) 'The Auto Oil Programme: A Critical Interim Assessment', *European Environmental Law Review*, 7(4), 104–12.

Gahrton, P. (1997) *Vill Sverige bli län i EU-stat?*, Lund: Gröna Böcker.

Galtung, J. (1964) 'Foreign Policy Opinion as a Function of Social Position', *Journal of Peace Research*, 1, 206–31.

Gidlund, J. and Jerneck, M. (2000) *Local and Regional Governance in Europe: Evidence from Nordic Regions*, Cheltenham: Edward Elgar.

Gilljam, M. (1996) 'Det kluvna Sverige?', in M. Gilljam and S. Holmberg, *Ett knappt ja till EU. Väljarna och folkomröstningen 1994*, pp. 167–210, Stockholm: Norstedts Juridik.

Gilljam, M. and Holmberg, S. (1993) *Väljarna inför 90-talet*, Stockholm: Norstedts Juridik.

Gilljam, M. and Holmberg, S. (1995) *Väljarnas val*, Stockholm: Norstedts.

Gilljam, M. and Holmberg, S. (eds) (1996) *Ett knappt ja till EU. Väljarna och folkomröstningen 1994*, Stockholm: Norstedts.

Goldmann, K. (1988) *Change and Stability in Foreign Policy: The Problems and Possibilities of Détente*, Princeton: Princeton University Press.

Goldmann, K. (1991) 'The Swedish Model of Security Policy', in J.-E. Lane (ed.), *Understanding the Swedish Model*, pp. 122–43, London: Frank Cass.

Gould, A. (1993) *Capitalist Welfare Systems*, Harlow: Longman.

Gould, A. (1994) 'Pollution Rituals in Sweden: the Pursuit of a Drug Free Society', *Scandinavian Journal of Social Welfare*, 3(2), 85–93.

Gourlay, C. and Remacle, E. (1998) 'The 1996 IGC: The Actors and Their Inter-action', in K. A. Eliassen (ed.), *Foreign and Security Policy in the European Union*, pp. 59–93, London: Sage.

Government Bill (1997/98) *Developing Cooperation between Neighbouring Countries* (1997/98: 70), Stockholm: SOU.

Government Communication (1994/95) *Det svenska miljöarbetet i EU – Inriktning och Genomförande* (1994/95: 167), Stockholm: Ministry of the Environment.

Government Paper (1997/98) *Euro-atlantiska partnerskapsrådet och det fördjupade Partnerskap för fred-samardetet* (1997/98: 29), Stockholm: SOU.

Government Report (Ds) (1997a) *Det svenska miljöarbetet i EU – Uppföljning av 1995 örs strategi* (Ds 1997: 68), Stockholm: Ministry of the Environment.

Government Report (Ds) (1997b) *Remissyttranden över betänkandet Sverige och EMU* (Ds 1997: 22), Stockholm: Finansdepartementet.

Government Report (Ds) (1998) *Svensk säkerhetspolitik i ny omvärldsbelysning* (Ds 1998: 9), Stockholm: Swedish Government.

Gradin, A. (1997) 'EMU är bra för Sverige', *Dagens Nyheter*, 23 January.

Gustavsson, J. (1998) *The Politics of Foreign Policy Change: Explaining the Swedish Reorientation on EC Membership*, Lund: Lund University Press.

Haas, E. B. (1958) *The Uniting of Europe*, Stanford, Calif.: Stanford University Press.

Haas, E. B. (1971) 'The Study of Regional Integration: Reflections on the Joy and Anguish of Pre-Theorizing', in L. Lindberg and S. Scheingold (eds), *Regional Integration: Theory and Research*, Cambridge, Mass.: Harvard University Press.

Haas, E. B. and Schmitter, P. (1964) 'Economics and Differential Patterns of Political Integration: Projections about Unity in Latin America', *International Organization*, 41, 491–517.

Haas, P. (1992) 'Introduction: Epistemic Communities and International Policy Coordination', *International Organization*, 46(1), 1–35.

Hagelin, B. (1997) 'Sweden', in P. Gummett and J.-A. Stein (eds), *European Defence Technology in Transition*, pp. 219–59, Amsterdam: Harwood Academic Publishers.

Hajer, M. (1995) *The Politics of Environmental Discourse*, Oxford: Oxford University Press.

Hakovirta, H. (1988) *East–West Conflict and European Neutrality*, Oxford: Clarendon.

Handelsbanken Markets (1999) *Economic Macro Forecast: Euroland Lagging Behind the US*, Stockholm: Handelsbanken Markets.

Hanf, C.-H. and Böckenhoff, G., (1993) *Food Industries in the Transition from Domestic Predominance to International Competition*, SNS Occasional Papers No. 50, Stockholm: SNS Förlag.

Hegeland, H. (1999) 'Den svenska riksdagen och EU', in K.-M. Johansson (ed.), *Sverige i EU*, pp. 95–112, Stockholm: SNS Förlag.

Hegeland, H. and Mattson, I. (1995) 'Att få ett ord med i laget – En jämförelse mellan EU-nämnden och Europaudvalget', in *Statsvetenskaplig tidskrift*, No. 4, 435–57.

Hegeland, H. and Mattson, I. (1996) 'To Have a Voice in the Matter: A Comparative Study of the Swedish and Danish European Committees', *Journal of Legislative Studies*, 2(3), 198–215.

Hegeland, H. and Mattson, I. (1997) 'The Swedish Riksdag and the EU: Influence and Openness', in M. Wiberg (ed.), *Trying to Make Democracy Work: The Nordic Parliaments and the European Union*, pp. 70–107, Stockholm: The Bank of Sweden Tercentenary Foundation.

Héritier, A. (1999) 'Elements of Democratic Legitimation in Europe: an Alternative Perspective', *Journal of European Public Policy*, 6(2), 269–83.

Héritier, A., Knill, C. and Mingers, S. in collaboration with R. Barrett (1996) *Ringing the Changes. Regulatory Competition and the Transformation of the State. Britain, France, Germany*, Berlin: Walter de Gruyter.

Hermann, C. F. (1990) 'Changing Course: When Governments Choose To Redirect Foreign Policy', *International Studies Quarterly*, 34(1), 3–21.

Hermansson, J. (1993) *Politik som intressekamp. Parlamentariskt beslutsfattande och organiserade intressen i Sverige*, Stockholm: Norstedts Juridik.

Herolf, G. and Lindahl, R. (1996) *Av vitalt intresse. EU:s utrikes- och säkerhetspolitik inför regeringskonferensen* (SOU: 1996: 7), Stockholm: Fritzes.

Hinnfors, J. (1997) 'Still the Politics of Compromise? Agenda-Setting Strategy in Sweden', *Scandinavian Political Studies*, 20(2), 159–77.

Hinnfors, J. (1998) 'EMU: Marknadens politik' in S. Holmberg and L. Weibull (eds), *Opinionssamhället*, pp. 207–17, Göteborg: SOM Institutet.

Hobson, B. (1997) 'Kön och missgynnande: Svensk jämställdhetspolitik speglad i EG-domstolens policy', in A. Stark (ed.), *Ljusande framtid eller ett långt farväl?* (SOU 1997: 115), Stockholm: SOU/Swedish Government.

Hoffmann, S. (1966) 'Obstinate or Obsolete? The Fate of the Nation State and the Case of Western Europe', *Daedalus*, 95, 862–915.

Holmberg, S. (1996) 'Partierna gjorde så gott de kunde', in M. Gilljam and S. Holmberg (eds), *Ett knappt ja till EU. Väljarna och folkomröstningen 1994*, pp. 225–36, Stockholm: Norstedts.

Holmberg, S. (1998) 'The Extent of European Integration', in A. Todal Jenssen, P. Pesonen and M. Gilljam (eds), *To Join or Not to Join. Three Nordic Referendums on Membership in the European Union*, pp. 269–83, Oslo: Scandinavian University Press.

Hubel, H. (1999) 'The European Union, the Baltic States and Post-Soviet Russia: Theoretical Problems and Possibilities for Developing Partnership Relations in the North Eastern Baltic Sea Region', in O. F. Knudsen (ed.), *Stability and Security in the Baltic Sea Region*, pp. 241–56, London: Frank Cass.

Huldt, B. (1994) 'Sweden and European Community-Building 1945–92', in S. Harden (ed.), *Neutral States and the European Community*, pp. 104–43, London: Brassey's.

Industriförbundet (1996a) *Swedish Industry and the European Union. A Policy Overview January 1996. Industrial Competitiveness*, Stockholm: Industriförbundet.

Industriförbundet (1996b) *Industriåret 1995/96*, Stockholm: Industriförbundet.

Industriförbundet (1997) 'EMU kan ta oss ur massarbetslösheten', *Tidningen Näringsliv*, No. 3, Stockholm: Industriförbundet.

Industriförbundet (1998a) *Storföretagen och EMU – en enkätundersökning*. Arbetsrapport 17, Stockholm: Industriförbundet.

Industriförbundet (1998b) *EMU-förberedelser i små och medelstora företag*. Arbetsrapport 19, Stockholm: Industriförbundet.

Industriförbundet, SAF and Grossistförbundet Svensk Handel (1995) *Näringslivet och EU:s regeringskonferens 1996*. Stockholm: Industriförbundet.

Ingebritsen, C. (1998) *The Nordic States and European Unity*, Cornell: Cornell University Press.

Iversen, I. (1996) 'Power, Flexibility, and the Breakdown of Centralized Wage Bargaining: Denmark and Sweden in Comparative Perspective', *Comparative Politics*, 28(4), 399–436.

Jacobsson, B. (1987) *Kraftsamlingen. Politik och företagande i parallella processer*, Lund: Studentlitteratur.

Jacobsson, B. (1999) 'Europeiseringen och statens omvandling', in *Politikens internationalisering*, Lund: Studentlitteratur.

Jacobsson, B. and Mörth, U. (1998) *Paradoxes of Europeanisation – Swedish Cases*, SCORE Working Paper, No. 1998: 2, Stockholm: SCORE.

Jacobsson, K. (1997) *Så gott som demokrati. Om demokratifrågan i EU-debatten*, Umeå: Borea Bokförlag.

Jahn, D. (1992) 'Nuclear Power, Energy Policy and New Politics in Sweden and Germany', *Environmental Politics*, 1(3), 383–417.

Jahn, D. (1993) *The New Politics of Trade Unions*, Aldershot: Dartmouth.

Jahn, D. and Widfeldt, A. (1996) 'The Stoney Path to Europe', in Ian Hampsher-Monk and Jeffrey Stanyer (eds), *Contemporary Political Studies 1996, vol. 1*, pp. 417–23. Exeter: Political Studies Association of the UK.

Jenssen, A.T., Pesonen, P. and Gilljam, M. (eds) (1998) *To Join or Not to Join: Three Nordic Referendums on the membership in the European Union*, Oslo: Scandinavian University Press.

Jerneck, M. (1993) 'Sweden – the Reluctant European?', in T. Tiilikainen and I. Damgaard Petersen (eds), *The Nordic Countries and the EC*, pp. 23–42, Copenhagen: Copenhagen Political Studies Press.

Johansson, A. W. and Norman, T. (1986) 'Den svenska säkerhetspolitiken i historiskt perspektiv' (Swedish Security Policy from a Historical Perspective), in B. Hugemark (ed.), *Neutrality and Defence: Perspectives on Swedish Security Policy 1809–1985 (Neutralitet och försvar: Perspektiv på svensk säkerhetspolitik 1809–1985)*, pp. 11–43, Stockholm: Militärhistoriska förlaget.

Johansson, K. M. (1998) 'Book Review', *Cooperation and Conflict*, 33(3), 334–6.

Johansson, S. (1997) 'Ekonomisk galenskap, Persson', *Dagens Nyheter*, 19 January.

Jonasson, L. (1993) *Mathematical Programming as Prediction*, Stockholm: Institutionen för ekonomi. Sveriges Lantbruksuniversitet.

Jørgensen, K. E. (1998) 'PoCo: The Diplomatic Republic of Europe', in K. E. Jørgensen (ed.), *Reflective Approaches to European Governance*, pp. 167–80. Basingstoke: Macmillan.

Karlsson, M. (1997) *Organisationerna och internationaliseringen*, Research report 97: 1, Stockholm: ÖCB.

Karlsson, M. (1999) 'EU och organisationsväsendet', in K.-M. Johansson (ed.), *Sverige i EU*, pp. 169–88, Stockholm: SNS Förlag.

Karvonen, L. and Sundelius, B. (1987) *Internationalization and Foreign Policy Management*, Aldershot: Gower.

Karvonen, L. and Sundelius, B. (1990) 'Interdependence and Foreign Policy Management in Sweden and Finland', *International Studies Quarterly*, 34, 211–27.

Karvonen, L. and Sundelius, B. (1996) 'The Nordic Neutrals: Facing the European Union', in L. Miles (ed.), *The European Union and the Nordic Countries*, pp. 245–59, London: Routledge.

Katz, R. S. and Mair, P. (1994) *How Parties Organize*, London: Sage.

KEMI (1997) Various Reports, Stockholm: National Chemicals Inspectorate (KEMI).

Kinnwall, M. (1996) *Should Sweden Join the EMU? How High is the Value of Waiting?* Unpublished manuscript, Stockholm: Handelsbanken Markets.

Kite, C. (1996) *Scandinavia Faces EU – Debates and Decisions on Membership 1961–1994*, (Diss.), Umeå: Umeå University, Department of Political Science.

Knopf, J. W. (1993) 'Beyond Two-Level Games: Domestic–International Inter-action in the Intermediate-Range Nuclear Forces Negotiations', *International Organization*, 47(4), 599–628.

Kohler-Koch, B. (1996) 'Catching up with Change: The Transformation of Govern-ance in the European Union', *Journal of European Public Policy*, 3(3), 359–80.

Kola, J., Rabinowicz, E. and Hofreither, M. (1999) *Recent Experiences of Entering the EU: Austria, Finland and Sweden*, Proceedings of the 66 EAAE Seminar/NJF Seminar No. 301, Tallinn, Estonia, 20–22 May 1999.

Kronsell, A. (1997), 'Sweden: Setting a Good Example', in M. S. Andersen and D. Liefferink (eds), *European Environmental Policy: The Pioneers*, pp. 40–80, Manchester: Manchester University Press.

KU (1998/99) *Granskning av statsrådens tjänsteutövning och regeringsärendenas handläggning* (1998/99: 10).

Lane, J.-E. (1991) 'Interpretations of the Swedish Model', in J.-E. Lane (ed.), *Understanding the Swedish Model*, pp. 1–7, London: Frank Cass.

Lane, J.-E. (1993) 'Twilight of the Scandinavian Model', *Political Studies*, XLI, 315–24.

Lantis, J. S. and Queen, M. F. (1998) 'Negotiating Neutrality: The Double-Edged Diplomacy of Accession to the European Union', *Cooperation and Conflict*, 32(2), 152-182.

Lapins, P. (1995) 'Flygande start för facket', *LO-Tidningen*, No. 33.

Larsson, T. (1995) *Governing Sweden*, Stockholm: Statskontoret.

Lawler, P. (1997) 'Scandinavian Exceptionalism and European Union', *Journal of Common Market Studies*, 35(4), 565–93.

Letter of Intent (LoI) between Ministers of Defence from France, Germany, Italy, Spain and Sweden *Concerning Measures to Facilitate the Restructuring of European Defence Industry*, July 1998.

Liefferink, D. and Andersen, M. S. (1998a) 'Strategies of the 'Green' Member States in EU Environmental Policy-making', *Journal of European Public Policy*, 5(2), 254–70.

Liefferink, D. and Andersen, M. S. (1998b) 'Greening the EU: National Positions in the Run-up to the Amsterdam Treaty', *Environmental Politics*, 7(3), 66–93.

Lindahl, R. (1995) 'Towards An Ever Closer Relation – Swedish Foreign and Security Policy and European Integration', in R. Lindahl and G. Sjöstedt (eds), *New Thinking in International Relations: Swedish Perspectives*, pp. 163–82, Stock-holm: Swedish Institute of International Affairs.

Lindahl, R. (1996a) 'The Swedish Debate', in J. Janning, F. Algieri, F. Rodrigo, R.

Lindahl, H. Grabbe and K. Hughes, *The 1996 IGC – The National Debates (2)* pp. 37–50, London: Royal Institute of International Affairs.

Lindahl, R. (1996b) 'En folkomröstning i fredens tecken', in M. Gilljam and S. Holmberg (eds), *Ett knappt ja till EU. Väljarna och folkomröstningen 1994*, pp. 149–67, Stockholm: Norstedts.

Lindahl, R. (1998) 'EU-opinionen efter tre års medlemskap', in S. Holmberg and L. Weibull (eds), *Opinionssamhället*, pp. 183–206, Göteborg: SOM Institutet.

Lindahl, R. (1999a) 'Schweden', in W. Weidenfeld and W. Wessels (eds), *Jahrbuch der Europäischen Integration 1998/99*, Bonn: Europa Union Verlag.

Lindahl, R. (1999b) 'Mångtydig EU-opinion', in S. Holmberg and L. Weibull (eds), *Ljusnande framtid*, pp. 371–86, Göteborg: SOM Institutet.

Lindahl, R. and Nordlöf, T. (1989) 'EG-frågan i svensk opinion', in S. Holmberg and L. Weibull (eds), *Åttiotal. Svensk opinion i empirisk belysning*, pp. 161–74, Report No. 4, Göteborg: SOM Institutet.

Lindbeck, A., Molander, P., Persson, T., Petersson, O., Sandmo, A., Swedenborg, B. and Thygesen, N. (1994) *Turning Sweden Around*, Cambridge, Mass.: MIT Press.

Lindberg, L. N. and Scheingold, S. A. (1971) (eds) *Regional Integration: Theory and Research*, Cambridge, Mass.: Harvard University Press.

Lindh, A. and Lejon, B. (1999) 'Så skall vi arbeta för ökad öppenhet inom EU', *Svenska Dagbladet*, 23 March.

Livsmedelsekonomiska Samarbetsnämden (LES) (1997) *Utvecklingen inom jordbruk, livsmedelsindustrin och handel under de senaste åren*, Stockholm: Department of Agriculture.

LO (1995) *Verksamhetsberättelse 1994*, Stockholm: LO.

Luif, P. (1995) *On the Road to Brussels: The Political Dimension of Austria's, Finland's and Sweden's Accession to the European Union*, Wien: Braumüller.

Lundquist, L. (1997) 'Sweden', in M. Jänicke and H. Weidner (eds), *National Environmental Policies. A Comparative Study of Capacity-Building*, pp. 45–71, Berlin: Springer.

Lundquist, L. (1998) 'Sweden: from Environmental Restoration to Ecological ModerNisation', in K. Hanf and A.-L. Jansen (eds), *Governance and Environment in Western Europe*, pp. 230–53, London: Longman.

Marks, G., Hooghe, L. and Blank, K. (1996) 'European Integration from the 1980s: State-Centric v. Multi-Level Governance', *Journal of Common Market Studies*, 34(3), 341–78.

Mény, Y., Muller, P. and Quermonne, J.-L. (1996) (eds) *Adjusting to Europe. The Impact of the European Union on National Institutions and Policies*, London: Routledge.

Micheletti, M. (1995) *Civil Society and State Relations in Sweden*, Aldershot: Avebury.

Miles, L. (1995) 'Enlargement of the European Union and the Nordic Model', *Journal of European Integration*, 19(1), 45–71.

Miles, L. (1996) (ed.) *The European Union and the Nordic Countries*, London: Routledge.

Miles, L. (1997a) *Sweden and European Integration*, Aldershot: Ashgate.

Miles, L. (1997b) 'Sweden and Security', in J. Redmond (ed.), *The 1995 Enlargement of the European Union*, pp. 86–124, Aldershot: Ashgate.

Miles, L. (1997c) 'Swedish Priorities for the IGC', *Current Sweden*, No. 415, Stockholm: Swedish Institute.

Miles, L. (1998a) ' "Diamonds are Forever": Sweden and the IGC', CEUS Research Paper 3/98, Hull: Centre for European Union Studies, The University of Hull.

Miles, L. (1998b) 'Sweden and the IGC: Testing the "Membership Diamond" ', *Cooperation and Conflict*, 33(4), 339–66.

Miles, L. (1999) 'Scandinavian Regionalism: The Case of Sweden', in P. Wagstaff (ed.), *Regionalism in the European Union*, pp. 130–39, Exeter: Intellect Books.

Miles, L. (2000) 'Making Peace with the Union? The Swedish Social Democratic Party and European Integration', in R. Geyer, C. Ingebritsen and J. Moses (eds), *Globalization, Europeanization and Scandinavian Social Democracy*, pp. 218–39, London: Macmillan.

Miles, L. and Kintis, A. (1996) 'The New Members: Sweden, Austria and Finland', in J. Lodge (ed.), *The 1994 Elections to the European Parliament*, pp. 227–36, London: Pinter.

Miljan, T. (1977) *The Reluctant Europeans*, London: Hurst & Co.

Ministry of Finance/Riksdagen (1991) *Finansplanen, Bilaga 1, Budgetpropositionen*, Stockholm: Ministry of Finance/Riksdagen.

Ministry of Finance (1997) *The Swedish Budget 1998*, Stockholm: Ministry of Finance.

Ministry of Foreign Affairs (1997a) Address by The Swedish Minister for Foreign Affairs, Mrs. Lena Hjelm-Wallén, at the Think-Tank Seminar on Hard and Soft Security in the Baltic Sea Region, The Åland Island Peace Institute, 29 August 1997, Stockholm: UD.

Ministry of Foreign Affairs (1997b) *The Council of the Baltic Sea States – A Survey*, Stockholm: UD.

Ministry of Foreign Affairs (1998a) *Nordic Foreign Policy Cooperation and Joint Action – A Survey*, Stockholm: UD.

Ministry of Foreign Affairs (1998b) *A Good Neighbourhood: Sweden's Cooperation with Central and Eastern Europe*, Stockholm: UD.

Ministry of Foreign Affairs (1998c) Statement by Anders Bjurner, Deputy State Secretary for Foreign Affairs, Sweden in Warsaw on 7 March 1998 at the Nordic Forum for Security Policy on 21st Century Challenges for the Baltic Sea Region and European Security, Stockholm: UD.

Ministry of Foreign Affairs (1998d) *An Enlarged EU – Opportunities and Problems – A Summary of the Reports on the Consequences of Enlargement of the EU*, Stockholm: UD.

Ministry of Foreign Affairs (1998e) *Developing Cooperation Between Neighbouring Countries*, UD Info, No. 2, March 1998, Stockholm: UD.

Ministry of Foreign Affairs (1998f) Statement by Gunnar Lund, State Secretary for European Union Affairs, at Groningen, 26 November 1998 – 'Sweden's Current Position in the European Union', Stockholm: UD.

Ministry of Foreign Affairs (1999a) *Statement of Government Policy in the Parliamentary Debate on Foreign Affairs, 10 February 1999*, Stockholm: UD.

Ministry of Foreign Affairs (1999b) *Baltic Sea – Sea of Opportunities*. Speech by Mr Leif Pagrotsky, Minister for Trade, Sweden, at the Baltic Sea Region Investment Conference in Stockholm, 8 June 1999, Stockholm: UD.

Ministry of Foreign Affairs (1999c) *Extract from Swedish Government Bill 1998/99: 1*, Stockholm: UD.

Ministry of Foreign Affairs (1999d) *Increased Support to Development Cooperation with Russia*, Press Release, 14 October 1999, Stockholm: UD.

Ministry of Foreign Affairs (1999e) Opening Statement by Foreign Minister Anna Lindh at the conference 'Russia and Europe', 13 October 1999, Stockholm: UD.

Ministry of the Environment (1997) *Sweden's Second National Communication on Climate Change. Under the United Nations Framework Convention on Climate Change* (Ds 1997: 26), Stockholm: Government Offices, Ministry of the Environment.

Misgeld, K. (1997) *Den fackliga europavägen: LO, det internationella samarbetet och Europas enande 1945–1991*, Stockholm: Atlas.

Molin, K. (1999) 'The Role of Sweden in EU Environmental Policy', *European Environmental Law Review*, 8(8/9), 243–51.

Moravcsik, A. (1991) 'Negotiating the Single European Act', in R. O. Keohane and S. Hoffmann (eds), *The New European Community. Decision-making and Institutional Change*, pp. 41–84, Boulder: Westview Press.

Mörth, U. (1996) *Vardagsintegration – La vie quotidienne – i Europa. Sverige i EUREKA och EUREKA i Sverige*, PhD Dissertation, Stockholm: Department of Political Science, Stockholm University.

Mörth, U. (1998a) 'Policy Diffusion and RTD – No Government is an Island', *Cooperation and Conflict*, 33(1), 35–58.

Mörth, U. (1998b) *EU Policy-making in Pillar One and a Half – The European Commission and Economic Security*, Research Report, Stockholm: The Swedish Agency for Civil Emergency Planning (ÖCB).

Mörth, U. and Sundelius, B. (1993) 'Dealing with a High Technology Vulnerability Trap: The USA, Sweden and Industry', *Cooperation and Conflict*, 28(3), 303–28.

Mörth, U. and Sundelius, B. (1995) 'Sweden and the United Nations', in K. Krause and W. A. Knight (eds), *State, Society, and the UN System: Changing Perspectives on Multilateralism*, pp. 101–31, Tokyo/New York/Paris: The United Nations University Press.

Mouritzen, H. (1997) *External Danger and Democracy: Old Nordic Lessons and New European Challenges*, Aldershot: Dartmouth.

National Institute for Economic Research (1997) *The Swedish Economy*, November, Stockholm: National Institute for Economic Research.

Niedermayer, O. (1995) 'Trends and Contrasts', in O. Niedermayer and R. Sinnott (eds), *Public Opinion and Internationalized Governance*, pp 53–72, Oxford: Oxford University Press.

Niedermayer, O. and Sinnott, R. (1995) (eds) *Public Opinion and Internationalized Governance*, Oxford: Oxford University Press.

Nilsson, Y. (1995a) 'Sociala frågor sällan socialpolitik', *Svenska Dagbladet*, 15 May.

Nilsson, Y. (1995b) 'Passionerade svenskar i motvind', *Svenska Dagbladet*, 15 June.

Nilsson, Y. (1996) '"Förmånsturism" i EU skall stävjas', *Svenska Dagbladet*, 30 March.

Nye, J. (1971) *Peace in Paris: Integration and Conflict in Regional Organization*, Boston, Mass.: Little Brown.

Nye. J. (1990) *Bound to Lead – The Changing Nature of American Power*, New York: Basic Books Publishers.

Nye. J. and Owens, W. (1996) 'America's Information Edge', *Foreign Affairs*, 75(2), 20–36.

OECD (1996) *Sweden, Environmental Performance Reviews*, Paris: Organization for Economic Co-operation and Development.

OECD (1997) *Review of Agricultural Policies: Latvia*, Paris: Organization for Economic Co-operation and Development.

Olsson, C. (1997) 'Ja-övervikt endast vid folkomröstningen', *Välfärds Bulletin*, No. 1.

Oscarsson, H. (1996) 'EU-dimensionen', in M. Gilljam and S. Holmberg (eds), *Ett knappt ja till EU. Väljarna och folkomröstningen 1994*, pp. 237–68, Stockholm: Norstedts.

Oskarson, M. and Ringdal, K. (1998) 'The arguments', in A. Todal Jenssen, P. Pesonen and M. Gilljam (eds), *To Join or Not to Join. Three Nordic Referendums on Membership in the European Union*, pp. 149–67, Oslo: Scandinavian University Press.

Parliamentary Committee on Foreign Affairs (1995/96) *Summary of Report 1995/96: The EU Intergovernmental Conference* (1995/96: UU130), Stockholm: Riksdagen.

Persson, G. (1999) 'Vi kommer inte att ge upp alliansfriheten' (We will not abandon non-alignment), *Svenska Dagbladet*, 2 June.

Pesonen, P., Gilljam, M. and Todal Jenssen, A. (1998) 'Postscript: Developments after the EU Referendums', in A. Todal Jenssen, P. Pesonen and M. Gilljam (eds), *To Join or Not to Join. Three Nordic Referendums on Membership in the European Union*, pp. 327–39. Oslo: Scandinavian University Press.

Pesonen, P., Todal Jenssen, A. and Gilljam, M. (1998) 'To Join or Not to Join', in A. Todal Jenssen, P. Pesonen and M. Gilljam (eds), *To Join or Not to Join. Three Nordic Referendums on Membership in the European Union*, pp. 13–36, Oslo: Scandinavian University Press.

Peterson, J. (1992) *The Politics of European Technological Collaboration. An Analysis of the Eureka Initiative*, PhD Dissertation, London: London School of Economics and York University.

Peterson, J. and Sharp, M. (1998) *Technology Policy in the European Union*, London: Macmillan.

Petersson, O. (1982) *Väljarna och världspolitiken*, Stockholm: Norstedts.

Petersson, O. (1994) *Swedish Government and Politics*, Stockholm: Publica.

Pierre, J. and Widfeldt, A. (1994) 'Party Organizations in Sweden: Colossuses with Feet of Clay or Flexible Pillars of Government?', in R. S. Katz and P. Mair (eds), *How Parties Organize: Change and Adaptation in Party Organizations in Western Democracies*, pp. 332–56, London: Sage.

POLARM document (11/98).

Pontusson, J. and Swenson, P. (1996) 'Labor Markets, Production Strategies, and Wage Bargaining Institutions, *Comparative Political Studies*, 29(2), 223–50.

Promemoria (1999) 'SB:s organisation för EU-arbetet samt internationella frågor', *Statsrådsberedningen*, Stockholm: Regeringskansliet.

Putnam, R. (1988) 'Diplomacy and Domestic Politics: The Logic of Two-Level Games', *International Organization*, 42(3), 427–60.

Rabinowicz, E. (1993) *Konsekvenser av EG-medlemskapet för jordbruket och livsmedelssektorn*. Billaga 3 till EG-konsekvensutredningen, Samhällsekonomi.

Rabinowicz, E. (1999) 'EU Enlargement and the Common Agricultural Policy: Finding Compromise in a Two-level Repetitive Game', *International Politics*, 36: 397–417.

Rabinowicz, E. and Bolin, O. (1998) 'Negotiating the CAP – the Nordic Experience', *Swedish Journal of Agricultural Research*, 28 sid., 5–15.

Raiffa, H. (1982) *The Art and Science of Negotiations*, Boston: Harvard University Press.

Randqvist, M. (1995) 'Regeringskonferensen 1996', *LO-Tidningen*, No. 33.

Redmond, J. (ed.) (1997) *The 1995 Enlargement of the European Union*, Aldershot: Ashgate.

Regeringens proposition (1998/99) *'Förändrad omvärd – omdanat försvar' (Changed External Environment – Restructured Defence)* (1998/99: 74), Stockholm: Riksdagen.

Regeringens skrivelse (1995/96) *Berättelse om verksamheten i Europeiska unionen under 1995 (Story of the Activities within the European Union during 1995)* (1995/96: 190), Stockholm: Riksdagen.

Regeringens skrivelse (1996/97) *Berättelse om verksamheten i Europeiska unionen under 1996* (1996/97: 80), Stockholm: Riksdagen.

Regeringens skrivelse (1997/98) *Berättelse om verksamheten i Europeiska unionen under 1997* (1997/98: 80), Stockholm: Riksdagen.

Regeringens skrivelse (1998/99) *Berättelse om verksamheten i Europeiska unionen under 1998* (1998/99: 60), Stockholm: Riksdagen.

Riksdag och Departement (1994) Tydlig klassröstning i EU omröstningen, No. 37.

Riksdag och Departement (1995a) Mer sparande för svensken för att komma med i EMU, No. 22/3.

Riksdag och Departement (1995b) Sverige vill sätta Europa i arbete, No. 37.

Riksdagskommitten (1999) *EU-bevakningen på kort och lång sikt – källor och informationsinhämtning*, PM 05–10.

Ringdal, K. and Valen, H. (1998) 'Structural Divisions in the EU referendums', in A. Todal Jenssen, P. Pesonen and M. Gilljam (eds), *To Join or Not to Join. Three Nordic Referendums on Membership in the European Union*, pp. 168–93, Oslo: Scandinavian University Press.

Rometsch, D. and Wessels, W. (1996) *The European Union and Member States: Towards Institutional Fusion?*, Manchester: Manchester University Press.

Rothstein, B. (1998) 'Breakdown of Trust and the Fall of the Swedish Model'. Paper delivered at the 1998 annual meeting of the American Political Science Association in Boston.

Ruin, O. (1974) 'Participatory Democracy and Corporativism: The Case of Sweden', *Scandinavian Political Studies*, 9, 171–84.

Ruin, O. (1982) 'Sweden in the 1970s: Policy-Making Becomes More Difficult', in J. Richardson (ed.), *Policy Styles in Western Europe*, pp. 141–67, Boston: Allen and Unwin.

Ruin, O. (1990) 'The Duality of the Swedish Central Administration: Ministries and

Central Agencies', in A. Farazmand (ed.), *Handbook of Comparative and Development Public Administration*, pp. 67–79, New York: Marcel Dekker, Inc.

Ruin, O. (1997a) 'Suède', in J. Rideau (ed.), *Les états membres de l'Union Européenne Adaptations – Mutations – Résistances*, pp. 439–58, Paris: L.G.D.J.

Ruin, O. (1997b) *Folkomröstningar och parlamentarism. En jämförande analys av EU-folkomröstningarna i Norden hösten 1994* (SOU 56, bil.1).

SACO (1997) *Remissvar över SOU 1996: 158 Sverige och EMU*, Stockholm: SACO.

SACO, SAF and TCO (1999) *Utanförskapets konsekvenser. En rapport från den partsgemensamma EMU-gruppen*, Stockholm: SACO.

Sæter, M. (1996) *The Nordic Countries and the Perspective of a 'Core' Europe*, NUPI Working Papers, No. 558, Oslo: NUPI.

SAF (1997) *Remissyttrande över EMU-utredningens betänkande*, Stockholm: SAF.

Sahlin-Andersson, K. (1998) 'The Social Construction of Projects. A Case Study of Organizing of an Extraordinary Building Project – the Stockholm Globe Arena', in N. Brunsson and J. Olsen (eds), *Organizing Organizations*, pp. 89–106, Oslo: Fagbokforlaget.

Sally, R. (1996) 'Public Policy and the Janus Face of the Multinational Enterprise: National Embeddedness and International Production', in P. Gummett (ed.), *Globalization and Public Policy*, pp. 64–82, London: Edward Elgar.

Sandholtz, W. (1992) *High-Tech Europe – The Politics of International Cooperation*, Berkeley/Los Angeles/Oxford: University of California Press.

Sandholtz, W. and Zysman, J. (1989) '1992: Recasting the European Bargain', *World Politics*, XLII, 95–128.

Sandström, M. (1997) *The Changing Swedish Defence Industry*, Projektpapier No. 13, Striftung Wissenschaft und Politik, Ebenhausen/Isartal.

SCB (Swedish Central Bureau of Statistics), Stockholm and Örebro.

SCB (1997/98) *Statistiska meddelanden. EU- och EMU-sympatier*, Stockholm: SCB.

Schneider, M. (1997) *Fogen des EU-Beitritts fur die Österrische Landwirschaft*, Studie des Österischen Instituts fur Wirtschaftforschung im Auftrag des Bundesministeriums fur Landschaft und Forstwirschaft, February 1997, Vienna.

Schuck, J. (1997) 'Wibe sätter jobben främst', *Dagens Nyheter*, 11 October.

Schyman, G. (1995) 'EU hänvisar kvinnor till 'atypiska' arbeten', *Vi Mänskor* No. 3.

SEPA (1993) *Aktionsprogram Miljö 1993. Ett välanpassat samhälle*, Stockholm: Swedish Environmental Protection Agency.

Sifo (Swedish Institute for Opinion Research), Stockholm.

Sinnott, R. (1995) 'Bringing Public Opinion Back In', in O. Niedermayer and R. Sinnott (eds), *Public Opinion and Internationalized Governance*, pp. 11–32, Oxford: Oxford University Press.

Socialdepartementet (1998) *Välfärdsfakta social*, Stockholm: Socialdepartementet.

SOM Institute (Society, Opinion, Mass-media), Research Institute at Göteborg University, various surveys, Göteborg: SOM Institute.

SoS-rapport 1996: 16 *EG rätten och socialtjänsten*, Stockholm: Socialstyrelsen.

SOU (1993a) *EG och våra grundlagar. Betänkande avgivet av Grundlagsutredningen inför EG* (SOU 1993: 14), Stockholm: Statens Offentliga Utredningar/Swedish Government.

SOU (1993b) *EG kvinnorna och välfärden* (SOU 1993: 117), Stockholm: Social-departementet.

SOU (1994a) *Om kriget kommit... Förberedelser för mottagande av militärt bistånd 1949–1969. Betänkande av Neutralitetspolitikkommissionen (If War had Occurred. Preparations for the Reception of Military Assistance 1949–1969. Report from the Commission on Neutrality Policy)* (SOU 1994: 11), Stockholm: Statens Offentliga Utredningar/Swedish Government.

SOU (1994b) *Suveränitet och demokrati. Betänkande avgivet av EG-konsekvensutredningarna: Subsidiaritet* (SOU 1994: 12), Stockholm: Statens Offentliga Utredningar/Swedish Government.

SOU (1996a) *Av vitalt intresse. EU:s utrikes- och säkerhetspolitik inför regeringskonferensen (Of Vital Interest. The Common Foreign and Security Policy of the European Union before the Inter-Governmental Conference)* (SOU 1996: 7), Stockholm: Statens Offentliga Utredningar/Swedish Government.

SOU (1996b) *EMU-utredningens betänkande ('Calmforsrapporten')* (SOU 1996: 158), Stockholm: Statens Offentliga Utredningar/Swedish Government.

SOU (1997a) *Större EU – säkrare Europa. Betänkande av kommittén om EU:s utvidgning – säkerhetspolitiska konsekvenser (A Larger EU – A More Secure Europe. Report from the Committee on the Enlargement of the EU – Consequences for Security Policy)* (SOU 1997: 143), Stockholm: Statens Offentliga Utredningar/Swedish Government.

SOU (1997b) *Folket som rådgivare och beslutsfattare, Betänkande avgivet av Folkomröstningsutredningen* (SOU 1997: 56), Stockholm: Statens Offentliga Utredningar/Swedish Government.

SOU (1997c) *Samhällsekonomiska konsekvenser av EU intvidgningen* (SOU 1997: 151), Stockholm: Statens Offentliga Utredningar/Swedish Government.

SOU (1997d) *Mat och Miljö. Svensk strategi för EU:s jordbrukspolitik: framtiden* (SOU 1997: 102), Stockholm: Statens Offentliga Utredningar/Swedish Government.

Stålvant, C.-E. (1990) 'Rather a Market than Home, but Preferably a Home Market: Swedish Policies Facing Changes In Europe', in F. Laursen (ed.), *EFTA and the EC: Implications of 1992*, pp. 135–62, Maastricht: European Institute of Public Administration.

Statens Jordbrukverk (Swedish Board of Agriculture) (1993) *EG:s struktur- och regionala stöd på jordbrukområdet*. Statens Jordbrukverk.

Statens Jordbrukverk (Swedish Board of Agriculture) (1998) *Utvärdering av de regionala stöden till jordbruket*, Jönköping: Statens Jordbrukverk.

Statskontoret (1996) *EU-medlemskapets effekter på svensk statsförvaltning: Samordning, organisation och arbetsformer i statsförvaltningens EU-arbete, 7.*

Statsrådsberedningens skriftserie (1995) *Ett halvår I EU*, Statsrådsberedningens skiftserie No. 4. Stockholm: Regeringen.

Stenelo, L.-G. and Jerneck, M. (1996) (eds) *The Bargaining Democracy*, Lund: Lund University Press.

Stenlund, P. (1999) *Policies for the Northern Dimension*. Presentation to the UACES Northern Dimension Workshop, National Liberal Club, London, 5 February 1999.

Sterzel, F. (1993) (ed.) *EG och den svenska grundlagen – en förbundsstat i vardande?, 29 Rättsfondens skriftserie*.

Stütz, G. (1999) *Opinion 98*, Stockholm: Styrelsen för psykologiskt försvar, Meddelande 147.

Sundelius, B. (1982) 'The Nordic Model of Neighbourly Co-operation', in B. Sundelius (ed.), *Foreign Policies of Northern Europe*, pp. 177–96, Boulder, Col.: Westview Press.

Sundelius, B. (1989) (ed.) *The Committed Neutral: Sweden's Foreign Policy*, Boulder, Col.: Westview Press.

Sundelius, B. (1994) 'Changing Course: When Neutral Sweden Chose to Join the European Community', in W. Carlsnaes and S. Smith (eds), *European Foreign Policy: The EC and Changing Perspectives in Europe*, pp. 177–201, London: Sage.

Sundelius, B. and Wiklund, C. (1979) 'The Nordic Community: The Ugly Duckling of Regional Cooperation', *Journal of Common Market Studies*, XVII(1), 59–73.

Sundström, G. (1999) *Att tala med en röst. En studie av hur medlemskapet påverkar samordningen inom Regeringskansliet*, Stockholm: Statsvetenskapliga institutionen, Stockholms Universitet.

Surell, V. (1997) 'Skyll inte på EU', *Socialpolitik*, No. 1.

Svåsand, L. and Lindström, U. (1996) 'Scandinavian Political Parties and the European Union', in J. Gaffney (ed.), *Political Parties and the European Union*, pp. 205–19, London: Routledge.

Svenska Dagbladet (Swedish Daily), 7 July 1998.

Sveriges Riksdag (1995) *The Constitution of Sweden 1995*.

Swedish Government (1997/98) *Riktlinjer för Sveriges arbete med jordbruks och livsmedelspolitiken inom den europeiska unionen* (Prop. 97/98: 142), Stockholm: Swedish Government.

Swedish IGC 96 Committee (1996) *Sweden, the EU and the Future* (SOU 1996: 19), Stockholm: Fritzes.

Taggart, P. A. (1996) *The New Populism and the New Politics: New Protest Parties in Sweden in a Comparative Perspective*, Basingstoke: Macmillan.

Tallberg, J. (1999) 'Sverige och efterlevnaden av EU:s regelverk: ett samarbetsdilemma' in K.-M. Johansson (ed.), *Sverige i EU*, pp. 5–76, Stockholm: SNS Förlag.

TCO (1996) *Vad TCO vill i EU*, Stockholm: TCO.

TEMO (1997) *Svenska EU programkontoret – sysselsättningseffekten av växtkraft Mål 4*.

Thomas, A. H. (1996) 'The Concept of the Nordic Region and the Parameters of Nordic Co-operation', in Miles, L. (ed.), *The European Union and the Nordic Countries*, pp. 15–31, London: Routledge.

Thorgren, G. (1994) 'Vi ska inte ge upp', *Pockettidningen*, No. 2.

Tilton, T. (1991) *The Political Theory of Swedish Social Democracy*, Oxford: Clarendon.

Todal Jenssen, A., Gilljam, M. and Pesonen, P. (1998) 'The Citizens, the Referendums and the European Union', in A. Todal Jenssen, P. Pesonen and M. Gilljam, M. (eds), *To Join or Not to Join. Three Nordic Referendums on Membership in the European Union*, pp. 309–26, Oslo: Scandinavian University Press.

Todal Jenssen, A., Pesonen, P. and Gilljam, M. (1998) (eds) *To Join or Not to Join.*

Three Nordic Referendums on Membership in the European Union, Oslo: Scandinavian University Press.

Törnquist, S. (1996) *Politiska institutioner för västeuropeiskt försvarsmaterielssamarbete*, Stockholm: Swedish Defence Research Establishment.

Ugland, T. (1997) 'Europeanization of the Nordic alcohol monopoly systems', *Nordisk Alkohol och Narkotikatidskrift*, 14.

Utrikesfrågor (1991) *Offentliga dokument m.m. rörande viktigare svenska utrikesfrågor 1990 (Foreign Policy Issues. Official Documents etc. Concerning Important Swedish Foreign Policy Issues 1990)*, Stockholm: Utrikesdepartementet, 1991.

Utrikesfrågor (1992) *Offentliga dokument m.m. rörande viktigare svenska utrikesfrågor 1991 (Foreign Policy Issues. Official Documents etc. Concerning Important Swedish Foreign Policy Issues 1991)*, Stockholm: Utrikesdepartementet, 1992.

Utrikesfrågor (1993) *Offentliga dokument m.m. rörande viktigare svenska utrikesfrågor 1992 (Foreign Policy Issues. Official Documents etc. Concerning Important Swedish Foreign Policy Issues 1992)*, Stockholm: Utrikesdepartementet, 1993.

Utrikesfrågor (1994) *Offentliga dokument m.m. rörande viktigare svenska utrikesfrågor 1993 (Foreign Policy Issues. Official Documents etc. Concerning Important Swedish Foreign Policy Issues 1993)*, Stockholm: Utrikesdepartementet, 1994.

Utrikesfrågor (1995) *Offentliga dokument m.m. rörande viktigare svenska utrikesfrågor 1994 (Foreign Policy Issues. Official Documents etc. Concerning Important Swedish Foreign Policy Issues 1994)*, Stockholm: Utrikesdepartementet, 1995.

Utrikesfrågor (1996) *Offentliga dokument m.m. rörande viktigare svenska utrikesfrågor 1995 (Foreign Policy Issues. Official Documents etc. Concerning Important Swedish Foreign Policy Issues 1995)*, Stockholm: Utrikesdepartementet, 1996.

Utrikesfrågor (1997) *Offentliga dokument m.m. rörande viktigare svenska utrikesfrågor 1996 (Foreign Policy Issues. Official Documents etc. Concerning Important Swedish Foreign Policy Issues 1996)*, Stockholm: Utrikesdepartementet, 1997.

Utrikesfrågor (1998) *Offentliga dokument m.m. rörande viktigare svenska utrikesfrågor 1997 (Foreign Policy Issues. Official Documents etc. Concerning Important Swedish Foreign Policy Issues 1997)*, Stockholm: Utrikesdepartementet, 1998.

Værnø, G. (1999) 'Bridging the Nordic-Baltic Gap or – The Nordic Predicament in the Baltics', in O. F. Knudsen (ed.), *Stability and Security in the Baltic Sea Region*, pp. 183–203, London: Frank Cass.

Verdun, A. (1999) 'The role of the Delors Committee in the Creation of EMU: An Epistemic Community?', *Journal of European Public Policy*, 6(2), 308–28.

Vobruba, G. (1995) 'Tomorrow's Euro-corporatist Stage', *Journal of European Social Policy*, 5(4), pp. 303–15.

Wæver, O. (1992) 'Nordic Nostalgia: Northern Europe after the Cold War', *International Affairs*, 68(1), January, 77–102.

Wahlbäck, C. (1982) 'The Nordic Region in Twentieth-Century European Politics', in B. Sundelius (ed.), *Foreign Policies of Northern Europe*, pp. 9–32, Boulder, Col.: Westview Press.

Weale, A. (1992) *The New Politics of Pollution*, Manchester: Manchester University Press.

Wessels, B. (1995a) 'Development of Support: Diffusion or Demographic Replacement?', in O. Niedermayer and R. Sinnott (eds), *Public Opinion and Internationalized Governance*. pp. 105–36, Oxford: Oxford University Press.

Wessels, B. (1995b) 'Support for Integration: Élite or Mass-Driven?', in O. Niedermayer and R. Sinnott (eds), *Public Opinion and Internationalized Governance*. pp. 137–62, Oxford: Oxford University Press.

Wetterburg, G. (1995) 'Återförena Europa är den främsta uppgiften', *Tiden*, No. 3, Stockholm.

Widfeldt, A. (1996a) 'Sweden and the European Union: Implications for the Swedish Party System', in L. Miles (ed.), *The European Union and the Nordic Countries*, pp. 101–16, London: Routledge.

Widfeldt, A. (1996b) 'The Swedish European Election of 1995', *Electoral Studies*, 15, 116–19.

Widfeldt, A. (1997) *Linking Parties with People? Party Membership in Sweden 1960–94*, Göteborg Studies in Politics, No. 46, Göteborg: Göteborg University.

Widfeldt, A. (1998) 'The Swedish Parliamentary Election of 1998', *ECPR News*, 10(1), 18–19.

Wurzel, R. K. W. (1993) 'Environmental Policy', in J. Lodge (ed.), *The European Community and the Challenge of the Future* (second edition), pp. 178–99, London: Pinter.

Wurzel, R. K. W. (forthcoming) *Environmental Policy in the European Union*, London: Macmillan.

Wyn Rees, G. (1998) *The Western European Union at the Crossroads: Between Trans-Atlantic Solidarity and European Integration*, Boulder, Col./Oxford: Westview.

Yost, D. S. (1998) *NATO Transformed: The Alliance's New Roles in International Security*, Washington, DC: United States Institute of Peace Press.

Zetterberg, K. (1997) 'Introduction', in K. Zetterberg (ed.), *Hotet från Öster. Svensk säkerhetspolitik, krigsplanering och strategi 1945–1958 (The Threat from the East. Swedish Security Policy, War Planning and Strategy 1945–1958)*, pp. 9–15, Stockholm: Department of Strategic Studies, National Defence College.

Index

DATE DUE

JAN 0 8 2007			
			Printed in USA